VOID

Library of
Davidson College

THE REDEFINITION OF CONSERVATISM

THE REDEFINITION OF CONSERVATISM

Politics and Doctrine

Charles Covell

St. Martin's Press   New York

© Charles Covell 1986
All rights reserved. For information, write:
St. Martin's Press, Inc., 175 Fifth Avenue, New York, NY 10010
Printed in Hong Kong
Published in the United Kingdom by The Macmillan Press Ltd.
First published in the United States of America in 1985

ISBN 0-312-66725-6

Library of Congress Cataloging in Publication Data
Covell, Charles, 1955–
The redefinition of conservatism.
Bibliography: p.
Includes index.
1. Philosophy, English—20th Century. 2. Conservatism—England—History—20th century. I. Title.
B1615.C66 1986   320.5'2   85-8296
ISBN 0-312-66725-6

To my Father

Contents

Preface ix

1 Wittgenstein and Contemporary Conservatism 1
2 Two Wittgensteinians: John Casey 15
3 Two Wittgensteinians: Roger Scruton 43
4 Michael Oakeshott 93
5 Two Oakeshottians: Maurice Cowling and Shirley Robin Letwin 144
Conclusion: The Significance of Contemporary Conservatism 202

Notes 241
Name Index 254
Subject Index 259

Preface

The principal aim of this book is to provide a general introduction to the moral, aesthetic, cultural and political doctrines of five contemporary conservative thinkers. Accordingly, Chapters 2 to 5 provide a comprehensive reconstruction of their thought.

John Casey is considered as a conservative moralist whose cultural doctrine owed most to Arnold and Leavis, whose political doctrine owed most to Hegel, and whose ethical doctrine owed most to Aristotle and Aquinas. The work of Roger Scruton is regarded as progressing through three distinct phases: an initial Kantian phase represented by his first book, *Art and Imagination*; a politically charged Hegelian phase, represented by *The Meaning of Conservatism* (his most polemical book); and a liberal Oakeshottian phase, represented by his editorship of *The Salisbury Review*. Michael Oakeshott – easily the most important thinker discussed in the book – is treated principally in his relation to Hobbes. In this connection, the central text is *On Human Conduct* and the central preoccupation the theory of 'civil association' expounded in its second chapter. Mrs Letwin is included partly because her work is a very powerful extension of Oakeshott's. She is included chiefly, however, because her conclusions about Hume highlight certain ambiguities regarding the status of Oakeshott's theory. Maurice Cowling – the only historian amongst the thinkers – is discussed in three aspects: as a doctrinaire Oakeshottian; as a political historian whose conclusions about the functioning of democratic politics demonstrate the internal fragility of civil association; and as an historian of ideas whose conclusions about religion in his latest book, *Religion and Public Doctrine*, identify the major problems to which all five thinkers are responding.

The book does not claim that the thinkers are united in their doctrinal conclusions. It demonstrates, rather, that they are not. Thus, Maurice Cowling and Mrs Letwin are discussed together in Chapter 5 less because of any significant affinities between them than because of their common relation to Oakeshott. And more generally, it is suggested throughout that much of doctrinal importance divides the Hegelian authoritarianism of Scruton from the Hobbesian libertarianism of Oakeshott and the Thomism of Casey.

An underlying purpose of the book is to insist upon the *philosophical* character of the conservatism which the thinkers propound. This is why Chapter 1 is a summary account of the thought of Wittgenstein. It emphasises the very powerful implications of his later philosophy for conservative doctrine. His inclusion should not be understood to mean that Wittgenstein is being claimed for conservatism in either a political or historical sense. He is included, firstly, because his later philosophy exerted a profound influence upon Casey and Scruton and remains essential to any adequate understanding of their doctrinal intentions. He is included, secondly, because he provides a point of contact with the concerns of the mainstream academic philosophy in relation to which all the thinkers – especially Oakeshott – must be considered. He is included, lastly, because he illustrates the extent to which the thinkers are prepared to claim unfamiliar intellectual territory for conservatism. Indeed, there are crucial respects in which the most significant fact about their philosophical conservatism is its remoteness from the main intellectual traditions of English conservatism.

In his T. S. Eliot Memorial Lectures, *The Politics of Imperfection*,[1] Anthony Quinton traced a continuous tradition of English conservative thought stretching from Hooker and Clarendon, through Halifax, Bolingbroke, Hume, Johnson, Burke, Coleridge, Newman, to Disraeli, Salisbury and Oakeshott. Quinton argued that the tradition was based upon three underlying principles. Firstly, there was the principle of *traditionalism*, 'expressed in the conservative's attachment to, or reverence for, established customs and institutions'. Secondly, there was the principle of *organicism*, the doctrine that society was 'a unitary growth, an organised living whole, not a mechanical aggregate'. Thirdly, there was the principle of *political scepticism*, 'the belief that political wisdom ... is not to be found in the theoretical speculations of isolated thinkers but in the historically accumulated social experience of the community as a whole'.[2]

None of the thinkers discussed in this book disputes the importance to conservative doctrine of the three principles which Quinton enunciated. However, Casey and Scruton defend them from the European perspective of Aristotle, Aquinas, Hegel, Marx and Wittgenstein. Both are aligned with the tradition of German idealism and both reject the metaphysical assumptions of British empiricism. For Oakeshott and Mrs Letwin, the central influences are Hobbes and Hume rather than Hooker and Burke. Hooker, Quinton's point of reference, belongs to the classical tradition of natural law from which both depart in the direction of the voluntarism of Hobbes and the historicism of Hume. Oakeshott's traditionalism is grounded more in the scepticism of Montaigne and Hobbes than the organicism of Burke. Mrs Letwin differentiates the romanticism of Burke and Coleridge from the libertarianism of Hobbes and Hume; and identifies the tradition of romantic conservatism with the alien continental tradition of totalitarianism of Rousseau and Hegel. And Cowling's work undermines Quinton's conclusion that political conservatism in England has not depended upon positive religious belief. The general implication of this book, indeed, is that the philosophical doctrines of the thinkers are not exclusively English in inspiration and that, where they are English, they are not self-evidently conservative.

The book concludes with an estimate of the significance of the work of the thinkers. One very suggestive conclusion is advanced. Despite their remoteness from the conventional liberal conservatism represented by the historical work of Robert Blake, they share an ambivalent relationship with liberalism. On the one hand, they dissent from various forms of liberalism, especially those associated with the utilitarianism of Bentham, Austin and Mill. And they all seek to explore or reestablish the connections between law, morality and politics which utilitarianism undermines: Casey from the perspective of Thomism; Scruton from the perspective of Hegel; Oakeshott and Mrs Letwin from the perspective of the procedural natural law; and Cowling from the perspective of Christianity. On the other hand, the thinkers remain deeply implicated in the ruling ethical and metaphysical assumptions of the liberal tradition in virtue of alignments with Hobbes (Oakeshott and Mrs Letwin) and Kant (Casey and Scruton); and in virtue of a common polemically anti-Statist orientation. Whether their implication in the tenets of liberalism provides them with a secure doctrinal foundation for reestablishing the connections between law, morality and politics that most concern them is the question with which the book concludes.

* * *

For assistance in the preparation of the typescript of this book, the author is indebted to Dr Paul Binski of Gonville and Caius College, Cambridge; and for help in tracing an article, he is indebted to Mr David Cooper of Peterhouse, Cambridge. During a psychologically critical stage in the book's genesis the author was fortunate to enjoy the companionship of Dr Nicholas Cook and his wife Louise in idyllic surroundings. He remains grateful to them for indulging his self-indulgences.

For permission to refer to and quote from an unpublished typescript of his forthcoming book *Religion and Public Doctrine in Modern England, Volume II: Tensions*, the author is grateful to Mr Maurice Cowling of Peterhouse. And for permission to refer to and quote from his unpublished manuscript on the traditional virtues, he is grateful to Dr John Casey of Gonville and Caius College. Throughout the composition of this book, the author derived immense benefit from discussion with Mr Alexander Perkins of Jesus College, Cambridge – for this, he remains especially grateful.

Cambridge   CHARLES COVELL

1 Wittgenstein and Contemporary Conservatism

The purpose of this book is to reconstruct the moral and political doctrines of a number of contemporary conservative theorists and to establish the philosophical character of their conservatism. This underlying purpose explains why Wittgenstein is treated as central. He is central because with two theorists – Casey and Scruton – his influence was direct. His centrality is not diminished because his work exerted no direct influence upon the thought of the remaining theorists: Oakeshott, Cowling and Mrs Letwin. On the contrary, Wittgenstein's revolutionary conclusions in the philosophy of mind, action and language provided a basis for doctrinal resistance to the tradition of liberal rationalism deriving from Descartes which all three – particularly Oakeshott and Mrs Letwin – regarded as representing the principal challenge to the survival of conservative values.

i

It is well understood that Wittgenstein's later philosophy overthrew Cartesian assumptions in the philosophy of mind and action. It is also well understood that the presuppositions of his first book, the *Tractatus Logico-Philosophicus*,[1] were rationalistic in the full Cartesian sense. Not only did Wittgenstein assert that the proper idiom of human knowledge was that of the natural sciences; he concluded further that the discourse of science was the only language possessing logical significance. Ultimately, philosophy could do no more than vindicate the rational supremacy of the scientific idiom, the philosopher himself being left 'to say nothing except what can be said, i.e. propositions of natural science . . . and then, whenever someone else wanted to say something metaphysical, to demonstrate to him that he had failed to give a meaning to certain signs in his propositions'.[2] Throughout the *Tractatus* Wittgenstein identified the legitimate acquisition of knowledge with the application of the method of enquiry appropriate to the inductive sciences. The implication that the method possessed a universal applicability arose directly from Wittgenstein's assumption that all languages were governed by a single logical structure, the 'general form of propositions'.

The methodological presuppositions of the 'general form of propositions' were positivist, because the truth of any proposition was taken to consist in its correspondence with 'states of affairs in the world'. And its ontological presuppositions were realist, because knowledge was regarded as knowledge of a natural world which had a reality and structure independent of the ordering imposed upon it by the forms of human thought. On the one hand, the realist ontology of the *Tractatus* permitted a return to the knowledge of a natural world from which all distorting social and historical perspectives were eliminated. On the other, it sanctioned a purely 'private' knowledge of the world, expressed through an entirely private language and constructed in accordance with a method of enquiry which presupposed no social or institutional context for its appropriate application. In both respects, the ideological implications of the *Tractatus* were liberal and progressive in the sense that the book provided a method of enquiry capable of challenging the authority of all existing social convention and all received ideas.

The *Tractatus* was a polemically anti-metaphysical book. Its anti-metaphysical conclusions derived from its realist presuppositions in precisely the manner of traditional empiricism. Wittgenstein reiterated the Humean distinction between facts and values, for instance, in what was effectively a distillation of the arguments against the naturalistic fallacy: 'The sense of the world must lie outside the world. In the world everything is as it is, and everything happens as it does happen; *in* it no value exists – and if it did exist, it would have no value'.[3] As remorsely as Hume, Wittgenstein was denying that human values were sanctioned by a nonhuman reality and implying, to the contrary, that they expressed human attitudes to which the natural world was indifferent. The principal consequence of Wittgenstein's extreme antinaturalism was to sever the evaluative discourse appropriate to religion, morality and aesthetics from the discourse of factual propositions appropriate to science.

In one sense, the separation between science and ethics which the book imposed was a conciliatory stance. It tended towards the Kantian conclusion that questions of value had an autonomy which science was powerless to undermine and that this autonomy was a measure of their ultimate importance: 'We feel that even when *all possible* scientific questions have been answered the problems of life remain completely untouched'.[4] In another, stronger sense, the separation denied to the propositions of ethics, aesthetics and religion any cognitive significance whatsoever: 'So too it is impossible for there to be propositions of ethics. Propositions can express nothing that is higher';[5] 'It is clear that ethics cannot be put into words. Ethics is transcendental'.[6] What Wittgenstein was implying was that in matters of value the anarchy of subjectivism was inevitable. In expressing merely subjective preferences, the propositions of value conveyed no genuine knowledge about the world. And in all disputes about questions of value there were no significant or objective standards by which the claims of competing preferences could be resolved.

Wittgenstein's radical subjectivism in matters of value was intimately related to the most Cartesian assumption of the *Tractatus*: the assumption that knowledge was exclusively contemplative. So far from acknowledging the possibility of practical knowledge, the *Tractatus* affirmed that the metaphysical exile of the will from the world was absolute, that 'the world is independent of my will'.[7] The exile involved the classical difficulty associated with Cartesian dualism inasmuch as it reduced agency itself to the status of an illusion: 'Even if all that we wish for were to happen, still this would only be a favour granted by fate, so to speak: for there is no *logical* connexion between the will and the world, which would guarantee it, and the supposed physical connexion itself is surely not something that we could will'.[8] And it involved the classical difficulty associated with Kantian transcendentalism: the problem of the connection between the transcendental will as 'the subject of ethical attributes' about which it was 'impossible to speak', and the empirical will of a bodily person as 'a phenomenon ... of interest only to psychology'.[9] Throughout his later philosophy Wittgenstein accorded an increasingly prominent place to practical knowledge at the expense of the contemplative knowledge emphasised by

Descartes. In retrospect, the exile of the will from the world – and the disjunction between facts and values which it entailed – was a mark of Wittgenstein's commitment in the *Tractatus* to the fundamental aspiration of Cartesian rationalism: the reconstruction of a disinterested contemplative knowledge of the world, divested of all the partial practical perspectives underlying morality, religion, culture and social custom, and derived from the application of an ethically transparent method of enquiry in no sense harnessed to the exercise of the will. The pervasive implication of the later philosophy was that the Cartesian aspiration was illusory, that so far from there being an ethically neutral method of enquiry all knowledge was ideological in being the reflection of the social practices which embodied and transmitted it.

ii

It is well understood that Wittgenstein's later philosophy departed from the Cartesian assumptions of the *Tractatus*. Firstly, Wittgenstein abandoned the realist ontology of the earlier book. Instead of language being understood to correspond to a structure inherent in the natural world, Wittgenstein demonstrated that the structure of language was determined entirely by human convention. Although language was supported by underlying continuities of social practice, Wittgenstein implied that the linguistic and social conventions which together constituted the human world were guaranteed by no ground external to themselves. In this sense, Wittgenstein concluded that all that guaranteed the objectivity of human knowledge was the relative stability of the forms of social life which embodied it. Secondly, the insistence of the *Tractatus* upon a uniform structure of language gave way to an acknowledgement of the diversity of languages. The acknowledgement had the consequence that the scientific idiom was stripped of the rational supremacy assigned it in the *Tractatus*. In fact, the dethronement of the language of science served to close the gap between facts and values which had been opened up by the empiricism of the *Tractatus*: not only was science merely one language amongst many, but all human knowledge was ethical inasmuch as it reflected an implicit practical commitment.

Wittgenstein's departures from the positions enunciated in the

Tractatus were reflected in the concerns of the book with which his name is most commonly associated: *Philosophical Investigations*.[10] Throughout *Philosophical Investigations* Wittgenstein asserted that a language presupposed a social practice shared in common by its users – a 'language game' – and that a language had accordingly to be understood as 'part of an activity, or of a form of life'.[11] And he emphasised that there was a plurality of language games which was not reducible to any enduring preconventional foundation. Instead of the 'general form of propositions', all that united the multiplicity of language games were 'family resemblances', the 'complicated network of similarities overlapping and crisscrossing'.[12] Wittgenstein's emphasis upon linguistic diversity provided an antidote to the rationalist universalism of the *Tractatus*. An equally potent antidote was his denial that the significance of a language game derived from its correspondence to material reality. Thus Wittgenstein insisted that to construe the meaning of a word as the object which it signified was merely 'to confound the meaning of a name with the *bearer* of the name'.[13] On the contrary, not only had its meaning to be understood in terms of its conventional function within a language game, but the procedure of pointing to its 'bearer' was simply one convention amongst a multiplicity of different conventions.

In challenging the correspondence theory of truth to which the realist ontology of the *Tractatus* capitulated, the *Philosophical Investigations* made assumptions harmonious with the tenets of idealism. Wittgenstein's analysis of the phenomenon of 'aspect perception', for instance, endorsed the Kantian conclusion that the human mind was actively constitutive of the reality which it experienced. Thus Wittgenstein noticed that, unlike ordinary perception, the perception of aspects required 'imagination' and that, in consequence, 'seeing an aspect and imagining' were 'subject to the will'.[14] And he distinguished the perception of aspects from 'immediate perception' by reason of its being a cognitive experience: not only was the perception of an aspect 'half visual experience, half thought', but its verbal and pictorial representation was always 'the expression of a thought'.[15]

The details of Wittgenstein's analysis of aspect perception need not detain us, save to note that his conclusions were of cardinal importance in the defence of Kantian aesthetics conducted by Casey and Scruton. What must be understood, however, is that the analysis was a special application of two principles fundamental to the entire enterprise of *Philosophical Investigations*: first, that the criteria for the attribution of states of consciousness to the human subject were irreducibly public criteria; second, that his emotional and intellectual experience of the world was enhanced by his submission to the persuasive restraints of social education. These principles informed the three main themes of the book: the critique of dualism; the analysis of rules; and the critique of the illusion of private experience in the philosophy of mind.

The critique of dualism derived its inspiration from Wittgenstein's doctrine that 'an "inner process" stands in need of outward criteria'.[16] An expectation, for instance, was 'embedded in [the] situation from which it arises';[17] and that conventional context imposed conceptual limits upon what could be expected. Wittgenstein thus rejected the dualism whereby the connection between the state of expectation and its object was understood to be contingent. It was logically impossible to expect just anything and in any context, as it was logically impossible to have a 'feeling of ardent love or hope for the space of one second'.[18] Wittgenstein's expressionist conclusions about expectation and love were true by implication of feeling, seeing, thinking and learning. They were true also of willing and intention. The illusion that willing was 'an inner process', Wittgenstein concluded, arose from the mistake of construing 'willing as an immediate non-causal bringing-about';[19] whereas the truth was that 'willing, if it is not to be a sort of wishing, must be the action itself'[20] and that the knowledge of our intentions was not a matter of inference from the observation of our actions, in the sense that 'I do *not* say: "See, my arm is going up!" when I raise it'.[21] In contrast to his conclusions in the *Tractatus*, Wittgenstein was saying that the knowledge of our own intentions was a form of practical knowledge which lacked grounds.

Where rules were concerned, Wittgenstein concluded that the practice of subscribing to a rule was an intelligent act which both presupposed the rational autonomy of the agent and had to be understood in terms of his reasons for acting. Thus the imparting of a rule or formula was significantly different from the issuing of commands to perform particular actions, in the sense that it was a criterion of the pupil's mastery of a rule or formula that he could proceed to 'write it down independently'.[22] The implication was that all rules required interpretation, that none carried the conditions for its application on its face, and that the knowledge involved in their interpretation and application was a form of practical knowledge: 'The word "knows" is evidently closely related to that of "can", "is able to"; but also . . . to that of "understands"'.[23] Moreover, successful tuition in the application of a rule depended upon a qualitative transformation in the pupil's *'way of looking at things'*.[24] However, the criteria for deciding whether the pupil had mastered a rule were public criteria, in the sense that if he was never 'justified by success'[25] in his application of the rule it would be legitimately concluded that the 'pupil's capacity to learn [had] come to an end'.[26] Thus, although rules required subjective interpretation, the necessary measure of uniformity in their objective application was secured by the restraints of the social customs and institutions which any system of rules presupposed: '[A] person goes by a sign-post only in so far as there exists a regular use of sign-posts, a custom'.[27] And what ensured the stability of the social conventions supplementing a system of rules was the consensual agreement in thought, action and language which provided the ultimate foundation of the forms of social life, the 'agreement not only in definitions but also . . . in judgements'.[28] Ultimately, the justification for any particular interpretation of a rule had to connect with a 'way of acting' to the minimal extent that it be consonant with its social context: 'If I have exhausted the justifications I have reached bedrock, and my spade is turned. Then I am inclined to say: "This is simply what I do"'.[29]

The treatment of rules was an aspect of Wittgenstein's continuous argument in *Philosophical Investigations* against the possibility of a purely private language. It was, for instance, an illusion to suppose that 'obeying a rule' was 'something that it was possible for only *one* man to do, and to do only *once* in his life'.[30] The notion of a private language was defective, firstly, because it assumed the Cartesian principle that the connection between internal experiences like sensations and their expression in speech and conduct was contingent; whereas the connection was, Wittgenstein asserted, intrinsic. Thus it was a necessary truth, and not a contingent fact, that it remained impossible to attribute 'pain *only* to inanimate things';[31] 'look at a stone and imagine it having sensations';[32] or 'doubt someone else's fear or pain'.[33] The notion was defective, secondly, because it remained doubtful whether an exclusively private language was even an intelligible language. A private language embodied no criteria for deciding whether it was used correctly, or whether its user understood it: 'Whatever is going to seem right to me is right. And that only means that here we can't talk about "right" '.³⁴ And in the absence of any criteria for identifying a minimal consistency in its use, a private language remained a language which communicated nothing and influenced no one: 'A wheel that can be turned though nothing else moves with it, is not part of the mechanism'.³⁵

Wittgenstein's arguments about private experience implied that the traditional empiricism reflected in the *Tractatus* was defective in failing to yield an intelligible account of experience as such. In that sense they established the Kantian principle that human self-knowledge presupposed the subject's participation in a public world governed by objective concepts. As surely as Kant, Wittgenstein was implying that the necessary unity of consciousness, which functioned in *The Critique of Pure Reason* as the foundational principle of all objective knowledge, was the ungrounded precondition of experience rather than an inferential conclusion from subjective introspection: 'When I say "I am in pain", I do not point to a person who is in pain, since in a certain sense I have no idea *who* he is'.³⁶

Nowhere was the Kantian character of Wittgenstein's later philosophy more manifest than in the fragmentary remarks on ethics, aesthetics and religion: *Lectures and Conversations on Aesthetics, Psychology and Religious Belief*.³⁷ Wittgenstein's conclusions about the rationality of aesthetic experience were, for instance, entirely harmonious with the conclusions of Kant's *Critique of Judgement*. They also represented a retraction of the subjectivist conclusions about aesthetic judgements provided in the *Tractatus*. Thus Wittgenstein rejected the subjectivist implications of the analysis of aesthetic judgements as primitive interjections expressing arbitrary preferences. Not only were such expressions not central to aesthetic discourse; more strongly, aesthetic judgements were of 'the nature of further descriptions' of their object. Moreover, these descriptions were objective in the Kantian sense that divergent judgements in aesthetics were instances of genuine 'contradiction', to be settled in terms of reasoning about their object, rather than irreconcilable assertions of unargued preference. In this respect, Wittgenstein was affirming that aesthetic reflection was fully cognitive. That meant that aesthetic judgements were about 'ends' rather than 'means', in the sense that they were concerned with values which were reducible to neither the subjective state of the judger nor an hypothesis about the likelihood of the art-object stimulating such a state in others. It meant, secondly, that aesthetic experience had an autonomy which excluded the possibility of a science of aesthetics based upon the methods appropriate to experimental psychology. Not only were explanations in aesthetics distinct from the causal explanations appropriate to science; but the experience of, say, aesthetic discomfort and the discovery of its cause were not separable in aesthetic reflection, and the connection between them was to be explicated in terms of reasoning about the aesthetic object: 'There is a "why" to aesthetic discomfort not a cause to it. The expression of discomfort takes the form of a criticism and not "my mind is not at rest" or something'.[38]

Wittgenstein's antipathy towards the scientific understanding of human conduct informed his conclusions about the ultimate incoherence of the deterministic implications of both the doctrine of the unconscious and the procedure of free association essential to Freudian psychoanalysis. In fact, Freud was less a scientist engaged in establishing scientific hypotheses than an adept at 'speculation'; and his dream language was less 'a scientific explanation of the ancient myth ... [than] a new myth'.[39] What this meant was that the scientific status of psychoanalysis depended upon its persuasiveness, and that the validity of a psychoanalytical explanation derived from its therapeutic success. On the one hand, the successful interpretation of a dream hinged upon the recovery of what was unconscious in the conscious reflection of the patient, '[the] dreamer redreaming his dream in surroundings such that its aspect changes'.[40] On the other, the validity of the analyst's interpretation depended entirely upon his persuading the patient to accept it as a convincing explanation of his past. To that extent, Wittgenstein's critique of psychoanalysis upheld Kant's principle of the necessary unity of consciousness against the encroachment of the physical sciences.

To that extent also, Wittgenstein was implying that psychoanalysis had the authority of a modern religion rather than the status of an inductive science. In fact, Wittgenstein defended the rationality of religion in the same Kantian terms as he defended psychoanalysis. He insulated religion from the threat to it posed by the inductive sciences, in the sense that the agent's religious faith was an 'unshakable belief' manifested 'not by reasoning or by appeal to ordinary grounds for belief, but rather by regulating for all in his life'.[41] And he insulated it from the attacks of history, on the grounds that religious faith did not rest on 'an historic basis in the sense that the ordinary belief in historic facts could serve as a foundation'.[42] The defensive stance which Wittgenstein adopted towards religion did not depart from one Kantian assumption of the *Tractatus*: that religious belief was a practical attitude which yielded no access to the transcendent reality postulated by dogmatic theology. It departed from the *Tractatus* in implying that religious faith and practice had an objective foundation provided by the traditional continuities of the forms of social life in which it was enacted. This departure saved religious faith from the arbitrary subjectivism with which it had been associated in the *Tractatus*. It did not, however, alter the extent of the later Wittgenstein's decisive implication in the secularising tendencies of Kantian metaphysics.

iii

The remarks on aesthetics and religion did not lead to any systematic pronouncements upon art and morality. The notes comprising Wittgenstein's discussion of doubt and certainty – *On Certainty*[43] – were of more account. With the exception of *Philosophical Investigations* they represented Wittgenstein's most sustained critique of the assumptions of Cartesian rationalism.

Like *Philosophical Investigations*, *On Certainty* was an exercise in the analysis of ordinary language. Thus Wittgenstein attacked the principle of first-personal certainty implicit in Descartes's doctrine of the *cogito* by insisting that the grammatical formulation of the principle – the first-person indicative sentence 'I know that p' – had a specific role to play in a language game, and that its role was determined by its containing linguistic context. The book also attacked the entire Cartesian programme of reconstituting certain knowledge upon the foundations of systematic doubt. Doubting was, Wittgenstein emphasised, a quite specific intellectual procedure which invariably presupposed the certainty of a number of beliefs not themselves subject to rational doubt: 'If you tried to doubt everything you would not get so far as doubting anything. The game of doubting presupposes certainty'.[44] Moreover, the procedures of serious doubting depended upon the mastery of certain public conventions: 'When a child learns a language it learns at the same time what is to be investigated and what not'.[45] And in the total absence of his conformity to those conventions, the child's persistent doubting would be a sign merely that 'he was incapable of learning certain doubting language games'.[46]

What Wittgenstein was challenging in *On Certainty* was the Cartesian distinction between belief and knowledge underpinning the separation of ethics from science imposed by the *Tractatus*. In this respect, the book provided the basis for a defence of the rationality of religion on the Kantian grounds suggested in the *Lectures and Conversations*. It also diminished the rational authority of science by implying that the unquestioning trust underlying scientific enquiry was no different from the unquestioning faith underlying religious practice: 'It belongs to the logic of our scientific investigations that certain things are indeed not doubted'.[47] In both regards the book implied that there was no unconditional Cartesian point of departure in the construction of human knowledge from which all the practical assumptions constituting human belief could be expunged. On the contrary, it insisted that there were some beliefs about the world which were irreducibly certain, and which together formed a 'kind of mythology'[48] in the sense of constituting 'our frame of reference'.[49] Moreover, inasmuch as those beliefs formed the foundation upon which all intellectual enquiry was based, they were not, Wittgenstein concluded, capable of validation by the methodological procedures of inductive reasoning prescribed in the *Tractatus*: 'But I did not get my picture of the world by satisfying myself of its correctness. . . . No: it is the inherited background against which I distinguish between true and false'.[50] On the one hand, their status as certain beliefs derived from the actively constructive attitude of 'unshakable conviction' held by the believer. Thus, it was the criterion of Moore's belief that the existence of the earth predated his own birth being a 'fundamental attitude' that no further evidential reasons could be advanced in its support in the face of contradiction.[51] On the other hand, they constituted the ideological consensus of communal belief impregnating the otherwise 'ungrounded way of acting' which sustained the social forms of life.[52] In fact, so far from treating the satisfaction of personal doubt as the precondition of rational participation in forms of life, Wittgenstein concluded that forms of life rested upon nothing more rationally demonstrable than an arbitrary and unquestioning 'trust': '[A] language game is possible only if one trusts something (I did not say "can trust something")'.[53]

Wittgenstein's conclusions in *On Certainty* were Kantian conclusions in two important respects. In his discussion of the fundamental attitudes underlying certain beliefs, Wittgenstein was concerned with precisely those structural conditions inherent in the active construction of experience which Kant explored in *The Critique of Pure Reason*. Moreover, the fact that the propositions expressing certain beliefs had no *transcendent* objects was in strict conformity to the transcendental requirements of Kantian metaphysics. Wittgenstein diverged from Kant, however, in two crucial regards. Firstly, he avoided the analytical idiom adopted by Kant and, in consequence, imposed no formal limits upon the cultural and historical diversity of the structural conditions constituting experience. Secondly, he implied that the conditions were not merely formal principles of the understanding, but public concepts validated ultimately by the authoritative continuities of social practice. As surely as Hegel, Wittgenstein was asserting that the concepts of the understanding were not objectively given in the Kantian sense; but that they were the product of the human mind as it objectified itself in the social practices which constituted the historical world. Indeed, it was the emphasis upon the priority of public convention to individual experience, and the concomitant priority of practical experience to the theoretical understanding, that represented Wittgenstein's profoundest departure from the formalism of Kant in the direction of the historicism of Hegel.

iv

This book assumes that Casey and Scruton were largely justified in drawing out the affinities between Hegel and Wittgenstein which this chapter has suggested. It assumes further that the connections which they established were crucial in the development of their conservative doctrine. And it assumes lastly that these connections provide a context for certain of the concerns of Oakeshott and Mrs Letwin. The Wittgensteinian procedures which Casey adopted in *The Language of Criticism*, his first book, were intimately related to the cultural Hegelianism he propounded as editor of *The Cambridge Review* in the late seventies. Scruton's admirable history of philosophy, *From Descartes to Wittgenstein*, demonstrated the relation between Kant, Hegel and Wittgenstein, and suggested that a philosophical conservatism would have to be defined in opposition to Cartesian assumptions in the philosophy of mind. And both Casey and Scruton mobilised philosophical arguments derived from Wittgenstein in the rejection of the deterministic and materialistic presuppositions of classical marxism. The critique of liberal rationalism which Oakeshott developed in the forties and fifties was as persuasive an attack upon the epistemological, moral, cultural and political implications of Cartesian principles in the philosophy of mind and action as that of Wittgenstein's post-*Tractatus* thought. And the historicist conclusions which Mrs Letwin associated with the philosophy of Hume confirmed the principal conclusion of Wittgenstein's later philosophy: that the traditional continuities of social practice embodied an ordering of human experience which was ungrounded in any nonhuman foundation like the God of traditional Christian metaphysics or the nature of Aristotelian biology.

There were, of course, significant discontinuities between Hegel and Wittgenstein. Wittgenstein neither adopted the dialectical procedure essential to Hegel's logic nor assumed the historical teleology which Hegel's dialectical method established. Nor did Wittgenstein attribute to philosophy the status of Absolute Spirit which Hegel conferred upon it in *The Phenomenology of Mind*. In fact, so far from seeking to transcend the contradictions inherent in everyday experience by appeal to the critical synthesis provided by *reason*, Wittgenstein's method of ordinary language analysis was confined to the clarification of the ordinary concepts which, for Hegel, constituted merely empirical *understanding*.

Nevertheless, the continuities were impressive. The conservative implications of Wittgenstein's later philosophy provided arguments for the rejection not only of the abstract rationalism deriving from Descartes, but also of the ascendancy of liberal and utilitarian assumptions concerning the authority and justification of customary and institutional practices. The implications were *anti-liberal*, because Wittgenstein affirmed that cultural and moral values were inevitably embodied in the public forms of social life, and that they were, in consequence, legitimately imposed by social training and education. And they were *anti-utilitarian*, because Wittgenstein affirmed that the institutional and customary continuities constituting a form of life were justified ultimately by no end or ground external to themselves. In both respects, Wittgenstein provided a substantial basis in analytical philosophy for the politically authoritarian conclusions which Casey and Scruton derived from Hegel.

Throughout his later philosophy, and particularly in relation to rules, aesthetics, religion and psychoanalysis, Wittgenstein upheld the foundational Kantian principle of the autonomy of reason. However, the later Wittgenstein tended to imply that the rational autonomy which Kant treated in formal terms was realised only in virtue of the individual agent's participation in the public world of social practice. To that extent, Wittgenstein was implying that the forms of life belonged to the sphere of *objective freedom* in the fullest Hegelian sense. Indeed, Wittgenstein's assertion of the priority of forms of life to all individual experience paralleled the claims which Hegel made in the *Philosophy of Right* on behalf of the sphere of *Sittlichkeit*, the sphere of customary morality and institutional ethics. Just as Hegel concluded that *Sittlichkeit*, rather than empirical self-awareness or passive Cartesian self-knowledge, formed the minimum self-sufficient reality; so Wittgenstein concluded that all human experience was dependent upon incorporation within a containing form of social life and identification by the public criteria which it embodied. In this respect, Wittgenstein provided an analytical sanction for the rejection of the Kantian dualism which Casey and Scruton, following Hegel, associated with liberalism.

It is questionable whether the explanatory power of the continuities between Hegel and Wittgenstein actually warranted the polemically conservative cultural and political conclusions which Casey and Scruton derived from them. In turning to Casey and Scruton it is important to insist that their conservative preferences were at their most problematic in violating the historicist principles which they associated with Hegel and the later Wittgenstein. That was true of Casey, who defended ethical naturalism in Aristotelian and Thomist terms, in tacit defiance of the Hegelian conclusion as to the *conventionalist* status of all law and morality which Wittgenstein's post-*Tractatus* thought tended to endorse. And it was true of Scruton, whose doctrine culminated in a strident assertion of Oakeshottian liberalism which made universalist claims on behalf of an historically determinate constitutional tradition, in open departure from Wittgenstein's emphasis upon the irreducible plurality of forms of life.

2 Two Wittgensteinians: John Casey

John Casey is a lecturer in the English Faculty in Cambridge. As an undergraduate he read a non-philosophical subject – English – and drifted into philosophy in research because he became aware of the theoretical limitations of that subject. He stands therefore at a remove from the tradition of analytical philosophy which has provided the dominant idiom of contemporary professional philosophy. In consequence he has written in the recognition that philosophical reflection cannot be a narrowly professional exercise, but that it involves taking up connected positions upon an extensive range of social, moral, cultural and political issues. That recognition was manifest in the higher journalism Casey practised as editor of *The Cambridge Review* between 1975 and 1979, and in the broad version of the history of ideas which he has adopted in the teaching of *The English Moralists* and *The History and Theory of Criticism* papers in the Cambridge English Tripos. If he has an analogue in mainstream philosophy, it is arguably Stuart Hampshire, although Hampshire, unlike Casey, has retained firm liberal convictions in politics whilst questioning all those empiricist assumptions in ethics, metaphysics and the philosophy of mind with which such convictions are associated.

Casey is primarily an aesthetician who has progressed from a sophisticated philosophical Leavisism to a fully articulate brand of Hegelian expressionism. In relation to politics and, in certain senses, to ethics also Casey has succumbed to the Hegelian influence. Nevertheless, he has achieved nothing approaching Hegel's transparency about the legitimate claims which philosophy is entitled to make on its own behalf and has remained unconcerned to map out the different idioms of human self-knowledge in terms of a hierarchy of either a dialectical or an historical character. The doctrinal apex of his thought is probably an Hegelianised version of Arnold's doctrine about 'poetry', 'criticism' and 'general culture' and Leavis's doctrine about language and 'practical criticism'. This was not, however, the apex of Hegel's system and Casey does not always write as though he understood that that was so. Indeed, inasmuch as Casey's Arnoldianism has elevated the claims of poetry over those of philosophy, science and religion, it has aligned him with a tradition of romantic liberalism that would have been problematic for his conservatism had his historical grasp been surer.

Casey is also an ethicist for whom, despite some substantial deposits of Thomism, a problematic aesthetic preference for Nietzsche and an idiosyncratic admiration for Hume, the Aristotle of *The Nicomachean Ethics* has provided doctrinal foundation. Casey has sought to defend the Aristotelian scheme of the virtues and vices against the Kantian insistence upon the autonomy of ethics from nature on the one hand and the claim of utilitarianism that they are but contingently connected with the human good on the other. However, it has never been clear whether Casey has chosen between Hegelian historicism and Aristotelian naturalism or whether he regards them as representing mutually exclusive alternatives. This indecision has left it ambiguous whether Casey believes that in the promulgation of a coherent political philosophy capable of expressing his conservative intuitions, the challenge posed by liberal utilitarianism should be resisted in terms of an appeal to Hegelian objective spirit or in terms of an assertion of the natural law enunciated by Aristotle and Aquinas.

i

Casey effected the transition from English to philosophy via his doctoral thesis: *The Language of Criticism*[1]. *The Language of Criticism* was a vindication of the rationality of practical criticism in particular and of the procedures adopted in the Cambridge English faculty in general which established that each had defensible philosophical presuppositions. The vindication turned upon a denial of the claim that the rationality of critical procedure depended upon its appropriation of a scientifically coherent methodology. Casey criticised those aestheticians like

Northrop Frye who invoked schematic paradigms of literary form in order to develop a science of criticism. In this regard Casey was establishing that science had no monopoly upon rationality and that, if the matter were examined closely, scientific argument itself had much in common with the reasoning appropriate to aesthetics. The book argued further that whilst the element of personal 'response' had to be accorded its priority in the experience of literature, that priority entailed neither a retreat into 'subjectivism' nor the immunity of critical reasoning from the canons of rational argument.

As the title of the first chapter, 'Wittgenstein and the Philosophy of Criticism', indicated, the methodology of the book was an application of the procedures and doctrines of Wittgenstein's *Philosophical Investigations*. To this extent, the book reflected Casey's dissatisfaction with the identification of rational discourse with the natural scientific idiom which Wittgenstein had prescribed in the *Tractatus*. In rejecting the 'descriptive' paradigm of language, Casey was seeking both to remove aesthetics from the realm of the 'mystical' to which Wittgenstein had consigned it and to establish the precise character of its rationality in a spirit unavailable to the traditional empiricism of which the *Tractatus* was the culmination.

Casey made much of Wittgenstein's discussion of the practice of rule-following. No explanation of the practices of following a rule, series or formula could be adequately undertaken in causal terms. Although rules had necessarily to be interpreted by those who subscribed to them, and so required the indispensable element of intelligent self-ascription if they were to be followed, rule-following was a *public* practice and unavoidably subject to the restraints of public conventions. In its application to aesthetics, Wittgenstein's discussion provided justification for Casey's claim that there was an 'internal' relation between works of art and our response to them. Not only had that response to be explicated in terms of reasons rather than causes, but it was more or less appropriate in terms of its conformity to the public conventions embodied in a tradition of criticism.

In insisting that the aesthetic response was not a logically private state of the subject, Casey took up the main thrust of Wittgenstein's anti-dualist conclusions about the publicity of mental states. An intention could be recognised only in terms of its having been embedded in a complex of institutions and customs, and such experiences as 'having an expectation' were internally related to their appropriate circumstances. The point was that these states of mind could not be understood as private processes contingently attached to outward circumstances. The circumstances, appropriate or otherwise, provided fully public criteria for the attribution of such states of mind to the subject.

The Language of Criticism brought out the importance of Wittgenstein's post-*Tractatus* perception of the plurality of the different language-games together with its implication that the knowledge involved in the passage from one language-game to another was neither deductive nor inductive. Casey made full use of what Wittgenstein had concluded in the *Lectures and Conversations on Aesthetics, Psychology and Religious Belief* about the logic of psychoanalysis and aesthetics. The treatment of psychoanalysis represented a bridging of the gap between knowledge and ethics of which aesthetics was a branch. The knowledge in aesthetic appreciation rested not upon a set of arbitrary and irrational decisions but upon something approaching a fully 'cognitive' grasp of its object, a grasp objective to the extent that it was subject to adjustment in the light of education and rational persuasion. And it meant that there were public criteria for the identification of an 'appropriate response' towards works of art which could, in turn, give rise to the identification of genuine aesthetic grasp.

In the *Tractatus* Wittgenstein had recognised that ethics and aesthetics were ultimately both aspects of the central problem concerning the logic of judgements of value. Since *The Language of Criticism* marked a departure from the ideology of that work it was natural that Casey should find close parallels between the status of aesthetic judgements on the one hand and the status of moral judgements on the other. Hence the starting-point of the second chapter, 'Values', was the central distinction in Hume's ethics between facts and values. Discussing the distinction in Wittgensteinian terms, Casey questioned whether the Humean 'sentiment of approval' could legitimately be said to name an inner process to which the ethical proposition corresponded. And he considered the prescriptivism which R. M. Hare had propounded in *The Language of Morals* and *Freedom and Reason* and the naturalism which Philippa Foot had revived in the articles 'Goodness and Choice', 'Moral Beliefs' and 'Moral Arguments' in the light of Wittgenstein's location of human knowledge somewhere between the inductive and deductive ranges. Casey objected to Hare on the grounds that prescriptivism imported an abstract conception of decision into the moral life, that it derived the moral law and the human good from an unconditional exercise of free choice on the part of the agent which was deprived of all *moral* significance, and that, in consequence, it made it impossible to discuss the substantive ends of the moral life once certain formal – and highly Kantian – conditions had been fulfilled. By contrast, Casey agreed with Philippa Foot that there was little sense in which the human good could be chosen at will – it remained 'logically impossible to count certain things as beneficial in the sense that we would have to alter our concept of man in order to do so'.[2] Nevertheless, he insisted that such changes could take place and that it was the error of naturalism to imply that historical changes in morality were impossible. Taking up the Wittgensteinian leads developed in the first chapter, Casey demonstrated that there was an important sense in which ethics was concerned with making judgements about intrinsic values which needed no justification in terms of their relation to extrinsic properties. This truth he took as sufficient evidence to defeat Hare, whose ethics based such justification on the extrinsic property of the agent's choice. And it enabled Casey to attack consequentialist theories of moral reasoning on the ground that consequences too were subject to moral judgements about their intrinsic value.

What the chapter established was that moral reasoning was equipped to discuss human ends in a way that avoided retreat into the Humean subjectivism whereby judgements of value were only contingently connected with their objects. What the chapter left unclear was whether Casey intended to resist the threat posed by Humean subjectivism by recourse to Kantianism or naturalism. The negativity towards Hare suggested a corresponding negativity towards both Kant and those post-Kantian ethicists like Sartre, about whose closeness to Hare Casey was explicit, in virtue of their emphasis upon the autonomy of ethics and their subversion of all naturalistic foundations for human morality. Yet the utilisation of Wittgenstein and the modification of Mrs Foot's naturalism implicated Casey in a cultural Kantianism radically antagonistic towards ethical naturalism given its tendency to ground values upon human 'convention' rather than 'nature'. This tension between ethical naturalism and post-Kantian assumptions about the autonomy of the human from the natural world has remained a permanent feature of Casey's doctrine.

The aesthetic assumptions of *The Language of Criticism* were romantic and expressionist. The majority of the aestheticians discussed – Arnold, Leavis, Richards, Middleton Murry, Northrop Frye and Yvor Winters – provided a core of doctrine for those who adopted the procedures of practical criticism within the Cambridge English Tripos. If the book had a polemical implication it was that those procedures inherited the aesthetic assumptions of romantic expressionism. These assumptions were manifest in Casey's analysis of particular aestheticians. The Arnold of *The Study of Poetry* was important because in adopting an expressionist aesthetics which admitted of no ultimate separation between the quality of literary expression and the quality of the thought or feeling expressed, he established a relationship between morality and art which avoided a hollow aestheticism on the one hand and the fallacious didacticism that the mimetic tradition represented by Dryden, Addison and Johnson had imported into aesthetics on the other. And the assumptions informed Casey's defence of Leavis, whose account of the concept of 'sincerity' in the essay 'Thought and Emotional Quality' was treated as establishing an intimate connection between thought and expression that represented a triumph of both the moral and artistic imagination.

Although a book on aesthetics, *The Language of Criticism* had several conservative implications. It implied that empiricism in aesthetics went with utilitarianism in ethics and politics in reducing values to the status of means. In vindicating the central place which the experience of art occupied in human life, the book implied that comparable vindications could be undertaken on behalf of ethics and religion. Moreover the book was conservative in a deeply Wittgensteinian sense. Casey took the Wittgensteinian concepts of 'forms of life' and 'language game' as supporting the claim that anything of value in human knowledge – whether ethical, cultural, political or religious – had its life only in the context of the public world of institutions and language and that, accordingly, human knowledge was always subject to the restraints of education.

Although Kant was scarcely mentioned directly, the enterprise of *The Language of Criticism* was highly Kantian in spirit. Casey's attempt to locate the rationality of aesthetic experience between the scientific and the arbitrarily subjective confirmed Kant's conclusion in *The Dialectic of Aesthetic Judgement* of *The Critique of Judgement* that whilst aesthetic judgements were not susceptible to proof in the manner of scientific judgements they were nonetheless rational in a way that judgements of mere taste were not. Moreover, Casey's examination of the logic of aesthetic judgements corresponded to what Kant had claimed about their logic in the Third Critique as a whole: that aesthetics can be freed from science only if it can be shown that our judgements about the beautiful cannot be determined by the means of concepts of the understanding; that aesthetics can issue in judgements which, while not supported by objective and universal principles, nevertheless lay claim to objective status in possessing the element of 'subjective universal necessity' with which the assent of all rational beings is demanded; that the terms of aesthetic appreciation, such as the predicate 'beauty', must be regarded as genuine properties of their object even though they cannot be justified by reference to that object considered in its material aspect; and that the 'autonomy' of the aesthetic attitude, the Kantian counterpart to Casey's personal 'response', is the condition of all aesthetic judgement.

Casey's project was Kantian in two respects which combined logical preoccupations with cultural doctrine in more obvious senses. It was anti-utilitarian in its conclusion that works of art had to be regarded as 'ends' and not as 'means' to the satisfaction of private taste or pleasure. Secondly, it was anti-empiricist in the fullest Kantian sense: aesthetic judgements had to be understood in terms of reasons and not causes, and were judgements about their object rather than reports as to the state of the judger in some mysteriously contingent way attached to their object.

In the respects that aesthetic explanation was concerned with reasons and not causes, that it was concerned with its object as an 'end' and that the aesthetic character of that object was distinguishable from its material character, Casey's book was establishing important parallelisms between Wittgenstein and Kant. In this connection it had the general implication that Wittgenstein's doctrine could be harnessed to the tradition of

German idealism and that, taken together, idealism and Wittgensteinianism could furnish the foundations of a philosophical conservatism.

The concept of sincerity which Casey had explored in relation to Arnold and Leavis in *The Language of Criticism* was subjected to a fuller investigation touching upon its moral and aesthetic implications in a subsequent essay: 'The Autonomy of Art'.[3] The essay attacked the disjunction between 'sincerity' as a concept in art and 'sincerity' as a concept in life upon which Croce had insisted in his *Aesthetic*. Croce's disjunction was defective because the use of such terms as 'sincere' and 'sad' in aesthetics had to be brought into relation with the 'sincerity' and 'sadness' of human beings. Casey insisted upon the priority of the concept of expression for the understanding of emotion in life in terms recalling the later Wittgenstein and, derivatively, for the understanding of works of art: there was no understanding works of art without a simultaneous grasp of their expressive properties. And he argued that the central criterion for the understanding of what a man is feeling was 'the description under which he sees his situation'. The fullest implications of that criterion could be grasped only when it was understood that artistic expression enabled men to comprehend their feelings in an increasingly mature form by providing them with a more vivid means of self-expression. Works of art thus offered themselves as objects of human knowledge and Casey concluded the essay by stating that their proper understanding by human beings represented both a moral and cognitive achievement: not only did works of art 'clarify a feeling, while at the same time leaving it as in some sense the same feeling that it was before it was clarified or articulated', but works of art themselves represented a 'form of knowledge, but knowledge of something other than facts'.[4]

The essay reflected the anti-Cartesian thrust of *The Language of Criticism*. It insisted upon the necessary relationship between the possession of thoughts and feelings and the capacity to express them in public forms, a relationship intimate in relation to art and logical in relation to linguistic and behavioural expression. Nevertheless the essay marked a departure from the philosophical strategy of the earlier book. The intricacies of Wittgensteinian logic were gone and with them the preoccupation with the Kantian enterprise of justifying the rationality of aesthetic judgement. In their place was a recognition that the aesthetic presuppositions of Casey's position were expressionist and an acknowledgement that the philosophical tradition upon which such an aesthetic would draw would not be Wittgensteinian but idealist. Hence the most significant feature of the essay was the general cultural and historical claims which Casey made on behalf of idealism. The idealist tradition had made 'the notion of Culture . . . a central concept', had the advantage of an 'historical rather than individualist' approach and had developed an aesthetics which treated 'the modes of expression of a particular period as creating, in a real sense, the possibilities of feeling'.[5] Although the essay made much of the parallels between aesthetic experience and the kinds of 'practical' knowledge involved in such experiences as 'forming intentions', 'making decisions' and 'recognising aspects', it made no mention of Hegel and did not insist upon what Hegel had insisted: the supremacy of art as a medium of self-knowledge subordinate only to religion and philosophy.

The omission was duly rectified in the subsequent review of Knox's translation of Hegel's *Aesthetics*: 'Beauty, Truth and Necessity'.[6] Hegel was favoured because he provided a systematic philosophy of mind capable of according a central role to the experience of art in human experience whereas British empiricism had not. And, more importantly, he was favoured because, while sharing Kant's emphasis upon the contemplative character of aesthetic experience and its autonomy from practical desire, Hegel asserted, whereas Kant had not, a fully *cognitive* theory of that experience.

Casey made it clear that he did not accept the Hegelian metaphysic in its entirety and that it was not necessary to adopt the Hegelian idiom without qualification. What he claimed was that Hegel's leading ideas – his theory of the imagination together with his insistence that aesthetic experience was unique to rational beings in being an 'inevitable fact of their humanity' – possessed both a philosophical validity and a striking modernity when translated into a philosophical idiom distinct from Hegel's own. Hence Hegel's theory of the inseparability of the active imagination from the construction of human knowledge was defended in the light of Wittgenstein's doctrine of 'aspect perception'; and his thesis that aesthetic experience was unique to rational beings was defended on the ground that the criterion of the capacity for the contemplative reflection essential to that experience was the possession of the very linguistic capacity upon which Wittgenstein had insisted throughout *Philosophical Investigations*.

There was a clear sense, then, in which Casey was making Hegel available to a wider philosophical public. He was demonstrating the relationship between Hegelian idealism and Wittgensteinianism on the one hand and the connection between art and morality established by Arnold and Leavis on the other. More directly, Casey was implying that Hegelianism could assist in the unravelling of systematic connections. Self-knowledge was more complicated than Cartesian dualism allowed and its most adequate realisation would have to refer ultimately to the entire system of metaphysics which Hegel had adumbrated: religion, art, history, politics and philosophy.

Although a member of an English Faculty, Casey has produced no literary scholarship, and his contribution to literary criticism has been negligible. It was inevitable that the exception to this rule should have been a *Chatterton Lecture* devoted to the work of Eliot: 'T. S. Eliot: Language, Sincerity and the Self'.[7] It was inevitable not just because Eliot had idealist sympathies and propounded a cultural conservatism, but rather because his verse enacted Casey's philosophical preoccupations in respects epistemological, moral and political. This was true particularly of *Prufrock* which Casey read as the poetic intimation of an entire philosophical tradition. In that Prufrock was passive in relation to the sensations which overwhelmed him, he was the poetic embodiment of the philosophical subject of Hume's empiricism, inherently incapable of referring those sensations to himself at all. In that he was unable to organise his experience in such a way that it could possess meaning for him, he lacked exactly that unifying property of self-consciousness upon which Kant had insisted. In that he was merely acted upon he lacked a sense of himself and was in turn – a good Hegelian perception – unable to define himself in relation to others. And his failure to attribute significance to his experience was somehow connected with his failure to possess a language – a good Wittgensteinian principle. Casey's exposition of the subsequent poems in Eliot's canon need not detain us. What needs to be stressed is Casey's recognition of Eliot's achievement as explicable only in terms of a containing philosophical tradition uniting idealism with Wittgensteinianism.

ii

Casey has had an overall conservative doctrine. It was expressed as a dissenting and polemical doctrine during his editorship of *The Cambridge Review*[8] in four contexts: education; Roman Catholicism; national politics; intellectual and cultural affairs.

About education, there was some polemic against the prevailing consensus. In 'Half Measures'[9] Casey protested at the egalitarianism and social engineering implicit in conventional educational policy, offering the Swiftian analysis that the ideal of equality of opportunity entailed the dismemberment of the family itself. And in 'Mr Callaghan's Standards'[10] he condemned the socialist consensus in education for its betrayal of concrete educational standards. Ultimately, however, what Casey's treatment of education reflected was a doctrine about the *university* understood as an *institution*. In 'The Tyranny of Fashion',[11] Casey upheld the intrinsic value of the single-sex college, exposing the arbitrariness of the consensual assumption that co-educational principles stood in some necessary relation to the canons of 'social justice'. In 'College Stipends: Malign Neglect',[12] he protested at the erosion in value of college stipends. And in 'Fees',[13] he defended the system of collegiate supervision, challenging the right of central government to determine on political grounds the educational policy of the university through its control of funding.

The uniting principle of these articles was a clear sense that the university was a corporation, and that any threat to its corporate autonomy – of whatever political character – had to be resisted. Casey emphasised that corporate autonomy could not exist in a vacuum. It could be preserved only if financial and constitutional autonomy were secured in turn. What was wrong with the ideal of equality of opportunity was that it involved an assessment of the university in purely instrumental terms which undermined its autonomy. Casey's doctrine of the corporate autonomy of the university rested upon Hegelian foundations in three important respects. First, it implied that institutions embodied public ends and values, and thus possessed an authority transcending the private interests of their individual members. Second, it emphasised that the 'justice' of academic institutions was inherent in their constitution. Third, it recognised that their autonomy would not be preserved unless they possessed the political power to preserve it: there was no escaping the conclusion that since the university had a role to play in the exercise of power it mattered a great deal what kind of education it offered its members.

The principle that institutions possessed an internal validation was central to Casey's discussion of Roman Catholicism. There was little doubt that his catholicism was conservative both doctrinally and politically. In 'Catholics'[14] and 'The Archbishop and Vatican Power'[15] he bitterly attacked the suppression of the Tridentine Mass, condemning the New Rite as a 'liberal' consensus imposed upon the 'conservative' faithful from above. And in 'The New Pope',[16] written on the death of Paul VI, he registered his dissent from those who advocated the election of a 'third-world pope' whose 'office' would be 'essentially pastoral'. The full implications of Casey's conservatism were developed in his rejoinder to Norman St John Stevas's celebration of the pontificate of John Paul II: 'Papal Idolatry'.[17] Casey exposed the heresy inherent in Stevas's claim that a 'part' of Christ was embodied in the new Pope. On the contrary, the Pope's authority could not depend upon his possession of certain attractive human dispositions since '[when] the Pope has authority it is because of his "office" and nothing else'. He allowed that the Pope should exert political power but insisted that in exercising it he could claim no special authority in virtue of his authority over a Christian association. And Casey emphasised the corporate character of the spiritual authority which the Roman Church exercised over its members: 'There is no such thing as "moral authority" independent of a precise system of belief. The Pope can have authority only over those who recognise his authority and share his beliefs'. In a sense, the ecumenism and humanism which Stevas had attributed to John Paul represented for Casey a retreat into 'abstraction' in the full Hegelian implications of that term. The Catholic Church, Casey was saying, had to recognise that its identity depended upon the preservation of its public institutions and offices according to very precise constitutional principles.

In relation to national politics Casey was clear that the public presence of Enoch Powell was of central importance to the destruction of the liberal consensus. In 'Church and State'[18] Casey sided with Powell in his defence of the British constitution for its rejection of the 'concurrent authority' of the spiritual and secular, and expressed agreement with the Powellite intuition that 'ecumenism' in its erosion of the ecclesiastical polity coincided with 'Europeanism' in its erosion of the legal sovereignty of the British Parliament. As with his treatment of the Catholic Church, Casey was asserting that the relation between authority and obligation in Church and State depended upon precise principles which only an institutional framework could provide – and he was implying that Powell's precision – his philosophical and historical grasp of the British political tradition – was a function of that precision. In a subsequent editorial, 'High Church and Powell',[19] he examined Powell's stand on the racial question in the context of the amendment of the 1976 Act removing the requirement to prove 'mischievous intent' in cases of incitement to racial hatred. He mocked the complacency of the liberal consensus and affirmed that the racial issue was a genuinely political issue offering the same 'possibilities and limitations of rational discussion as do all other political issues', that the requirement to prove 'mischievous intent' was a safeguard of freedom of speech and that, whatever the intrinsic merits of Powell's position, it was a matter of political opinion which would be subjected to political censorship should that requirement be removed. What Casey was demanding was that the proposed amendment be understood in its properly illiberal character. In that respect the editorial was not without irony. An ironic strategy was persistent throughout Casey's editorship of *The Cambridge Review*. The irony enabled him to demonstrate in 'Humbug'[20] that the conservative moralist was better equipped than the liberal to justify legislation prohibiting child pornography, precisely because he rejected the legal fiction of 'consent' underpinning liberal theory in favour of absolute values like 'innocence'. The ironic strategy, designed to show the *arbitrariness* of liberal assumptions and the tyranny which they would exert if their exclusiveness was not made clear, reached its apotheosis in the controversial article 'Anti-Racialism'.[21]

The article argued that anti-racialism was a myth, that it was an ideology which did not reflect and often opposed 'the established practices and values of a community', and that it was a predominantly liberal myth which drew its theoretical inspiration from the liberal tradition culminating in the Nozickean conception of a 'minimal state' dissociated from language, community and history. It claimed that the myth did not reflect the actualities of the modern world since it ignored both the potency of nationalism in the contexts of Ireland, Israel and African decolonisation, and the fact that the post-feudal constitutions of modern Europe had tended towards nationalism in proportion as they had tended towards democratisation. More strongly it claimed that the liberal tradition was defective in its explanation of the citizen's attachment to the state itself since it ignored his patriotic allegiance to the 'continuity of institutions, shared experience, language, custom and kinship' which the state presupposed. What was pernicious about the anti-racialist consensus, Casey was saying, was that it had undermined such pieties and replaced them with a 'rootless individualism'.

Casey's defence of Powellism was not unproblematic. He certainly left it unacknowledged that Powell's Unionism was anti-nationalistic in its Irish, Welsh and Scottish contexts. And he did not consider that Powell's assertion of the national sovereignty of the United Kingdom in the contexts of immigration, defence and the Common Market represented a commitment to 'Little England' which conflicted with the brutal fact of post-war American ascendancy, and left ambiguous the role Britain was to assume within the international system in the nuclear age. The defence should most appropriately be understood as the establishment on Casey's part of powerful affinities between Powellism and Hegelianism. The affinities were everywhere apparent in a paper Casey delivered to The Conservative Philosophy Group in 1982, 'One Nation: The Politics of Race',[22] in which he left little doubt that Powell's insistence upon the connection between the racial and cultural identity of the nation and the legal sovereignty of the civil institutions through which the nation acquired statehood was harmonious with the Hegelian authoritarianism he had propounded in the essay 'Tradition and Authority'.

In relation to intellectual affairs Casey promoted an onslaught upon the loose thinking in morals and education propagated by Barthes, Laing and Castenada through the series 'Modern Charlatanism', written in collaboration with Roger Scruton. In 'The Pornographic Lobby',[23] for instance, he deplored the unquestioned status of the premises upon which the liberal debate on pornography had been conducted, exposing the partiality of the consequentialist presuppositions of that debate, implying the superiority of the account of moral reasoning derived from

Aristotle and Hegel which emphasised the priority of 'values' to 'rights', and establishing that in virtue of its degradation of the human consciousness and not merely in virtue of its harmful consequences the harm involved in pornography was *intrinsic*.

More impressive than the polemic was the obituary tribute to Leavis: 'F. R. Leavis'.[24] Leavis the exponent of practical criticism was placed squarely in the expressionist tradition of aesthetics. And Leavis the theorist was defended for having eliminated the Cartesian disjunction between 'the world of facts and the world of values' with a neo-Wittgensteinian doctrine about language. Above all, Leavis was the champion of literature understood as the fundamental manifestation of the 'collaborative' enterprise of civilisation itself. The endorsement of Leavisian humanism, with its familiar traces of Arnold, Hegel and Wittgenstein, summed up the presiding themes of the cultural conservatism enunciated by *The Cambridge Review* of those years: that human freedom required realisation in the public world; that the public world embodied the ends and values of artistic expression and institutional life towards which political indifference was impossible; and that the greatest sin of the liberal was to present his partial moral and political commitments as a form of enlightened neutrality.

However much political content was implied in the dissenting phase of *The Cambridge Review*, it could hardly be said that Casey had produced a systematic political philosophy. His most developed account of a conservative politics was the essay 'Tradition and Authority'[25] which appeared in the collection *Conservative Essays* edited by Maurice Cowling. 'Tradition and Authority' should be read as a modern restatement of Hegel's *Philosophy of Right*. Its starting-point was the antinomy between the rival Marxist and liberal accounts of the relationship between the institutional and traditional life on the one hand and individual freedom on the other. Casey expressed his agreement with those Marxists who claimed that 'rights' were intelligible only in terms of their concrete embodiment in the social and economic structure underlying the political arrangements of the state. Although he identified liberalism with the Lockean attempt to prescribe an ahistorical natural law, what Casey was resisting was utilitarianism, with its insistence that the authority of traditions and political institutions was always subject to critical analysis by the simple criterion of their propensity to realise the extrinsic end of private welfare. On the contrary, Casey claimed, traditions and institutions embodied the ends of life in the fullest Hegelian sense. Whatever canons of justice were applicable to them, those canons were internal to the traditions and institutions themselves and had to be insulated accordingly from the reductions implied in the unitary utilitarian criterion.

Although Casey explained allegiance to traditions and institutions in the Thomist terms of the virtue of *pietas*, his central point was that that allegiance was not a trivial matter of nostalgia or aesthetic preference. Allegiance had to be understood in the fully political terms which recognised both that traditions and institutions exercised coercive power and that, in consequence, the depoliticisation of their nature was implicated in liberal illusion. Protection from liberal illusion was what Marxism provided and Casey was in doubt as to its superiority over liberal theory. Marxism was nonetheless defective in its subjection of traditional and institutional life to a radical critique which divested it of 'right' and reduced to mere power the authority that it might otherwise claim. By adopting the concept of 'alienation', the Marxist could claim that institutions and traditions exerted a coercive power over their subjects going beyond their capacity for self-understanding. By contrast, it was the desire to establish that traditions and institutions did not 'positively darken human consciousness' that led Casey to embrace the Hegelian doctrine of 'objective spirit'. The realm of 'objective spirit', embracing history, culture, religion and language, traditional and institutional life, had to be seen as an essential element in human practical knowledge. And since that realm embodied the objects of human self-knowledge, it had to be understood in terms of human 'intention'. This did not mean that participation in traditional life presupposed the exercise of an unconditional freedom of choice on the part of the agent. On the contrary, Casey was clear that human autonomy was compatible with the agent's acceptance of his place in an objective order and that it required no capitulation to the Kantian formalism in which he acknowledged no moral restraints save those that he imposed upon himself through an act of arbitrary self-legislation. What it did mean was that Marxism had to be rejected on account of its engrossing causal claims in relation to human agency itself. The rejection left room for a conservative doctrine which preserved the connection between 'form and content' and insisted 'that our conscious loyalties to institutions, our conscious pieties, cannot be explained in terms alien to itself'.[26] In a deep sense Casey was affirming the 'necessary unity of consciousness' as the foundation of a conservative politics. He made Kantian points about the priority of self-ascription in the construction of human knowledge, and Wittgensteinian points about the priority of a public linguistic capacity to the attribution of thoughts and feelings to human beings. None of this excluded the possibility that the individual might be induced to assent to a fresh description of his conduct, by coming to understand his dependence upon the public world through the medium of Freudian therapy, the expressive capacities of an artistic tradition or the simple assent to authority presupposed by education itself. But it did exclude any crudely pseudo-scientific understanding of his conduct which reduced his traditional allegiances to mere blind determinism. The exclusion preserved exactly the element of conscious agency upon which Hegel had insisted throughout the *Philosophy of Right* and so imported into traditional life exactly the element of 'right' which the Marxist was obliged to reject.

Throughout the essay there was generous allusion to precedents from both the philosophy of mind and political philosophy. The allusion served notice that Aristotle, Burke, Hegel, Spinoza, Joyce, Strawson, Eliot, Hampshire, Wittgenstein and even a Marx divested of his mono-causal materialist assumptions could all be mobilised in the formulation of conservative doctrine. If it confirmed that Casey's conservatism rested upon secure philosophical foundations, the argument of 'Tradition and Authority' was nevertheless simple. Provided that autonomy was not construed in terms of unconditional freedom, participation in traditional and institutional life could not deprive the agent of his proper autonomy, because that participation had to be understood in terms of his reasons for acting and not of the external causes which compelled him to act. And since traditional life was manifestly *historical* in character, there could be no universal or systematic explanation of its authority: both natural right and natural law were ultimately ideological abstractions, and the attempt to prescribe an ideal model of justice external to the plurality of traditions a rationalistic illusion. In rejecting natural rights and natural law, however, 'Tradition and Authority' marked a departure from the ethical naturalism which Casey had defended previously.

iii

The Language of Criticism had established that naturalism was preferable to prescriptivism in moral theory and that morality itself had to be insulated from the subversions of consequentialism in the name of intrinsic values. Those conclusions were developed in the essay 'Actions and Consequences' which appeared in the collection of ethical studies *Morality and Moral Reasoning* published under Casey's editorship in 1971.[27] Casey discussed neither the 'naturalistic fallacy' directly, although he gave reasons why the central Humean distinction between fact and value was not of ultimate importance; nor Kant's doctrine of the autonomy of ethics, although the essay implied that Kantian formalism could be discarded in favour of a concrete scheme of moral values. Nor was Aristotle mentioned by name, although the essay went far in providing a structure of moral reasoning upon which the Aristotelian scheme of the virtues could be reconstructed.

What the essay did defend was the doctrine of ethical absolutism. Ethical absolutism held that certain traditional virtues such as justice and courage were absolutely good irrespective of the harmful consequences of the actions which instantiated them. Absolutism was defended against the doctrine of ethical consequentialism in which any scheme of moral values possessed authority in virtue of its conduciveness to the realisation of some final good like happiness; and which, accordingly, promised a criterion for the criticism of existing moral codes in the light of 'a changing reality' and for the resolution of those conflicts between ultimate values which absolutism entailed but could not settle.

Casey did not claim that consequentialism was necessarily wrong, only that the consequentialist could not demonstrate that absolutism rested upon a mistake about the logic of moral reasoning. Far from resting upon a neutral model of moral reasoning, the consequentialist's attack made ideological assumptions about the superiority of an exclusive moral code. Whatever structure of moral reasoning we adopt, Casey was saying, we are unavoidably committing ourselves to a certain picture of human ends and implicitly expressing a moral preference.

Casey developed his defence of absolutism in the context of arguments drawn from the theory of action. He recognised that there was an area of conduct in which the unintended consequences of an action could be legitimately attributed to the agent in the assessment of his responsibility. But he denied that there was a general 'moral equivalence' between 'deliberate killing' and 'letting die' in cases where there was no question of negligence or inadvertence. There was a point – which the consequentialist was unable to specify coherently – at which the attribution of responsibility to the agent for the unintended consequences of his actions had to come to an end, even in cases where those consequences were foreseeable.

Casey argued that that point could be reached only by a consideration of the agent's conception of the responsibilities attaching to his occupation of a particular social role. The doctor whose operation to save the life of the unborn child had the foreseen consequence of causing its mother's death neither intended her death nor could be relevantly described as having 'let her die'. And the priest who did not report a crime to the authorities divulged to him in confession did not intend that the criminal should escape. What had to be considered in the assessment of their responsibility were the descriptions which the doctor and priest would be prepared to offer of their actions, descriptions capable of incorporating their sense of occupying a particular role: 'So not only will our conception of a man's responsibilities govern what we can properly describe him as doing . . . but *his* conception of his role and its duties will determine the description for him under which he acts. However much we may wish to redescribe his actions in terms of some reformist view of his role, *his* conception of his role can govern what he can be said to intend in acting as he does'.[28] What Casey was saying was that the assignment and possession of roles did not represent a pre-moral stage in social life and that, in consequence, the values embodied in a 'role-morality' were invulnerable to assessment in terms of extrinsic ends. He implied that the agent's conformity to his social role involved no 'passive' surrender to the external authority of society conflicting with the Kantian requirement of autonomy. He attacked as mere dogmatism Jonathan Bennett's association of ethical absolutism with the unthinking conservatism that clouded the 'normal moral conscience' by its failure to 'do [its] own moral thinking'. And he rejected Rawls's doctrine of the 'ideally rational man . . . "seeking case by case to realise the best on the whole"' as an ideological preference. Casey thus insinuated objections both to the procedures which Rawls was to adopt throughout *A Theory of Justice* and to his assumption that the 'original position' recovered an ethically neutral core of human nature.

Having rejected consequentialism, what remained problematic was the justification of absolutism itself. Casey's solution to the problem reflected his indebtedness to Wittgenstein. An absolutist scheme of moral values had an *internal* justification. And the agent's assent to the values embodied in his social role was ultimately inseparable from his very participation in the entire culture in which such roles had their validation, in much the way that the rules of Wittgenstein's language-games had no justification external to the practice of rule-following itself: 'In looking for the justification of such a principle as "it is always wrong to kill the innocent, whatever the consequences of not doing so", we might take account of its scope, its richness, the place it has in a particular scheme of values. This would bring out its meaning for the people who adhere to it – and perhaps its role in a particular culture'.[29]

Casey did not discuss whether an absolutist scheme of values ultimately enjoyed its status in 'naturalistic' or 'conventionalist' terms. His preference for the traditional virtues suggested naturalism. But he was not explicit whether the authority of the absolutist scheme was contingent upon the particular roles assigned men in the culture in which they were born, which would tend to subordinate values to historical variation, or whether it reflected an unchanging core of natural law. Nor did he consider whether a complete doctrine of ethical absolutism required the specification of a substantive theory of human nature capable of explaining the human needs which cultural roles must satisfy if their authority is to be justifiable or whether social and political authority could legitimately be resisted by appeal to the natural law itself. Casey's ambiguity on this point was of a piece with the parallel ambiguity in 'Tradition and Authority' of how, in the absence of any external criterion of justification, the authority of the state could be distinguished from its power. The ambiguity was exacerbated by the fact that 'Actions and Consequences' intimated the Hegelian direction in which Casey would proceed subsequently. The essay suggested that public institutions embodied the ends of life through their provision of determinate roles and stations in the fullest Hegelian sense; and it implied that the technical issue of 'action-description' had significant precedents in the Hegelian tradition in the doctrines of 'concrete universal' and 'objective spirit'. Yet in both respects 'Actions and Consequences' posed a central problem which it did not resolve and which Casey has not resolved since: how Hegelianism, implicated as it was in anthropocentric historicism, could reestablish the objectivity of morality upheld by the traditional natural law in the absence of the metaphysical teleology of Aquinas and the naturalistic biology of Aristotle.

In a subsequent essay, 'Human Virtue and Human Nature',[30] Casey embraced the naturalistic alternative without qualification, arguing that the traditional scheme of the virtues derived from an 'unchanging core of human nature' possessing complete immunity from ideological fashion. Certain values were not subject to historical variation since, as he claimed, 'people could no more cease to feel fear or desire, love or hatred, pleasure or anger, than they could cease to think; and ... could no more cease to be brave or cowardly than they could cease to have intentions'. However, the essay provided no discussion of the place of social roles in the moral life and did not develop the implications for political philosophy of its theory of human nature.

iv

That Casey has propounded a conservative doctrine is not in doubt. What is in doubt is the exact *sense* in which it is a conservative doctrine.

Central to Casey's conservatism has been a doctrine about culture. He has defended the values of traditional culture, particularly those of humane learning, and the autonomy of the corporations which perpetuate them against the creeping philistinism inherent in social engineering. In a recent article, 'Attacking Scholarship',[31] he reaffirmed what he had expressed in *The Cambridge Review*: that the goods embodied in the traditional academic disciplines should be preserved even at the cost of imposing limitations upon their equal and universal distribution; and that it was the duty of the universities 'simply to offer the best education possible ... to their members and not to indulge in large-scale social or political judgements about who ought to be their members'. Casey has been right to challenge Rawlsian assumptions about the priority of distributive justice and statist subversions of the independence of subordinate corporations alike and to expose the culturally authoritarian consequences of egalitarian educational policy. He has, however, implied that the values of traditional culture do not reflect exclusive moral and cultural preferences and that their preservation does not require a fully political commitment. To this extent his cultural doctrine has represented a significant liberal recession from the Marxist intuitions of 'Tradition and Authority'.

The Hegelian identification of state with culture proposed in 'Tradition and Authority' certainly left it unclear upon what basis the power of the state was *actively* to promote cultural uniformity given the diversity of traditional continuities and cultural allegiances which the modern state inevitably comprehends. If the power was not to be understood in the Marxist terms of class antagonism nor was it to be exercised in the confessional idiom appropriate to an established religion. On the contrary, the cultural doctrine, deriving its inspiration from Arnold, Mill and William Morris as much as from Burke and Coleridge, implicated Casey in the tradition of romantic liberalism that had undermined precisely the ecclesiastical religion upon which the strongest connections between culture, morality and the state have been established. In this respect, Casey was remote from Oakeshott, whose Hobbesian dissociation of state from community represented a substantial concession to cultural pluralism, and from Cowling, whose grasp of the historical centrality of the Church-State question within English conservatism left little doubt that romanticism was what had to be resisted.

Casey's allegiance to romantic liberalism was clear too from his aesthetic doctrine. In the recent paper 'Emotion and Imagination',[32] the most systematic statement of his aesthetics, Casey defended the 'traditional view' of literature as the enactment of 'human values' against the materialist assumptions of the structuralists. He repudiated the charge of the Marxists that the critical tradition of Arnold, Leavis and Richards associated with the 'traditional view' reflected 'ideological or moral preferences'. On the contrary, it was grounded upon the idealist philosophy of mind and the 'corresponding idea of failure and success in expression' which Hegel and Collingwood had made central to 'the expression theory of art'. Nevertheless, the Marxist point remains very well taken to the extent that Casey's defence of expressionism inevitably involved him in highly partial ideological assumptions.

The traditional view made assumptions about the aesthetic, restricting the procedures of practical criticism too narrowly to romantic poetry and the nineteenth century novel and leaving it unclear in what sense they had application to pre-romantic literature and the formalism of modernist literature.

More centrally, the traditional view made assumptions about morality itself. On the one hand it prescribed a relationship between art and morality that avoided didacticism in either its mimetic or structuralist variants on the ground that the values expressed in art could not be 'extracted from a work and presented as its moral content'. On the other, it postulated an association between artistic expression and the notion of practical knowledge derived from the ethical ideals of Aristotle's *phronimos* and Spinoza's active freedom. The implications of the relationship were clear: what had been received as a matter of Wittgensteinian logic was confirmed by the doctrines of expressionist aesthetics and Aristotelian and Spinozistic rationalism: morality was not a matter of conformity to an externally imposed ethical code since moral excellence consisted ultimately in 'the self-awareness that goes with a coherent pattern of wishes, feelings and intentions'.

Whether it associated morality with Leavisian 'sincerity', Arnoldian 'seriousness', Coleridgean 'imagination', Humean 'sympathy' or Nietzschean 'transvaluation', the proposed relationship between morality and art bound Casey to the ethical assumptions of romantic liberalism. The relationship was, in fact, profoundly subversive of *objective* morality, particularly of the objective authority of the rules and sanctions essential to law and society upon which both the Hegelian conservative and the Thomist would generally insist. It left unacknowledged the tension between the cultural uniformity which society inevitably imposes through the restraints of education, and the spirit of liberal comprehension conveyed through Arnold's ideal of 'poetry' as a 'criticism of life' and Leavis's ideal of the 'common reader' understanding 'literature by entering into it imaginatively, bringing his values to bear upon it whilst . . . allowing them to be instructed and modified by it'. And the relationship tended to overthrow the claims of traditional Christianity in favour of those of culture. The invocation of Aristotelianism associated Casey with a pagan ethics antagonistic towards both the Christian virtues and the dogma of fallen nature integral to a Christian conservatism. Even if Aristotle was an acceptable precedent for political conservatism, it was not obvious that Spinoza could be enlisted for conservatism at all. Not only did Spinoza's *Ethics* express an ideal of enlightened rationalism subversive of the superstitions of supernatural and legalistic Christianity on the one hand and of the traditional authority of law and social morality on the other; but the ethics were intimately related to a politics in which Spinoza asserted the priority of natural right and rejected the authority of the natural law in accordance with the spirit of Hobbesian liberalism.

Casey may deny that these conclusions follow from his doctrine. But the tensions remain and his doctrinal eclecticism has served merely to accentuate the problematic status of his conservatism.

Despite its eclecticism, a great deal can still be claimed on behalf of Casey's work in philosophy. His work in aesthetics has suggested important continuities between Wittgenstein's empiricism and the idealism of Kant and Hegel and established that both traditions possess serious implications for the formulation of conservative doctrine. In relation to ethics – where Casey is developing his most coherent statement of position[33] – his work had been strikingly original for its defence of the traditional virtues in terms of the anti-Cartesian assumptions in the philosophy of mind inherited from Hegel and Wittgenstein. It is clear from unpublished versions of the defence that Casey believes that there is a continuum from the agent's possession of the traditional virtues of temperance, *phronesis*, justice and courage as elaborated by Aristotle to his participation in the public realm of 'objective spirit' as elucidated by Hegel. The rational ordering of the appetitive and emotional life reflected in the life of virtue, Casey is suggesting, will find its full expression in the Hegelian realm in which 'all of human nature, from the human body, to all the human emotions, to man's ability to have a history and to express himself in institutions and practices . . . is expressive of man's nature as rational agent'. Certainly Casey's insistence that 'man's essence can be found only in his embodiment of the historical idea' provides evidence that the ethical naturalism sketched in 'Human Virtue and Human Nature' will not remain unadulterated by Hegelian historicism.

Whatever the results of Casey's work in ethics, what is required to transform his enterprise from striking originality into a coherent achievement is an explanation of how in making the Hegelian passage from abstract right to the state, in which the Aristotelian virtues will play an indispensable role, Casey can provide the state itself with its proper legitimation in the natural law that Aristotle and Aquinas treated as the complement to a naturalistic ethics. What the enterprise requires will be a dissociation of Hegelianism from the historicism which it initiated and the historical materialism into which Marx transformed it on the one hand; and from the tradition of natural right of Hobbes, Locke, Spinoza and Kant on the other, a tradition of which the *Philosophy of Right* was the culmination and which marked a departure from the natural law systems of Aristotle and Aquinas.

In his review of Alasdair MacIntyre's *After Virtue*[34] Casey recognised that such an enterprise would be difficult. He implied that Nietzschean amoralism was perhaps the only position available to the contemporary moralist. And he was explicit that the modern age could not return to a 'golden age when a blend of Aristotelianism and *Sittlichkeit* made certain ethical theories impossible', a 'golden age' which, as Casey correctly noticed, had little of the foundation in historical reality that MacIntyre claimed was indispensable to ethical coherence and which in the Benedictine form that MacIntyre prescribed simply 'ignored the world as it is now'. Whether the same reservations are to be entertained about Casey's project remains the central question since they challenge, at both a philosophical and historical level, the viability of his conservatism.

In the context of one public statement the reservations cannot be avoided. In a lecture delivered to the Royal Institute of Philosophy – 'The Noble'[35] – Casey defended the importance attached to the virtue of courage in the ethics of Aristotle and Hume. In asserting that the virtue of courage was intimately related to the fully political virtue of 'the noble', Casey challenged the widespread assumptions about morality deriving from Kantian ethics. The concept of the noble collapsed the Kantian dualism between rational autonomy and the heteronomy of natural necessity. Nobility was not simply a matter of the 'good will' or 'good intentions'. Rather, it presupposed a fortuitous 'success in acting upon the world' and the occupation by the agent of a 'public role' within a 'social practice'. Moreover, inasmuch as the noble was both a moral and aesthetic concept, it blurred the distinction between the moral and non-moral qualities upon which Kant had insisted with its implication that moral merit depended in part upon the contingencies of natural and social endowment.

Casey did not deny that the concept of the noble had far-reaching political consequences, and his challenge to the democratic assumptions of Kant's ethics must be understood as a resistance to the democratic, liberal and egalitarian assumptions in politics to which Kantianism had given rise. In a contemporary context Casey was dissenting from the dualistic 'original position' from which Rawls developed his highly Kantian model of social democratic justice in *A Theory of Justice*, and from the dissociations of state from public morality and citizenship from virtue entailed by the 'minimal state' prescribed by Nozick in *Anarchy, State and Utopia*. And in the widest historical context Casey was dissenting from the tenets of the post-Reformation polity, particularly from the tradition of natural right, which had sundered the legal and constitutional arrangements of the modern state from the public morality embodied in the social order, made an improper attribution of ethical neutrality to those arrangements and abandoned teleological justifications of their authority in favour of utilitarian justifications of their regulatory power. Throughout the lecture Casey was explicit that the ethics of nobility had no application in the 'open' and 'competitive' societies of bourgeois, liberal democracy. And he was clear that what had happened to bring about that state of affairs was the occurrence since the Renaissance of an 'important shift of criteria . . . as to what is to be included within the notion of a man's self' which made it impossible to reconstitute the relationship between the political realm and the moral practices in which the ethics of the noble had once had a natural place. What had been decisive in causing the shift had been the increasing predominance of the empiricist assumptions in the philosophy of mind initiated by Descartes: that predominance had sold the pass to the dualisms between reason and nature, individual and society, upon which Kant's ethics turned by postulating the self as subject to 'descriptions uniquely identifying it without bringing in social, political or cultural concepts'. And what had been lost in the shift was the teleological structure of Aristotelian ethics with its insistence that the essence of man's selfhood was ultimately the 'idea of being-in-the-world, of one's self being fulfilled in a social role or function, and of an identification of oneself with a public world'.

Casey was not explicit whether the aristocratic arrangements of the pre-Reformation polity could be reconstituted in the modern age, in defiance of the fact that the advent of mass democracy in the nineteenth and twentieth centuries had destroyed the political power of the aristocracy. And yet the tenability of Casey's conservatism must depend finally upon the answer to exactly that question.

In the absence of a positive answer, it is hard to avoid two conclusions: that the concept of the noble survives ultimately as a matter of *aesthetic sentiment*, rather than as a fully political morality; and that what Casey is prescribing is the perpetuation of the aristocratic ideal as an intensive form of personal morality within the framework of political arrangements in which it no longer possesses a social correlative. Neither the sentiment nor the prescription was without precedent. In certain senses Burke's defence of the aristocratic constitution expressed a nostalgic romantic sentiment in the face of the prevailing democratic and revolutionary movements. In a stronger sense, Oakeshott retained the aristocratic ideal as 'self-enactment', a personal ethic of motive and sentiment enabling the virtuous citizen to transform the fulfilment of his civil obligations into the expression of his individual fidelity. Oakeshott also made the ideal central to the understanding of Hobbes's theory of political obligation. Nevertheless, Oakeshott grasped the vulnerability of the ideal in a way that Casey did not. Indeed, Oakeshott took as its political correlative the post-Reformation polity. Not only were *its* social and political presuppositions precisely those which Casey rejected; but Oakeshott defined it largely in opposition to the seigneurial arrangements of feudalism which, Casey implied, provided the preconditions for the ethics of nobility. And lastly there was the precedent of Nietzsche, whose celebration of the noble virtues undoubtedly furnished Casey with an attractive model of dissent from the egalitarian and democratic assumptions of Kantian liberalism, but whose ethics were nonetheless profoundly *individualistic* and anarchically subversive of exactly the objective moral authority of social practices upon which Casey claimed that the ethics of nobility depended. If Nietzsche held out the promise of an Aristotelian alternative to Kantianism, then the promise was largely empty given that Nietzsche's invocation of the Aristotelian virtues carried none of the teleological claims of the Aristotelian *polis*. Indeed, Nietzsche's remoteness from Aristotle and Hegel served only to underline the nature of Casey's problem: that in the modern age the aristocratic virtues rested upon no more than an appeal to aesthetic sentiment and a preferred form of individual morality. In Casey's treatment, both the sentiment and the personal ethic were impressive. Yet they not only 'ignored the world as it is now' – they left it unclear in what sense the conservative moralist could reestablish the relationship between morality and the state which liberalism had destroyed in terms that engaged with the political legacy of that liberalism.

There we should leave Casey: the propounder of a multifaceted philosophical conservatism, notable for its disengagement with contemporary political reality yet powerful in its concern for values that command immediate respect when transmitted by a writer capable of Casey's sophistication. This summary judgement may leave the impression that Casey's achievement is comparatively slight. The impression would be unfortunate and it should be reaffirmed that much has been justly claimed on Casey's behalf. However, it remains the case that several of the more suggestive implications of his work have not been developed to their fullest extent. For an assessment of one attempt to provide them with systematic coherence we must turn from Casey himself to his former pupil, a philosopher who displays no doubts as to the contemporary relevance of philosophical conservatism: Roger Scruton.

3 Two Wittgensteinians: Roger Scruton

Unlike Casey, Roger Scruton is a trained philosopher. He is unusual for a philosopher nurtured in the analytical tradition in possessing a very wide range of intellectual interests and developing the connections between them. His works include: a formal treatise on aesthetics: *Art and Imagination*;[1] a more accessible analysis of architecture: *The Aesthetics of Architecture*;[2] two volumes of critical essays and philosophical articles: *The Politics of Culture*[3] and *The Aesthetic Understanding*;[4] a politics: *The Meaning of Conservatism*[5] supplemented with *A Dictionary of Political Thought*;[6] two contributions to the history of ideas: *From Descartes to Wittgenstein*[7] and *Kant*;[8] and a novel: *Fortnight's Anger*.[9] As his writing has developed since *Art and Imagination* it has acquired an increasing fluency such that he no longer writes as an analytical philosopher in bondage to the professional conventions of his discipline but, rather, as a cultural critic whose province is as extensive as that claimed for philosophy by the intellectual giant who has become his touchstone: Hegel. Indeed, *philosophy* for Scruton is now less an academic enterprise than an instrument for the propounding of a comprehensive moral, cultural and political doctrine. It is an instrument which has lent itself effectively to the journalism with which, as editor of *The Salisbury Review* and *Times* weekly columnist, Scruton has expounded his philosophical conservatism as a public doctrine. About the substantive content of Scruton's doctrine it is necessary to say that it was avowedly conservative and that its conservatism rested upon two assumptions which it shared with Casey's: that continuities could be established between idealism and Wittgensteinianism and that those continuities had farreaching conservative implications for aesthetics, morality and politics.

i

Like Casey's, Scruton's conservatism has reflected an intellectual progression from Kant to Hegel. However, Scruton has lacked Casey's Thomist perspective and written without his allegiance to ethical naturalism. In fact, his early contribution to *Morality and Moral Reasoning*, 'Attitudes, Beliefs and Reasons',[10] upheld Moore's arguments concerning the 'naturalistic fallacy' and defended an ethical theory radically antagonistic towards naturalistic ethics: emotivism. Not only were there no 'truth-conditions' governing the application of moral judgements to the natural world, but there inevitably existed 'ultimate disagreements in ethics' in exactly the sense which naturalism denied since the agent was under no logical compulsion ever to 'admit that he [was] wrong in a moral judgement'. Emotivism, by contrast, provided a more convincing analysis of the 'actual structure of moral language' precisely because it distinguished, as naturalism did not, between 'reasons for acting' and 'reasons for believing'. It recognised both that 'moral beliefs' expressed attitudes incorporating a 'reactive content' not itself reducible to beliefs, and that moral attitudes themselves possessed a social aspect of 'normativity' expressing less the agent's beliefs about the natural world than his 'desire for conformity of attitudes' on the part of others. Second, emotivism provided a solution to the problem of the *justification* of moral attitudes, which naturalism simply evaded by ignoring the 'reactive' element of normativity. Whereas naturalism implied that it was a contingent matter that 'believing something to be good' furnished 'reasons for following it', emotivism acknowledged that the relation between the belief and the reason was one of entailment. The relation of entailment did not, however, suffice to close the gap between facts and values in the manner of naturalism. On the contrary, it remained 'a matter of fact if human beings have attitudes to certain states of affairs and hence ... a matter of fact if these states of affairs can provide people with reasons for acting in a certain way'. Indeed, Scruton concluded by affirming that it was the chief virtue of emotivism to have culminated in the anti-cognitivist insight that 'although we can give sense to our claims to know moral propositions, we can never know them'.[11] Naturalism was wrong, Scruton was saying, because inasmuch as it expressed the practical attitudes of the agent morality did not embody an object of human knowledge at all.

Although it presupposed an absolute distinction between factual discourse and moral language, the essay had the corrective purpose of vindicating the *rationality* of moral reasoning from the emotivist perspective. It established that emotivism could be rehabilitated without the reduction of moral argument to the mere assertion of arbitrary subjective preference which had been the principal defect of the neo-Humean ethics of Ayer and Stevenson. In moral argument the element of 'subjectivity' imported by the 'reactive content' of moral attitudes was 'suspended'. Moral argument was necessarily conducted on the Kantian presumptions that the 'adducing of reasons' in practical disputes presupposed 'some further agreement', that 'agreement [was] somewhere to be discovered', and that theoretical reason was incapable of demonstrating the necessity of 'ultimate disagreement about what could count as a reason for an attitude'. Nevertheless, the objectivity of moral judgement guaranteed by the suspension of 'subjectivity' did not compromise the Kantian principle of the autonomy of morality from nature, since the suspension was for the sake of 'a moral judgement that [could not] be objectively true'.

'Attitudes, Beliefs and Reasons' was, then, a highly Kantian essay. It asserted the priority of the practical to the theoretical reason and grounded the moral law and the human good upon the autonomous will of the rational agent as expressed through his choices and attitudes. It excluded the derivation of the moral attitudes from knowledge of the natural world, including human nature itself. And it excluded their derivation from knowledge of the transcendent realm since, as the essay implied, the dogmatic claims of traditional religion to provide knowledge of the supernatural world were irrelevant as grounds of human morality. Religion has not been central to Scruton's conservatism. What has been central – cultural romanticism, Wittgensteinian conventionalism and Hegelian historicism – has been consistent with the anthropocentric foundation for morality established in 'Attitudes, Beliefs and Reasons'; although it was not inevitable that the Kantian formalism to which the essay ultimately capitulated should have culminated in Hegelian conservatism rather than a political formulation of the Kantian liberalism with which it was equally consistent. The essay was not, however, harmonious with either a naturalistic ethics or the invocation of the substantive natural law to justify the authority of the state.

To say that Scruton adopted a Kantian position subversive of the natural law will seem paradoxical in the light of recent statements in *The Salisbury Review* invoking the canons of natural justice. Nevertheless, neither the authority which those canons have been intended to confer upon the state nor the connections between law and morality which they have presupposed have necessitated an accompanying reformulation of the naturalistic ethics which the early essay rejected. In fact, their naturalistic status has been problematic in virtue of their very compatibility with the liberal and relativistic implications of the essay.

After 'Attitudes, Beliefs and Reasons' Scruton made few contributions to ethical analysis. What the essay led to was an aesthetics which inherited both its anti-cognitivism and formalism.

Art and Imagination was a version of the doctoral thesis which Scruton wrote under Casey's influence. It developed the concerns of *The Language of Criticism* in two directions. First, its procedures were those of applied Wittgenstein. Thus Scruton rejected emphatically the phenomenological aesthetics of Sartre, Dufrenne and Ingarden, on the Wittgensteinian grounds that such concepts as the 'aesthetic attitude' and 'aesthetic experience' had to be 'elucidated in terms of their criteria, the observable states of affairs that warrant their application'.[12] Second, the book upheld Kant's enterprise in *The Critique of Judgement* by defending both Kant's assertion of the objectivity of aesthetic judgements, together with his conclusion that the rationality proper to aesthetic judgement was significantly distinguishable from the rationality proper to science. Whereas the defence of Kantianism had been merely implicit in Casey's book, Scruton's was doctrinally explicit.

Scruton began by saluting the centrality which idealists like Hegel and Croce had assigned to aesthetic experience. Idealism provided an alternative to the empiricist aesthetics of Hutcheson and Hume, which had trivialised the experience of art by explaining it in 'affective' and 'sentimental' terms, reducing aesthetic 'taste' to an 'isolated and segmented part of human psychology' and by treating its exercise as the mere assertion of arbitrary and irrational preference. Scruton did not deny that the philosophy of mind upon which Hegel and Croce had relied was defective. Yet he insisted that the doctrines of Ryle and Wittgenstein were equally defective in offering no sustained analysis of aesthetic experience. To the extent that he was providing such an explanation, Scruton was seeking to rehabilitate idealism in general and Kantianism in particular within the firm analytical framework of modern empiricism.

Kant provided the principal source of inspiration for Scruton because, in upholding the objectivity of aesthetic judgements and distinguishing the 'material' from the 'aesthetic' object of those judgements, Kant had assumed the ultimate inseparability of 'aesthetic judgement' from 'aesthetic appreciation'. Scruton developed the implications of that assumption in Wittgensteinian terms by taking up the critique of the descriptive paradigm of language provided in *Philosophical Investigations*. He allowed that it was fundamental to our conception of truth that some at least of our sentences were true in virtue of their correspondence with states of affairs, their truth-conditions being 'identified ostensively, by pointing to observable features of the world'. Nevertheless, he insisted that the model of ostensive definition was inadequate to explain the nature of human knowledge itself. Learning a language presupposed both a natural understanding of the states of affairs with which the judgements expressed through sentences were correlated; and the context of the 'unarticulated background' of the Wittgensteinian 'forms of life' embodying exactly the 'necessary and sufficient conditions' for the truth of particular judgements that the model of bare ostensive definition alone could not yield. The insight that human judgements possessed a contextual appropriateness explained the importance which Scruton attached to Wittgenstein's doctrine of the 'criterion'. In establishing that human understanding involved a conceptual relation between sentences and the public criteria for their correct application, the doctrine had a particular application to Kant's principal theses: that the objectivity of aesthetic judgements consisted not in correspondence with their objects determinable by means of concepts of the understanding, but in the universalised form of their assertion; and that reference to those objects considered in their empirical character was incapable of resolving disputes in issues of aesthetic judgement. The application implied that whilst aesthetic judgements were fully 'public', there were important senses in which they could not be 'true' or 'false'. It was the truth of that conclusion which substantiated Scruton's underlying thesis that the logic of aesthetic judgements had to be understood in terms of the conditions not of their 'truth' but of their 'acceptance'.

Art and Imagination was a highly technical book and much of it remains accessible only to the specialist philosophical readership to which it was addressed. Two observations need to be made however. First, in making Kant central, Scruton was serving notice that the Kantian principles of *autonomy* and *objectivity* would be key elements in his doctrine, thus permitting him to assert the priority of the 'public' to the 'individual' and to resist utilitarianism in matters of moral and aesthetic value. The book's pivotal chapter, 'The Aesthetic Attitude', defended Kant's claim that the judgement of taste was universalised in exacting 'agreement from everyone'. Extending the analysis of normative attitudes provided in 'Attitudes, Beliefs and Reasons', Scruton demonstrated that aesthetic judgements were fully normative, differing from the moral attitudes discussed in the essay only inasmuch as the latter were legitimately concerned with the *punitive* 'enforcement of a code of conduct', whereas the former were confined to the *educative* 'development of a particular capacity for enjoyment'. As with the moral attitudes, the element of 'subjectivity' in aesthetic response was 'suspended' for the sake of a practical attitude since the normativity of aesthetic reasoning presupposed 'a search for agreement' constituted 'in reason and not in the mere convergence of opinion'. Both moral and aesthetic judgements had a stable propositional form that was not reducible to the mere assertion of personal taste. And in expressing them it was necessary to offer reasons for their justification and eccentric to remain indifferent to the divergent judgements of others. In asserting the normativity of aesthetic judgements, Scruton concluded – after Kant and Wittgenstein – that they were essentially judgements about ends and not means. In consequence, he sought also to substantiate Kant's conclusion that art pleases 'apart from all interest' and is to be enjoyed 'for its own sake' as an end with no 'rationale external to itself'. Aesthetic enjoyment was distinguishable from practical interest in general and 'animal desire' in particular. Whereas 'animal desire' could be satisfied by an unlimited range of objects, aesthetic enjoyment could be satisfied only by the enjoyment of the particular work of art considered in its uniqueness. And aesthetic enjoyment had an intellectual element absent from 'animal desire' in which 'the desire to continue looking at x . . . [was] founded on the thought of x, in that the thought . . . [provided] one with the reason for one's desire . . . and "for no other reason" '.[13]

Art and Imagination thus confirmed that art possessed an autonomy and the reasoning concerned with it a public status. Whilst these conclusions provided Scruton with a basis for resistance to liberal utilitarianism and liberal individualism alike, it should not be thought that *Art and Imagination* was a doctrinally conservative book. It established no connections between aesthetics and politics whatsoever and contained little to imply the cultural conservatism which Scruton later defended. On the contrary, the second observation to be made about the book is that in *restricting* himself to Kant, Scruton left unresolved two questions of critical importance for the cultural conservative: in what sense aesthetic experience yielded *knowledge* of the world; and in what sense Kant's formalism presupposed a substantial public world in which the normative aspirations of aesthetic judgement achieved concrete fulfilment. In these respects, the book inherited the Kantian dualism of 'Attitudes, Beliefs and Reasons' between the knowledge of the natural world expressed in the factual discourse of science and the human attitudes expressed in the discourse of ethics and aesthetics. It was precisely this dualism which Scruton rejected throughout his subsequent Hegelian phase.

A substantial part of the second section of *Art and Imagination* was devoted to defending Kant's thesis that the aesthetic imagination was 'free' of concepts yet fully rational in being bounded by the laws of the understanding. Developing Wittgenstein's remarks about aspect-perception, Scruton argued in the chapters on the imagination that the experience of 'seeing as' central to aesthetic experience was an activity of the imagination and not of the judgement, and that, in consequence, it did not involve genuine beliefs about the literal truth of its objects. Imagination shared enough in common with thought for it to be fully rational. It was 'intentional' in being internally related to its object. And the criterion for its attribution was verbal, with the implication that animals could not, as a matter of logical truth, 'see aspects . . . [or] form images'. However, it was unlike thought in being subject to the will. Thus, whereas the command to believe the truth of a proposition was nonsensical, it was perfectly intelligible to obey an order to imagine something since compliance required 'not believing something, but rather entertaining propositions unasserted'. This meant that in aesthetic experience the unasserted thoughts entertained by the imagination were not ascribed to their objects as 'true beliefs' about them. And it established a distinction between the place of imagination in aesthetic experience on the one hand and its exercise in ordinary perception on the other. Whereas in ordinary perception the experience of 'seeing as' was not subject to the will and the sensory beliefs upon which it rested were held to be internally related to true and asserted beliefs about its objects, the unasserted thoughts involved in imagination always went 'beyond what is believed . . . [and] given in ordinary prediction and belief'.[14]

The analysis of the imagination was fundamental to Scruton's entire thesis. The element of rationality in aesthetic experience which he was concerned to defend was defined almost exclusively in terms of the 'category of unasserted thought'. The definition implied that aesthetic judgement was neither cognitive nor directed towards literal truth. These implications were developed throughout the third part of *Art and Imagination*. Although he acknowledged that representation and expression were the central cases of aesthetic interest, Scruton denied that they necessitated a cognitive theory of art. On the contrary, they were forms of 'imitation' the understanding of which derived from imagination and not belief. Indeed, Scruton attacked those aesthetic doctrines which treated art as 'an instrument of knowledge' and the aesthetic attitude as concerned with the discovery of 'facts, whether about the work of art or about the world to which [art] "refers" '. In particular he challenged the continuum between the 'aesthetic and scientific attitudes' assumed by the semantic theories of Nelson Goodman and Susanne Langer. The semantic theories were questionable from the Kantian perspective in two respects. First, they denied that *aesthetic interest* was stimulated by the work of art considered in its uniqueness, as the 'object of a particular experience', and hence that the work was an end. They reduced art to a means of conveying knowledge about the world to which it referred or the feeling which it expressed of no more intrinsic aesthetic significance than ordinary language itself. And in so reducing art, the theories obscured the essential difference between the meaningfulness of art, which always went beyond its conformity to rules, and the meaningfulness of language, which presupposed a logical structure providing rules of truth and reference. Second, they denied that *aesthetic experience* was autonomous and irreducible. The experience of art was not reducible to a propositional truth expressible in some other medium. On the contrary, the knowledge gained from the work of art was 'direct', and inseparable from the 'experience of the work itself'. In a sense, this insight reflected concurrence on Scruton's part with Hegel's definition of art as the 'sensuous embodiment' of ideas expressible in no other form. Nevertheless, it is vital to understand that *Art and Imagination* was not an Hegelian book and that it sanctioned none of the claims of art and public culture to embody objective truth upon which Scruton's Hegelian conservatism was subsequently to depend.

ii

The numerous reviews and articles which Scruton published after *Art and Imagination* provided evidence that he was moving towards an Hegelian position. In 'Philosophy and Literature'[15] he vindicated Hegel's association of the cognitive with aesthetic experience by affirming that art expressed a 'truth' available only in disinterested contemplation. In a review of Leavis, 'Sense and Sincerity',[16] he endorsed Leavis's expressionist conviction that 'our consciousness is created by our language', implying that literature was a vehicle of human self-knowledge in an Hegelian sense. In 'The Impossibility of Semiotics',[17] 'Deconstruction and Criticism'[18] and 'The Semiology of Music'[19] there were polemical attacks upon the efforts of the structuralists to establish a 'science' of aesthetic appreciation and to remove from it the primacy of aesthetic 'value'. And reviews of Adrian Stokes,[20] the Marxist architectural theorists[21] and David Watkin[22] established that architectural theory would be Scruton's instrument of aesthetic doctrine.

Scruton's book on architecture, *The Aesthetics of Architecture*, was impregnated with Hegelian assumptions. Its invocation of Hegel's doctrine of art as the embodiment of human practical knowledge accorded aesthetic experience a cognitive status and a moral and political significance unacknowledged in *Art and Imagination*. This is not to say that its analysis of architectural experience contradicted the conclusions of the earlier book. On the contrary, in the chapters 'Experiencing Architecture' and 'Judging Architecture' Scruton sought to demonstrate that the experience of architecture was rational, that it presupposed the voluntary exercise of 'imaginative' perception peculiar to the aesthetic attitude rather than the 'literal' perception characteristic of ordinary experience, and that the judgements about its aesthetic object were objective in the Kantian senses defended in *Art and Imagination*. Moreover, Scruton at no point compromised the spirit of Kant's insistence upon the autonomy of experience itself in either an epistemological, moral or aesthetic sense. Not only was he clear that the experience of art had to be mediated by a conscious understanding of its 'surface' meaning but he was everywhere concerned to refuse recognition to any theory which denied the principle that 'the superior understanding of a building induced by criticism [was] one with the improved way of seeing it'. He attacked semiological interpretations of architecture, on the ground that their generalising, pseudo-scientific terminology was vacuous at the points where they should properly have provided precise discriminations. He entertained comparable doubts concerning the Marxist theorists, whose endeavour to demystify the 'ideological distortions' inherent in cultural phenomena like buildings had proved incapable of qualifying negatively or positively the content of aesthetic experience itself. And he attacked the psychoanalytical theory of Adrian Stokes. By invoking the concept of the unconscious, Stokes had obscured the nature of aesthetic attention, and in reducing the value of architecture to that of a mere stimulus of unconscious feeling he had falsely construed it as a *means*. Moreover, Stokes had misrepresented the nature of psychoanalysis itself. Following Wittgenstein, Scruton insisted that its nature was essentially 'therapeutic' and that the only unconscious causes relevant to therapy were those 'salvaged' through the conscious recognition of the patient, the analyst inducing 'his patient to transform the "he" of observation into the "I" of self-knowledge'. Whether in the contexts of Semiology, Marxism or Freudianism, Scruton was upholding Kant against any reductive theory implicated in the empiricist's fallacy of making the relation between aesthetic object and aesthetic response 'causal' rather than 'internal'.

Nonetheless, for all its continuity with *Art and Imagination*, *The Aesthetics of Architecture* was written in the recognition that architecture posed a special problem for the Kantian aesthetician. Its principal significance was neglected by the romantic tradition of art in which 'aesthetic interest' was severed entirely from all practical considerations. However, Scruton was clear both that architecture was a form of art which could not be understood in isolation from its practical function, and that Collingwood's post-Kantian distinction between art and craft was manifestly inappropriate to its aesthetics. He rejected the trivial aestheticism of the 'sculptural attitude' in which attention to the 'decorative' element of architecture excluded all sense of its 'functional' elements. Not only did buildings have a function which satisfied the 'practical' needs of the 'normal man', but architecture itself – which demanded a movement away 'from the realm of high art towards that of common practical wisdom' – subverted the elitist pretensions of the 'sculptural attitude' with which the Kantian conception of aesthetic autonomy was associated.

In rejecting romantic aestheticism Scruton in no sense upheld the cause of architectural 'functionalism'. Functionalism, no less than the 'sculptural attitude', assumed an impoverished conception of practical reason. The need which architecture satisfied was not an 'animal preference' but the Aristotelian *eudaimonia*: the fulfilment of the rational agent in the end of practical activity itself. Accordingly, in 'Architecture and Design' Scruton attacked those functionalists who treated beauty as the incidental consequence of 'rational design'. The architect had both to satisfy the 'practical understanding' of those who inhabited his buildings, and to recognise that their 'aesthetic sense' was an essential ingredient of that understanding since practical reason included not merely knowledge of how to act, but also the knowledge of 'what is right and appropriate in matters of aesthetic judgement'. Indeed, the character of practical reason demonstrated a great truth about aesthetic experience which the functionalist ignored: the complexity of the relationship between ends and means. This truth established the ethical character of the aesthetic in senses only implicit in *Art and Imagination*. Thus, in the final chapter, 'Architecture and Morality', Scruton concluded that the utilitarian approach to architecture of functionalism failed, in the way that utilitarianism in morals and politics failed, to confront the critique of individualism – whether the individualism implicit in Benthamite hedonism or the individualism embodied in the Cartesian dualism – provided by Kant and Hegel. The inspiration of that critique was Kant's thesis of the 'transcendental unity of apperception', and its substantial core was provided by the Hegel of *The Phenomenology of Spirit*. The objective world, the existence of which Kant's formalism had merely implied, embraced ethical life, culture, tradition and the state, indeed the entire world of 'objective spirit' through which the 'self-realisation' of the agent was sought and achieved. Art had an indispensable role to play in the agent's 'spreading himself' on the objective world. Moreover, the aesthetic sense impregnated his experience of 'everyday life' itself and, inasmuch as its objects were given concrete embodiment in the architectural environment, it was the means whereby the agent discovered meaning and value in his world. Capitulation to functionalism in common with capitulation to utilitarianism in politics, Scruton was saying, would lead to an alienation of the agent from his public environment.

It was not clear in what senses *The Aesthetics of Architecture* was a conservative book. It was not obviously conservative in matters of architectural taste. Although Scruton expressed a preference for the classical style, he was clear that the *philosophical* demonstration of the necessity of style stood in no logical relation to any particular style reflecting an aesthetic preference. In this respect Scruton's project diverged from the project of David Watkin in *Morality and Architecture*,[23] whose invocation of the eighteenth century conception of 'taste' was all too obviously involved in a preference for the classical style, rooted in empiricist assumptions foreign to those of Scruton the Hegelian, and connected with a doctrine about the relationship between art and morality strangely impoverished in contrast with Scruton's attempt at a realignment on the Aristotelian lines suggested by the doctrine of practical knowledge. Ultimately the doctrine of *The Aesthetics of Architecture* was conservative in an Hegelian sense. It asserted that the public world embodied human ends and provided the precondition of individual freedom. And it implied that the retreat into the pluralism of 'subjective' preference represented a retreat into Kantian heteronomy on the aesthetic front and liberal illusion on the political front. The book thus brought Scruton to the Hegelian position which Casey had reached in 'The Autonomy of Art' and introduced a dimension lacking in *Art and Imagination*: that the experience of art was cognitive in reflecting human self-knowledge, just as public culture expressed the profoundest beliefs which men might entertain about themselves.

Since *The Aesthetics of Architecture* Scruton has continued to provide contributions to aesthetics. On occasions aesthetics has merged with literary criticism and Scruton's wider philosophical concerns, most notably in the fine essay 'Beckett and the Cartesian Soul'[24] in which he attributed Beckett's nihilism to the 'moral and metaphysical illusion' of Cartesian dualism and offered an Hegelian critique of Beckett's romantic contempt for 'habit, custom and social order'. Generally, however, the contributions have involved little modification of positions expounded in earlier works. Scruton has confirmed the conclusions of *The Aesthetics of Architecture*. In 'Aesthetic Education and Design'[25] he attacked 'aesthetic consequentialism', insisted upon the 'practical significance' of architecture and upheld the classical discipline imposed by the 'education of the orders'. And in 'Art History and Aesthetic Judgement'[26] he maintained that the discipline of art history presupposed aesthetic judgement; that the subjective element in aesthetic experience was the foundation of art historical method; and that the autonomy which that experience implied established both that the subject of art history was a 'revelation of intention' and, hence, the inappropriateness of the causal explanations adopted in Marxist historicism to its historical recovery. Elsewhere Scruton has confirmed the conclusions of *Art and Imagination*. In 'Recent Aesthetics in England'[27] he criticised the ahistorical assumptions of analytical philosophy for having deprived 'philosophy of its status as a humanity', and phenomenological aesthetics for its violations of Wittgenstein's prohibition upon 'first personal' analysis. He also prescribed a subject for future aesthetics – the questions touching the nature of 'aesthetic interest' made central by Kant – and a procedure for its investigation: the analysis of the 'aesthetic experience' stressed in phenomenology in a Wittgensteinian idiom capable of liberating the 'study of the imagination from the first-personal viewpoint'. In Scruton's case the prescriptions have not issued in significant new departures in aesthetics. There have been statements about photography, challenging its claims to the status of a genuinely 'representational art' on grounds provided by Kantian and Hegelian aesthetics and expressing moral objections to the cinema's fulfilment of 'fantasy interest' rather than 'aesthetic interest'.[28] And there have been statements about music, particularly a number of contributions to *The New Grove Dictionary of Music*,[29] fulfilling Scruton's demand that the defects of the traditional theory of musical expression be remedied by an analysis of musical understanding and the 'aesthetic interest' of musical experience. Nonetheless, save for the essay 'Musical Understanding',[30] there has been little work in this field. The fact remains that since *The Aesthetics of Architecture* aesthetics has yielded its central place to politics amongst Scruton's doctrinal concerns.

iii

That Scruton's work in aesthetics had implications for politics was obvious from the book on architecture. Throughout the seventies he developed these implications in a number of articles. He attacked liberalism wherever it prescribed an ideal of freedom abstracted from the constraints of social and institutional life. In 'The Ideology of the Market'[31] he attacked Mrs Thatcher's espousal of Hayekian liberalism and the Conservative Party's obsession with 'freedom'. In that the rhetoric of 'freedom' was propagated to defend liberal economic policy, it was merely an ideology which disguised the pursuit of a 'real interest' – and insofar as the Trades Unions recognised that fact they, and not Mrs Thatcher, were right. In 'Academic Freedom'[32] he denounced the Gould Report on academic freedom for its misunderstanding of the political nature of academic institutions. The real ideological battle in education, Scruton concluded, was not between liberal 'freedom' and Marxist 'indoctrination'. Rather, the battle was about the destruction and conservation of academic institutions; and it was one in which the Marxist had the advantage over the liberal in virtue of his readiness to recognise that the survival of academic institutions depended upon the exercise of political power in their defence. And in 'The Ideology of Human Rights',[33] he was polemical about the liberal foreign policy of Jimmy Carter. He insisted that the doctrine of 'human rights' was an abstraction from a highly parochial Western constitutionalist tradition. Moreover, its very parochialism was a measure of its failure to engage with the local traditions of the emergent nations in the defence of whose interests it was invoked. Scruton recognised that those nations would turn to Marxism and not liberalism in the future precisely because Marxism understood that national independence depended not upon an ideology, but upon the assertion of national power. Moreover, Scruton insisted upon the philosophical vacuity of the ideology itself. He demonstrated that 'human rights' reflected an appeal to the tradition not of 'natural right' but of natural law; that the ideology was juristically spurious in implying that there could be genuine rights in the absence of reciprocal duties imposed in positive law; and that it was politically naive in providing for no sovereign power against which the rights it asserted could be claimed. Whether because it embodied morality without power or rights without laws, Scruton was clear that the interest of 'humanity' was unacceptably abstract as an objective of foreign policy.

Like Casey, Scruton recognised both that the Conservative Party's association with liberalism exposed it to the charge of cultural philistinism and that what was required in response was a doctrine about culture and education which acknowledged that each expressed the *ends* of life. He emphasised the civilising mission of the humanities in the essay 'Humane Education',[34] defending them against the post-Baconian assumption of the priority of science to moral education. He did not deny that scientific progress was desirable nor that within its own house science was master, there being no 'parts of nature which lie beyond the purview of science'. He did, however, assert the permanence of the humanities and their absolute autonomy from science in terms which combined Arnoldian perceptions of their consolatory power with Kantian emphases upon the priority of the practical to the theoretical reason. 'Values', Scruton was saying, had a priority in the 'human world', and that world had to be mastered in terms of 'reasons' understood by its inhabitants rather than causes uniquely available to the scientist.

A polemical conclusion of the essay was that the real threat to the humanities came not from the sciences, but from those subjects like 'Black Studies' and 'Women's Studies' which tended to undermine the constraints imposed by the traditional disciplines of humane learning by demanding the strict relevance of education to contemporary political fashions. This conclusion did not mean that Scruton believed that politics bore no relation to culture. On the contrary he insisted that they were inextricably related, even affirming in 'Poetry and Politics'[35] that any political doctrine which failed the 'poetical test' by conflicting with man's aesthetic instincts had to be rejected. He was clear, nevertheless, that their relationship was deeply complex. Scruton sought to unravel the complexities in the important essay 'The Politics of Culture'.[36]

'The Politics of Culture' should be read as a conservative defence of traditionalism. It distinguished 'high culture' from both the so-called St Petersburg view, in which culture was merely the 'entertainment of the leisured classes', and the Leninist identification of high culture with the ideology of the ruling class. Notwithstanding the dissociation from Leninism Scruton accepted the Marxist recognition that political arrangements expressed an underlying cultural process. He rejected only the Marxists's denial of the rational autonomy of those immersed in that process. Men, he claimed, had reasons for their actions. Although these reasons were not always articulate, there was, in principle, a description of their participation in society to which they could give their assent and in which they would recognise that their individual intentions and projects had been realised. Where these were to be realised was in the political process itself. Adopting the great distinction in Kant's ethics between ends and means Scruton affirmed that social and political arrangements were ends in their own right. And following Hegel and Marx he affirmed that political ends were the object of *practical* rather than *theoretical* certainty. These ends presupposed principles of political association extending far beyond the narrowly circumscribed limits of the liberal state since they were instantiated ultimately in the historical continuities of the traditions of 'high culture' itself: 'Among the claims that have been made for high culture . . . are the claims that it embodies a shared moral experience, and that it conveys a sense of historical continuity. . . . By a "sense of historical continuity" it is not intended to refer to any accumulation of factual knowledge, of dates, battles, policies and kings, but rather to an intuitive understanding of how *this* arrangement, with which one is . . .

inextricably mingled, has developed in time, and of what it contains by way of potentiality, not just for the future, but for the past'.[37] From the vantage-point of high culture Scruton attacked those liberals who held that the state could be neutral in issues like pornography, and the 'social engineering' which they had promoted in advocating functionalist architecture. This was because he wanted to avoid the philistine view that aesthetic values were merely a matter of individual taste. Inasmuch as they affected the entire quality of the community's life, the aesthetic values embedded in a culture were ends in themselves and the object of practical certainty for the citizen.

Scruton did not suggest that the diversity of cultural continuities and allegiances represented a political problem, that the liberal polity and the democratic constitution had any advantages in accommodating the diversity nor that that diversity was an admirable feature of the modern state. Instead he bemoaned the 'rot of pluralism' and professed his faith in a cultural elite to provide the appropriate articulation of cultural uniformity: 'It is not absurd . . . to rule out of consideration a great many of a man's professed desires and reasons. Nor is it absurd in the case of society. An expression may be disregarded if it contains no serious attempt to understand or articulate the experience which compels it'.[38] In essence this faith reflected an effort to *politicise* the expressionism which Casey had propounded in 'The Autonomy of Art'. What it left unclear was the *political authority* of the elite responsible for the articulation of high culture.

That the doctrine of 'The Politics of Culture' was deeply philosophical and anti-liberal was confirmed in a subsequent essay, 'The Significance of Common Culture',[39] in which Scruton spelled out that the notion of practical knowledge had its origins in Aristotle, and that the working-out of its political implications in Burke and Hegel had issued in profoundly anti-individualistic conclusions. That it was a conservative doctrine was, however, less obvious – it was plainly not a Burkean doctrine lacking, as it did, any appeal to a prescriptive natural law. But that the cultural doctrine conveyed *conservative* intuitions Scruton was entirely convinced, since they were given formal promulgation in a full-length book: *The Meaning of Conservatism*.

The Meaning of Conservatism was a systematic defence of conservatism on a broad philosophical front and it should be read as an extended restatement of the position Casey had reached in 'Tradition and Authority'. The greater part of the book was a sustained critique of the liberal tradition represented by Hobbes, Kant and Mill. It was also – and pre-eminently – a celebration of Hegel in general and *The Philosophy of Right* in particular. As such it departed from the formalism of *Art and Imagination* by asserting a principle essential to conservatism that was radically opposed to Kantian liberalism: 'There is no autonomy that does not presuppose the sense of a social order, and if the order may be ideal, this is only because it was once experienced as real'.[40] The celebration of Hegel reached its mystical culmination in the concluding chapter, 'The Public World', in which the nation-state was upheld as the 'realisation of full political "self-consciousness" ', the statesman urged to embody 'the public voice of the nation' in the manner of Hegel's constitutional monarch and in which the 'private life of the citizen' was stripped of its claim to 'indefeasible right' and consumed entirely by the public world of the nation which it presupposed. And it was everywhere apparent in the much reduced role which Scruton assigned to 'private property' in conservative politics. Property was defended neither in Lockean terms as that to which the citizen had a natural and unconditional right nor in Smithian terms as a concomitant of wealth-creating market capitalism, but in those Hegelian terms in which property was at once a form of individual 'self-realisation' and a manifestation of 'right' itself: '[a] . . . a part of the process whereby man frees himself from the power of things, transforming resistant nature into compliant image'.[41]

As the first chapter made clear, 'The Conservative Attitude' was defined in sharp opposition to the liberal temper and the tradition of natural right which had provided its principal doctrinal inspiration. Not only did the citizen possess no natural right which transcended his obligation to be governed, but there was no 'unconditional' freedom in the sense intended by the natural right theorists. In dissociating conservatism from the natural right tradition, Scruton expressed grave philosophical reservations concerning the fiction of the social contract which had been that tradition's chief theoretical metaphor. What the fiction obscured was the relationship between freedom and political life: freedom was the *consequence* and not the *precondition* of submission to the order imposed by civil and institutional life, of which subordination to the civil authority of government (the legitimacy of which the social contract was invoked to justify) was but a small part.

For all his anti-contractarianism, Scruton nonetheless shared the liberal's conviction that political arrangements had to respect individual freedom in the crucial respect that he was opposed to the imposition of the 'purposive' idiom upon the civil life. Political arrangements were not to be understood as providing the means to some further end not presupposed in themselves. Rather, they had to reflect the internal moral authority which Kant had claimed on behalf of the 'kingdom of ends', Aristotle had claimed on behalf of friendship and *polis* association, and which Oakeshott conveyed in the ideal of 'civil association'. What conservatism opposed was the imposition of ends upon the citizen by government which, in failing to secure his consent and approval, involved a lapse into Kantian heteronomy, Aristotelian tyranny or Oakeshottian 'enterprise association', and the destruction of that reciprocity between ruler and ruled expressed in the principles of 'just dealings between men' conducted in the spirit of 'friendship'. Scruton did not explain why the 'purposive' idiom was not to be resisted in terms of the specification of rights brought into being by the social contract itself in the manner of Hobbes and Locke, or sanctioned by the prescriptive natural law in the manner of Aquinas and Hooker. Instead, he was clear that resistance required simply an application to legal morality of the central Hegelian doctrine that institutional morality was essentially non-instrumental. The application of Hegel provided persuasive reasons for concluding that the utilitarianism of Bentham, Austin and Mill was unable to explain the internal connections between morality and the administration of justice. It was at its least convincing in explaining how opposition to the 'purposive' idiom was to be sustained in the context of the modern democratic state given the undoubted political fact that governments necessarily pursue policies incapable of securing the approval of all their subjects, and in the imposition of which upon them law and the judicial establishment remain very powerful instruments. This consideration raised wider questions concerning the *legitimacy* of the power that law and the state unavoidably exert which Scruton's conservatism implied were nonsensical given his Hegelian identification of right with existing social convention, and his anti-utilitarian determination to eschew the purposive justifications of its exercise without which any answers were impossible. The implication was not merely unfortunate — it challenged the success of his enterprise in re-establishing the connections between politics and morality which Scruton claimed had been broken by the liberal tradition.

The critique of natural right and liberalism informed his discussion of law and constitutional government. In connection with law Scruton dissented from the view developed by Hobbes and Kant, and enshrined by Mill, that a system of law was subordinate to the requirements of individual liberty, that its justification was 'protective' and that the freedom of the individual was to be realised in some sphere lying beyond the constraining obligations imposed by the positive law. Scruton insisted that the view had to be resisted on the Hegelian ground that there was no genuine autonomy in the absence of a social order more substantial than that created by a common system of law. The natural right tradition was defective because it took the fiction of the 'consenting adult' as its premise and the justification of government as its conclusion, whereas the truth was that the 'consenting adult' possessed no freedom in abstraction from the social and economic order which law and government presupposed. As Scruton stressed, the fiction was not even reflected in English law: the laws of obscenity, libel and blasphemy established that the criminal law was directly concerned with private and public morality; the law imposed restraints upon trade and commercial contract; and it recognised no indefeasible right to dispose of private property. In the last resort 'the autonomous individual' of liberal theory was 'the product of practices . . . [designating] him as social'. Ultimately it was the identity of law and society which provided the firmest guarantee that the state commanded the allegiance of its subjects. Accordingly, every area of civil society concerning morality, education and commerce was legitimately subject to the jurisdiction of the positive law. Thus Scruton was saying that the content of a given legal system embodied a *political* commitment to certain exclusive substantive ends, and that it was the error of the liberal to pretend otherwise by detaching 'from the law the image of a particular social arrangement'. In this commitment the law had its role to play not in protecting natural rights held by the citizen against the state itself, but in legitimising the exercise of state power by subordinating it to the moral requirements of the rule of law. Consequently, what constrained the state in its exercise of legitimate power was the basic core of natural justice reflected in the procedural elements of the English Common Law.

In relation to the constitution of state Scruton was clear that there was no ideal type of constitution, that every constitution was the product of contingent historical circumstances and that none could be constructed at will to accord with some independently premeditated model. In contrast with the liberal, the conservative was acutely aware of both the political consequences of *historical relativism* – since what commanded his respect were always the constitutional arrangements of 'a particular country, a particular history, a particular form of life' – and the cultural diversity of those arrangements. The truth was that 'to the extent that there are arrangements that have been proved in social life, and which have the power to command the loyalty of their participants, to that extent is there variety among the forms of conservative politics'.[42] Thus not only did the prescription of 'human rights' in isolation from the settled traditions of constitutional government which had generated the morality unique to the English Common Law involve a retreat into abstraction – it had the pernicious consequence, entirely unwelcome to the conservative, of conferring the universal moral authority once claimed by the 'imperial and ecclesiastical supremacy' upon the parochial traditions of Western democracy.

What informed Scruton's conservatism was the Hegelian principle that the constitution of state was inseparable from the traditions of civil society, supported by the conclusions of the later Wittgenstein. The constitution was not a mere 'body of rules' since rules had no existence apart from a complex background of custom and social convention. In claiming that it was, liberalism was the 'political survival of the Cartesian theory of mind', which sought 'to represent the mind of society as functioning in accidental relation to its body'. Moreover, in justifying the authority of civil society in terms of a pre-social act of consent liberalism was flawed in exactly those respects exposed by Hegel and Wittgenstein since it denied the truth that 'without social order the very notion of an individual committing himself through a promise would not arise'.[43]

Scruton was entirely right to insist upon what liberalism obscured: the *political* implications for the structure and quality of civil society of the character of the law and constitution of the state. He made, however, an improper inference from the necessity of those implications to an assumption of communal and cultural homogeneity within any existing state. He criticised much social democratic and socialist legislation, for instance, on the ground that it severed the traditions of civil society from the state. And he justified the independent judiciary on the ground that it imposed the restraints of natural justice upon the wilful pursuit of 'social justice' by government. The criticism assumed – what was politically untrue – that socialist aspirations were not themselves nourished by legitimate political traditions belonging to civil society. It assumed also – what was constitutionally questionable – that the political momentum of civil society required no exercise of legislative sovereignty for its articulation in law that was not to some degree arbitrary and controversial. The justification neglected the political character of the judiciary itself, the extent to which the cause of social justice could be promoted through a legitimate exercise of sovereignty in accordance with the rule of law, and the extent to which the restraints of natural justice had the inevitable political consequence of *preserving* the *existing* distribution of economic and political power within civil society. In virtue of this neglect Scruton tended to confer the authority of natural law upon political arrangements which were the product of history in breach of the very Marxist dogmas he readily invoked against liberalism.

Like Casey, Scruton claimed both that conservatism was not necessarily anti-Marxist and that it was closer to Marxism than to *laissez-faire* liberalism. What was defective about Marxism, Scruton argued, was its materialism and determinism which had led Marxists to obscure a principle upon which conservatives would generally insist: 'that the political activity of the citizen is determined by his own conception of his social nature'.[44] It was nonetheless the virtue of Marxism that it rejected the abstraction of natural rights in the name of the socio-economic order which political arrangements presupposed. Marxism thus provided a doctrinal precedent for the rejection of the atomistic individualism implicit in the social contract for its exclusion of all the mediating institutions and forms of life of civil society through which the subject identified himself with the state as a matter of allegiance. Marxism thus acknowledged, as liberalism did not, the existence of what the conservative held to be desirable: the existence of an extensive political establishment through which the otherwise abstract authority of the state could be made tolerable to the citizen. Any association, like trades unions or the church, which provided a focus of allegiance for the citizen within civil society had a political significance and it was, in consequence, the duty of government to ratify it to ensure that the 'power of the state links itself and becomes one with the power of society'. Thus Scruton argued in favour of an established church as a reinforcement of 'the attachment of the citizen to the forms of civil life'; urged a realistic attitude towards trades unions in which the legal establishment of their de facto power would entail their answerability to the state; and he defended the integrity of class loyalties not as a consequence of the 'varying relations to the means of production', but as a focus of cultural identity which was not to be sacrificed in the cause of the classless egalitarian society.

The Meaning of Conservatism was not a liberal book. Nor was it an Oakeshottian book. Whilst Scruton made an Hegelian affirmation of the bonds connecting state and civil society, Oakeshott tended to make a Hobbesian affirmation of their mutual distinctness. Scruton upheld the claims of community against the narrowly legalistic conception of the state which had inspired Oakeshott's 'civil association', insisting that a common legal culture was an abstraction in the absence of a social order comprising a national culture shared by all its subjects, and a political establishment including church, class and corporative life far more extensive than the strictly 'civil' establishment of Oakeshott's *respublica*. Moreover, whereas Oakeshott explicitly claimed allegiance to the natural right tradition of Bodin, Hobbes, Spinoza and Kant, Scruton was a self-confessed Hegelian critic of that tradition and, in consequence, tended towards a teleological justification of civil authority which Oakeshott scrupulously excluded. In these respects Scruton had less sense of the plurality of cultural and traditional allegiances, little of Oakeshott's sceptical recognition of their inevitable diversity and was less exercised by the moral difference between the voluntary character of corporative association and *sittlich* relations on the one hand and the compulsory character of the state on the other. If Scruton was shrewder than Oakeshott in acknowledging the extent of the political power vested in the public realm of state and civil society, he was considerably less troubled about the entitlement of the state to exercise it in the coercion of the individual citizen. Whether we stress Oakeshott's libertarian disdain for compulsion or his concern to establish the 'positive' extent of the citizen's legal obligations, we are stressing that Oakeshott, both tonally and doctrinally, placed an absolute moral value upon freedom whereas Scruton obviously did not.

iv

Both Casey and Scruton developed their conservative doctrine with a bulk of evidential support from the history of ideas. The significance of *From Descartes to Wittgenstein* was that it provided a sustained historical gloss on that doctrine. The book was a general introduction to modern philosophy. It nonetheless had a clear doctrine about the development of post-Cartesian philosophy which sought to restore Kant and Hegel to their proper pre-eminence by demonstrating their relation to Wittgensteinianism.

Scruton began with Descartes. Descartes's achievement had been to subordinate metaphysics to epistemology and to establish the ascendancy of empiricist assumptions within epistemology itself. This ascendancy rested upon Descartes's assertion of the 'priority of the first-person case'. That priority established that the knowledge which the self possessed of its own mental states was the 'paradigm of certainty' and that it had an authority which its knowledge of other minds and the material world lacked. The 'priority of the first-person case' together with the mind-body dualism which it entailed had issued in two principles concerning the nature of human knowledge: that its true idiom was that of the 'natural sciences' and that knowledge was essentially 'contemplative' rather than 'practical'. All Scruton's preferences amongst subsequent philosophers were for those who qualified these Cartesian principles. The most important were Kant, Hegel and Wittgenstein.

Kant was the 'greatest philosopher since Aristotle', and his masterpiece, *The Critique of Pure Reason*, laid claim to greatness for its replacement of epistemology with metaphysics and the decisive rejection of the 'first-person privileges' in the argument of 'The Transcendental Deduction of the Categories'. The 'transcendental' status which Kant attributed to the subject in 'apperception' meant that it was possible to explain – in a way unavailable to empiricists like Hume who stood in the Cartesian tradition – in what sense the experience of the self had a unity beyond the mere collection of its present thoughts and feelings. The self-knowledge which was peculiarly subjective, to which Descartes had assigned the privilege of certainty, was possible only because the self possessed an enduring identity in the objective world.

It was natural – given his intellectual development from Kant to Hegel – that Scruton should interpret Hegel as fulfilling the Kantian metaphysical enterprise, and as enjoying his status as 'the towering presence in modern philosophy' in virtue of his qualification of Kantianism at all those points where it was least acceptable to the conservative theorist: its realism; its formalism; its failure to associate the 'objective' dimension introduced by the categories of human understanding with the social and institutional world of human practices.

Scruton acknowledged the still widespread anti-metaphysical disillusionment with Hegel characteristic of Moore, Russell and the early Wittgenstein. Nevertheless, he emphasised that Hegel could be rehabilitated by demonstrating the continuities between his extension of Kant and the spirit of modern philosophy. This was true supremely of *The Phenomenology of Mind*. The *Phenomenology* extended what had been implicit in Kant's Transcendental Deduction. Thus it amalgamated the practical and theoretical reason; insisted upon the 'publicity' of human self-knowledge; and demonstrated that the 'pure' subject of Cartesian psychology achieved knowledge of itself only when the objectivity of the world which it inhabited was postulated. In affirming that the self acquired self-knowledge only through its active participation in the public world of ethical and political institutions, Hegel had demonstrated the priority of *practical knowledge* within the enterprise of establishing the 'third-person case' denied in the Cartesian model of 'contemplative' knowledge and obscured by the formalism of Kant's transcendentalism.

In this connection the discussion of Wittgenstein's later philosophy at the conclusion of the book was of great importance. Scruton stressed both the anti-positivism and anthropocentric dimension of the post-*Tractatus* thought. What was 'given' in his later thought was not the sense-data of the positivists, but the 'forms of life' of Kantian anthropology. And he brought out the familiar tenets of late Wittgenstein: its hostility towards the scientific idiom; its vindication of the Kantian principle that the world was to be understood under the aspect of 'meaning' and human conduct understood in terms of reasons and not causes; and its emphasis upon the 'publicity' of sense which explained why the subject's participation in a 'language-game' necessarily excluded the consequences of Cartesian 'privacy'. All this was well known. What was striking were the claims which Scruton made on behalf of Wittgenstein *vis-à-vis* Kant and Hegel. Wittgenstein's philosophy, Scruton argued, was the justification in an unparasitic idiom of the Kantian enterprise initiated in the 'Transcendental Deduction'. With such arguments as those against the possibility of 'private languages', Wittgenstein had demonstrated conclusively that the first-person case could yield nothing knowable about the world, since first-personal knowledge was contingent upon a capacity to speak a 'public' language. Moreover, Wittgenstein fulfilled the ambition of Hegel himself and Scruton concluded the book with a judgement on his greatness which serves as an epigraph to his and Casey's achievement: 'The assumption that there is a first-person certainty which provides a starting-point for philosophical enquiry, this assumption which has led to the rationalism of Descartes and to the empiricism of Hume, to so much of modern epistemology and so much modern metaphysics, has been finally removed from the centre of philosophy. The ambition of Kant and Hegel, to achieve a philosophy which removes the "self" from the beginning of knowledge so as to return it in an enriched and completed form at the end, has perhaps now been fulfilled'.[45]

In relation to political philosophy Scruton provided interpretations of the central theorists which confirmed the doctrine of *The Meaning of Conservatism*. With Hobbes, Scruton stressed neither the 'authoritarianism', the 'nominalism' nor the relation between his contractarianism and liberalism upon which Oakeshott had placed most emphasis. Indeed, Hobbes emerged only barely distinguishable from Hegel himself. It was because Hobbes had distinguished the 'unconditional authority' of the sovereign from his 'absolute power' that he had made *legitimacy* the central question in political theory. His voluntarist perception that there was ' "no obligation on any man which ariseth not from some act of his own" ' Scruton took to establish that the legitimacy of civil government was created by the 'consent' of its subjects and that the participation in the state which civil obligation imposed was fully 'intentional'. Hobbes was limited, however, because his adherence to contractarianism left the liberty which was the converse of civil obligation unacceptably negative and abstract. Rousseau's *Social Contract* represented an advance upon *Leviathan*. But whilst Scruton emphasised the importance of the fiction of the 'General Will' in establishing that moral and political freedom was the result of man's admission to civil society he left the impression, ultimately, that Rousseau was but an introduction to Hegel.

Scruton's exposition of Hegel left no doubt that Hegel was profoundly right about politics. First, Hegel had recognised that the state was a *person* in its own right and that, accordingly, it had to be understood as an end and not a means. Second, the distinction between state and civil society of *The Philosophy of Right* demonstrated that the state could not arise from a contract and that, in consequence, the appeal to a freedom existing in the state of nature was an illusion. Third, Hegel brought political philosophy into relation with a philosophy of mind vastly superior in its ethical implications to that of the liberal tradition of Bentham and Mill. Fourth, he extended the concept of legitimacy which had been intimated in Hobbes by showing that legitimacy transcended the 'natural right' of the individual and so arose through neither 'contract' nor 'tacit consent'.

About Scruton's discussion of Hegel it is necessary to say only that it confirmed the claims of *The Meaning of Conservatism* at every turn. It demonstrated that political self-knowledge presupposed the public realm of institutions and that the positive freedom achieved through participation in that realm could not be understood in utilitarian terms.

About *Kant* it is necessary to say less. *Kant* was a traditional – and highly Strawsonian – interpretation which brought out Kant's contribution to the overthrow of Cartesian dualism and the emergence of his critical philosophy as a transcendence of Hume's empiricism and Leibniz's rationalism. But ultimately it should be read as a reiteration of what Scruton had argued in other contexts: that Kant's was a defence of the *objectivity* of human knowledge.

V

Since assuming the editorship of *The Salisbury Review* in 1982 Scruton has been transforming his philosophical conservatism into an articulate public doctrine. In effecting the transformation Scruton made three assumptions. First, that the 'ruling socialist' consensus dominating post-war British politics had collapsed. Second, that that consensus had lacked any serious account of 'what a society without class, privileges and private ownership of the means of production would be like'.[46] Third, that the stance of 'pragmatic adjustment' adopted by the Conservative Party during the post-war phase of resistance to socialism was no longer adequate and that, accordingly, the party in government should be prepared to consider 'radical measures' so that 'radical measures [would] be the norm'.[47]

It is questionable how radical were the measures which Scruton himself proposed for the new ideological conservatism. Most of them had been acceptable conservative orthodoxies during the Butskellite consensus and none called into serious question the principal achievement of that consensus: the welfare state. He made statements on substantive issues about national defence, celebrating the Falklands victory, stressing the Soviet menace and upholding the American alliance;[48] about immigration, advocating voluntary repatriation and full integration;[49] about conservation, demonstrating that the cause was not an 'exclusively left-wing issue' and that regimes exercising 'social ownership' had failed to fulfil its objectives, and urging conservative governments to adopt 'interventionist measures' transcending 'the merely legal restraints upon a market economy' to solve the problem of environmental control in the nuclear age;[50] about capital punishment, adopting an Hegelian position about the unique morality of the retributive principle of punishment and a Hobbesian position on the right of the state to inflict capital punishment as a necessary concomitant of its possession of full sovereign power;[51] about fiscal policy, prescribing the abolition of capital taxation[52] and regretting the transfer of stately homes from 'public to private ownership' resulting from the imposition of death duties;[53] about education, upholding the classical disciplines[54] and condemning the subordination of the 'ends' of collegiate life to 'the shibboleths of social policy'.[55] And he made statements about the desirability of preserving social privileges, not as ends in themselves, but as the necessary condition of other values, arguing that the hereditary principle was a 'major safeguard of the national wealth';[56] that a diversity of privately administered 'schools and colleges' alone provided a 'standard against which the officially sanctioned "education" [could] be judged';[57] and that privilege was an unavoidable consequence of the principle of freedom of association which offered the best defence for civil society against the tyrannical abuse of power by the state that constituted the most indefensible 'privilege' of all.[58]

The majority of these statements need not detain us. Save for some conciliatory remarks about the 'free market',[59] they were crystallisations of positions implicit in *The Meaning of Conservatism*. They should be understood primarily as attempts to establish the philosophical defensibility of the 'sentiments of the people' which Scruton claimed had been belittled by the unargued consensual prejudices of the media, universities, professions and Parliament.[60] In some cases – capital punishment and immigration – left-liberal victories gained in earlier battles were merely confirmed by conservative inaction after 1979. With others – fiscal policy, private education and social privilege – battles won for conservatism after 1979 were to be explained partly in terms of left-liberal irresolution after 1964. And with one issue, the Falklands war, Scruton conferred a retroactive coherence of governmental principle upon a fortuitous political triumph, neglecting the unclarity of governmental intention preceding it and the political possibilities for pragmatic opportunism which it provided.

That the statements were marginal to the political phenomenon which they were intended to legitimise is easily established. In issuing them Scruton assumed that 1979 marked a significant departure from the consensus which preceded it. He thus minimised the extent to which the Thatcher years, in respect of the growth of public spending and domestic demand, the fall in industrial production and of the continuing imbalance of payments, have reflected trends fully continuous with trends first established in the 1950s. And in assuming that Thatcherism was a politics whose ideological commitments were other than gratuitous, Scruton minimised the extent to which the conditions for its initial success in 1979 had been created as much by the Labour Party's reluctance to implement socialist solutions to the problems of inflation and impending unemployment after 1966 as to the persuasiveness of the monetarist critique of statism and Butskellism; and the extent to which the landslide endorsement of 1983 was a consequence of electoral opportunism as much as ideological vindication.

The remoteness of Scruton's philosophical conservatism from Thatcherism is neither surprising – given the Hegelian positions he had adopted during the middle seventies – nor intrinsically important – given that the conservatism which he has propounded since 1982 has conveyed greater moral conviction than political judgement. The truth remains that the ideological foundations of his conservatism have not been Thatcherite: its liberalism has not been economic but constitutionalist, and its conservatism has been grounded upon an appeal to a doctrine about law and morality which Scruton has treated as fundamental to the traditions of western constitutionalist government.

In upholding the constitutionalist traditions of the west Scruton made four polemical claims. First, that western governments were united in alone having acquired the moral authority conferred by constitutional legitimacy. Second, that the chief tenets of western constitutionalism established connections between law and morality fulfilling at least some of the aspirations of the traditional natural law. Third, that there existed an absolute ideological division between the constitutional governments of the free west and the governments of the communist east and third world whose purposive engagements were incompatible with the provisions of the natural law. Fourth, that the nature of both western unity and the ideological division was generally misunderstood owing to the obsession of western liberals with democracy, human rights and distinctions between left- and right-wing political affiliations.

In a *Salisbury Review* article, 'Turkey and the West',[61] Scruton made it clear that those obsessions had obscured the fundamental harmony between western constitutionalism and General Evren's military government. Since 1980 General Evren had governed according to a constitution which adhered faithfully to the Ataturkist principles of 'representative, secular and constitutionalist government' upon which the post-Ottoman Turkish state had been established. In consequence, not only was Evren's Turkey a strategically indispensable ally of the west in providing a bulwark against Islamic revolutionary theocracy and Soviet expansion – it was also a natural ideological ally in upholding a 'European rule of law'. The fundamental principles of the harmony between Turkey and the west were threefold: constitutionality; succession; consensus. Western governments had acquired constitutionality because they respected the principle of 'judicial independence' which represented the condition of the rule of law rather than the rule of arbitrary government. Second, they maintained a tradition of constitutional law which established authoritative rules of succession for the legitimate occupation of offices and imposed an absolute distinction between the authority of the civil office and the personal attributes of its various occupants. Finally, western governments had acquired legitimacy because their adherence to constitutional rule had generated a consensus in their favour on the part of their subjects which conferred an authority upon them in excess of the mere power that they commanded.

In spelling out the tenets of constitutional rule Scruton was scrupulous in emphasising what constitutionality did not require. It did not require the provision of a 'written' constitution. The greatest legacy of the British Empire to the newly independent nations had not been the gift of written constitutions, Scruton argued, but a 'developed legal system, with elaborate common law rights . . . supported by a system of natural justice'.[62] Nor did constitutionality presuppose any particular form of economic order. In one *Salisbury Review* editorial[63] Scruton denied that constitutional government was bound to promote the economic conditions of the 'free market'. The liberties peculiar to the free market depended finally upon the 'wider questions of social and political equilibrium' settled by law and civil society. Not only had constitutional government the right to intervene in the economy in the interests of preserving that equilibrium, but the attempt by government to *impose* the conditions of the free market upon societies such as Britain which possessed a settled tradition of 'mixed economy . . . [and] a settled expectation of employment' represented a dangerous and unconservative retreat into ideological politics. If Scruton dissociated constitutionalism from economic liberalism, he nonetheless dissociated it firmly from the welfare socialism which bound governments to provide substantive benefits for their subjects. Thus in another *Salisbury Review* editorial[64] he questioned the philosophical coherence of the principle of the 'right to work' prescribed in the soviet constitution. Whereas a right existed only where there was a reciprocal duty and power to enforce it, the 'right to work' imposed a self-contradictory duty upon government to provide work in economic conditions which made it impossible for it to do so. Not only was there no guarantee that governmental intervention could remedy unemployment, but the attempt by government to secure the 'right to work' in conditions of recession compromised the rights which its subjects indisputably possessed under constitutional rule, through the creation and exercise of coercive powers by the state.

Above all else, Scruton was clear that constitutionalism did not require that government be constituted according to democratic principles. In fact he emphasised that the majoritarian principle of legitimacy had proved generally destructive of the principles of constitutional rule. He argued that it had been the maintenance of judicial independence which had preserved constitutional rule in South Africa whilst it had been its subversion under majoritarianism which had destroyed it throughout the greater part of Black Africa.[65] And in the British context he affirmed that the non-elected House of Lords and independent judiciary rather than the elected opposition imposed the genuine constitutional restraints upon the arbitrary exercise of sovereign power by the democratically elected parliamentary majority.[66]

Scruton's reservations about democracy were a measure of the strength of his belief that constitutional government was under threat in the modern world. He made statements about its principal enemies which left no doubt that there was little to separate Marxist–Leninism from German fascism and the revolutionary socialism of Angola, Zimbabwe, Vietnam, Cambodia and Mozambique, in their common antagonism towards the principles of constitutionalism. He wrote in the conviction that the systematic violation of constitutionalist principles throughout the phase of Stalinism was the natural consequence of the theoretical tenets of the Marxist–Leninism upon which Stalin had drawn and which had inspired revolutionary nationalism in the third world. This was so because Leninism sanctioned the systematic subordination of the law and constitution to the will of the ruling party in the name of socialist legality, the suppression of judicial independence in the interests of revolutionary justice, the absorption of all institutions into the state and the imposition of a 'command structure' by the ruling party upon the state, economy and civil society. In all these respects Leninism coincided with the spirit and practice of nazism. The 'racism' of Hitler's nazism paralleled the 'classism' of Leninism by substituting the fiction of collective responsibility for the reality of individual responsibility and so undermining the moral notions of agency and desert upon which the very idea of law was founded.[67] Moreover both had diverged from western constitutionalism in their failure to tolerate a lawful political opposition within the constraints of constitutional rule.[68] Scruton concluded that even those Marxists who had criticised soviet communism or developed the original Marxism in the face of political circumstances unforeseen by Marx himself had failed to revise Marxism in terms consistent with the requirements of constitutionality. He was clear that this had been the failing of Gramsci,[69] whose doctrine of the hegemony of the Marxist intellectuals failed to engage with the crucial political issue of the accommodation of opposition under the constitution and left unanswered the question of the legitimacy of their rule in the revolutionary state. And it was the failing of Rudolf Bahro,[70] whose critique of soviet practice had stopped short of attributing soviet tyranny to the structural requirements of state socialism itself and whose vision of redeemed bureaucratic communism retained the very principle of the 'one-party state' which had proved the greatest obstacle to the rule of law in post-revolutionary Russia.

For all its polemical conclusions about practical politics the ideological conservatism of *The Salisbury Review* was nonetheless inspired by sophisticated philosophical and jurisprudential convictions. This fact explains the importance of Scruton's *Dictionary of Political Thought*. The *Dictionary* was an admirable example of its genre and it remains arguably Scruton's most accomplished book. It is important because it provided a systematic *philosophical* elucidation of the legalistic and constitutionalist conservatism defended in the *Review* and *Times*. In this connection it is necessary to say, first, that the book manifested the increasing influence of Oakeshott, and second, that it implied that the tradition of liberal constitutionalism rested upon surer connections between law and morality than those established by modern liberal theory. The *Dictionary* made statements about *Natural Right, Natural Law, Human Rights* and *Natural Justice*. These statements established that the truth contained in traditional natural law doctrine lay not in the prescriptions of a 'substantial' moral law but in the core of formal natural justice reflected in the two principles governing the procedures of adjudication: 'that no man shall be judge in his own cause' and 'that each side be heard and no one condemned unheard'. They vindicated the strong sense in which the natural right to adjudication was fundamental given that the existence of all positive rights presupposed the existence of a 'legal procedure whereby to uphold them'. And they clarified the confusions surrounding the modern conception of human rights by drawing attention to the truth that the right to due process of law was the only genuine human right commanding universal assent. The book also made statements about constitutional government. These asserted that the model upon which western constitutionalism was based had been provided by neither Locke nor Montesquieu but by the *Politics* of Aristotle. And they filled out the senses in which the very notions of constitutionality and the rule of law entailed respect for the canons of procedural justice. This meant not simply that the constitution of the state declare the supremacy of law and that the power of the state be exercised through offices in accordance with established law. It meant, more strongly, that the law be enforceable in open court by the private citizen against the state itself for the unlawful acts of its officers. In the absence of the 'judicial independence' which alone made that enforcement possible, Scruton insisted, there was neither a genuine separation of powers nor a genuine constitution, since if the state and its officers had an exclusive power to enforce the constitution then the constitution itself provided for no legal constraints upon their actions.

The *Dictionary* was at its most powerful in the continuities it suggested between ethics, political philosophy, jurisprudence and legal practice. It made statements about the English law which demonstrated that the connections between law and morality were stronger than either the natural right, utilitarian or Marxist traditions allowed. The entries on *Crime, Tort, Contract, Common Law, Statute, Equity, Adjudication* and so on conveyed Scruton's dissatisfaction with both the tradition of legal positivism of Hobbes, Bentham, Austin, Kelsen and Hart, in which the connections were held to be merely contingent, and the ethical presuppositions of Kantian liberalism with which that tradition was ultimately associated. Scruton qualified the doctrine common to those positivist jurists that the model of positive law was the paradigm of all law; and his entries on law implicitly challenged their voluntarist assumptions that the source of all valid law was the *will* of the sovereign legislator and the source of all valid legal obligation was the *consent* of its subjects. Thus whilst he acknowledged that the law of contract reflected the Kantian notion of the 'autonomous moral agent who puts himself under an obligation through his voluntary act', Scruton insisted that the principles governing contractual relations were not constitutive of most forms of legal order. They underlay neither the general obligation 'to refrain from harming another' imposed by the law of tort, nor the authority of those non-contractual associations like the family and the state whose obligations arose from their 'autonomous nature and not from the agreement of the parties'. They failed to account for the Common Law crimes of murder, theft and rape which corresponded to 'antecedent moral intuitions' about substantive moral values grounded in human nature itself. And they were incapable of explaining the tradition of Equity which provided judicial remedies in the absence of positive remedies in the Common and Statute law. Where Equity was concerned, Scruton did not deny that express legislative enactment was a source of law nor that statute law possessed a supreme authority within the jurisdiction of English law. But he emphasised that statute law was merely a part of the law, the greater part of which was derived from the legal customs of the Common Law generated by continuous adherence to 'entrenched judicial precedent'. Moreover, inasmuch as statute law presupposed an independent judiciary authorised to apply it, it was constrained by the principles of natural justice governing judicial interpretation which were not themselves revocable by the determinations of the sovereign legislator. The principles of mens rea, the priority of proven offence to punishment and of the intuitive injustice of retrospective legislation and strict liability enshrined in the criminal law, for instance, reflected the extent to which those principles of natural justice entered into judicial interpretation. And the precedence of Equity over the Common Law indicated the extent to which those principles were constitutive of English law as such.

At times Scruton has adopted the perspective of ethical naturalism in matters of morality to complement the legal naturalism which the *Dictionary* associated with the traditions of English law. He has made anti-Kantian assumptions about the ultimate derivation of the moral law in order to insist that certain values are grounded in human nature and do not arise from the autonomous exercise of human choice. Thus he attacked the ethics of 'authenticity' of Laing and Sartre;[71] heart transplant and sex change operations for having undermined the values of 'love, loyalty and friendship' derived from 'the natural condition of men';[72] and feminism for its corruption of 'human nature'[73] and reduction of sexuality to a mere 'animal function' liberated from 'the restraints of family life, sexual roles, modesty and chastity'.[74] Moreover, he has argued for both the legitimacy and desirability of the state's enforcement of the moral law, insisting upon the fully political character of 'sexual love and family life'[75] and defending the legal prohibition of paedophilia on the grounds that liberal pluralism was an illusion and that no society could survive in 'a state of moral insensibility'.[76]

It is unquestionable that Scruton's sophisticated legal naturalism was persuasive as a polemical instrument in the exposure of liberal shallowness. It established that the relation between law and morality was more complex juristically and of greater political consequence than liberals complacently assumed. Nevertheless Scruton did not confront a fundamental question posed by the liberal tradition itself: whether the enforcement of morality by the state conflicted with the values of legal morality which he upheld. Nor was Scruton explicit about the source of the moral law, which the state had a duty to enforce, in a predominantly secular age. Save for a polemic against the liberal churchmen which denied any necessary connection between Christian doctrine and the unavoidably partial opinions about human morality and politics[77] he was deafeningly silent about ecclesiastical religion in general and the Church-State question in particular. And in the context of Ataturkism he made it clear that the tradition of western constitutionalism had been admirably secular in its ethical presuppositions. Ultimately it has to be concluded that his naturalistic perspective involved Scruton in no important doctrinal departures from the Kantian ethical principles first sketched in 'Attitudes, Beliefs and Reasons' and the Hegelian association of law with the prevailing conventions of social morality defended in *The Meaning of Conservatism*. On the contrary, with the exception of the criminal law prohibitions on murder, rape and theft, Scruton's conception of the connection between law and morality reflected a commitment on his part to a procedural natural law in service to liberal values profoundly antagonistic towards any employment of legal means by the state in the enforcement of substantive ends. About that commitment it is necessary to raise two questions: in what senses it diverged from the spirit of *The Meaning of Conservatism*; and in what senses the divergence implicated Scruton in a backsliding alliance with liberalism.

Scruton's invocation of the procedural natural law obviously involved a recession from the Hegelian *etatisme* expressed in *The Meaning of Conservatism* towards the liberal constitutionalism embodied in Oakeshottian conservatism. To the extent that the recession aligned Scruton with the anti-totalitarian stance of Hayek, Popper, Talmon and Oakeshott, it marked a departure from the mobilisation of Rousseau, Hegel and Marx that had been fundamental to his critique of liberalism throughout the seventies. Whereas Scruton had previously employed Marxist doctrines in a concerted attack upon the ascendancy of liberal utilitarianism, *The Salisbury Review* replaced the *political* onslaught upon liberalism with an *ethical* assault upon Marxism. Moreover, the negativities towards Islamic theocracy, Leninism, Stalinism, nazism and state socialism conveyed an hostility towards the political regulation of culture and civil society by the exercise of state control which had been demanded by the Hegelian positions adopted during the earlier phase.

In one sense, the liberal recognitions expressed in *The Salisbury Review* provided a retrospective gloss upon *The Meaning of Conservatism* in drawing attention to the fact that its Hegelianism had been deployed to defend *liberal* values. They left it clear that the civil society which Scruton had insisted that the state uphold was ideally a civil society rich in the liberal diversity of its institutions and cultural traditions; and that the ends to be realised in the political realm which he alleged that liberalism had reduced to the status of means were ultimately the ends of liberal, romantic culture. In another sense, the recognitions were fully continuous with the Hegelianism of *The Meaning of Conservatism* in their assumption of the conclusiveness of the Kantian distinction between man and nature. Although Scruton attacked the utilitarian separation of law and morality imposed by legal positivism to uphold the natural law, he did so in the name of liberal values derived from Kantian premises concerning the autonomy of rational nature itself. So far from reviving a naturalistic ethics,

SCRUTON's adherence to Kantianism precluded any derivation of the moral law from a determinate core of human nature abstracted from history which did not presuppose the intervention of the active, autonomous will, whether the individual rational will of Kantian liberalism or the historical will of Hegelian conservatism. The adherence to Kantianism was problematic since it tended to expose the precarious position of the natural law, which Scruton invoked to resist collectivism, social democracy, welfare economics and socialist redistribution, in a post-Kantian ethical context in which the pass had been sold in matters of personal and objective morality to all the liberalising, humanistic forces being resisted – Hegelian historicism included.

Despite his increasing indebtedness to Oakeshott, it should not be thought that Scruton's legal proceduralism was unequivocally Oakeshottian. His preference for the customary law of the English Common Law and his appeal to the legal model of Equity conflicted with much of what Oakeshott had inherited from Hobbes, particularly his voluntarist emphasis upon the priority of the positive to the natural law. Moreover, whereas Scruton's earlier high culturalism had been discordant with Oakeshott's libertarian tone, his assertion of the procedural natural law was marked by a tone of ideological rationalism entirely discordant with the spirit of Oakeshott's anti-rationalism. Indeed, in *universalising* the canons of procedural natural justice, in indifference to the diverse conventions of time and place upon which Oakeshott placed such weight, Scruton betrayed an absence of the historical relativism that, in his Hegelian phase, he had insisted was essential to the conservative attitude. In that respect he deviated not only from Oakeshott, but from the Marxist orthodoxies which he had earlier freely adopted in the battle against liberal rationalism.

The legal proceduralism which inspired Scruton's anti-Marxism conflicted with the Hegelian perspective of *The Meaning of Conservatism*. The legal formalism to which it reduced implied a severance of the legal order of the state from civil society, and placed the conditions of 'objective freedom' beyond the political realm in exactly the liberal senses which Scruton had previously condemned. It thus obscured the truths upon which Marxism had insisted: that a schedule of positive law does reflect the socio-economic interests of the political classes and that the rule of law tends inevitably to legitimise a social order which enshrines socio-economic inequalities between those classes. And it obscured the truth that the 'ascendancy of statute' and the concomitant subordination of the Common Law was an historical consequence of the conditions of economic and industrial development characteristic of the modern democratic state, conditions under which the state was necessarily 'managerial', the civil law necessarily an instrument of policy and the identification of legal and natural justice with the cause of social and distributive justice a necessary condition of the state's continuing to command the consent of its subjects. In obscuring those truths, Scruton's legal proceduralism diverted attention away from the *compulsory* character of the state and the irreversibility of the power which it exerts and left unanswered the question of the *justification* of the ends that law imposes and the coercive sanctions it inflicts upon its subjects. He thus left it unclear how that question could be answered on any grounds other than the utilitarian grounds he explicitly rejected; and in what respects other than those based upon unargued aesthetic or political preferences his legal proceduralism was *morally* distinguishable from the utilitarianism it was designed to supplant. Finally, Scruton's anti-Marxism involved him a failure to achieve transparency about the ideological assumptions of the legal proceduralism for which he claimed the status of natural law. Inasmuch as it was an abstract of the traditions of the English Common Law, it was a form of natural law grounded entirely upon the historical continuities manifested in the human world. Yet the source of its derivation tended to deprive it of both its 'naturalistic' and 'pre-conventional' character and to provide little defence against the Marxist charge that the canons of the procedural natural law were an ideological abridgement of the conventions of a determinate historical tradition, belonging to a particular culture on behalf of which none of the universalist claims associated with the natural law could be advanced.

The retreat into rationalism and liberal ideology which marked Scruton's anti-Marxist phase was of great consequence for his treatment of two political issues: international relations and British socialism.

vi

In both *The Times* and *The Salisbury Review* Scruton has defended NATO as providing international security for the constitutionalist west against the threat of ideological subversion posed by Soviet imperialism. His defence has rested upon the premises that the Soviet Union possesses aggressive intentions towards western Europe; that Soviet 'enmity towards our freedoms, our institutions, our customs, our religion and our ideals has existed unaltered since 1917';[78] and that Soviet aggression can be resisted only through the American alliance. Given the extent of the Soviet threat Scruton has been clear that the peace movement – in both its internationalist and pacifist sentiments and its multilateral disarming objectives – has constituted a menace to western security and the maintenance of peace itself: the movement ignored the unavoidable truths, upon which the deterrent theory insisted, that international peace required not 'the absence of weapons, but the absence of war' and that its preservation in Europe depended upon the west's 'matching the armaments and blocking the expansionist policies of the Soviet Union'.[79] Scruton has been clear also, however, that the arguments of isolationists like Enoch Powell have been equally flawed. In *The Salisbury Review* article 'Powell and the Alliance'[80] he denied that the undermining of Britain's national sovereignty through the continuation of the American alliance constituted a greater evil than Soviet hegemony in Eastern Europe. On the contrary, Powell's underlying assumption – his conviction that 'the nation . . . provides both the premise and the conclusion of coherent politics' – ignored the 'realities of modern politics' in which the nation was 'held in a web of international influence' and its independence remained a 'precious accomplishment' secured through participation in negotiated alliances. Moreover, his invocation of Britain's sovereignty was illusory, since the isolationism which he claimed it presupposed implied that Britain's future status would be one of either Finlandisation – which left it uncertain how the civil and economic institutions of the free west would survive an enforced neutrality subject to Soviet control – or Gaullism – which provided only for a 'precarious isolation' under American protection. Lastly, Powell's nationalism evaded the crucial questions of 'principle' governing the conduct of British foreign policy which the fact of American ascendancy has posed.

Scruton has not denied that the first duty of government is to pursue the national interest and he has defended the right of the United States 'to act in defiance of international law when its long-term interests are threatened by obeying it'.[81] Nevertheless he has been concerned to associate national self-interest with a commitment to moral values, and to endorse the ideological aspirations of western foreign policy. On the one hand, Britain and America were bound together not simply by mutual self-interest, but chiefly by shared constitutionalist affinities. The United States was Britain's natural ally because its leaders were committed to upholding a 'system of government bequeathed to it by the English Common Law'. On the other hand, Soviet expansionism was to be attributed to the ideological orientation of the Soviet regime together with the 'structural transformation' of Eastern Europe wrought by Soviet tyranny. The Soviet adoption of an 'aggressive foreign policy', for instance, was a 'structural requirement', arising from the instability of the regime created by its suppression of 'representative government, judicial independence, freedom of association and expression'.[82] Thus whereas NATO was a voluntary alliance of sovereign states subject only to the 'influence' of its dominant partner, the Warsaw Pact was an association not of 'natural allies' but of client states with 'slave armies' and 'puppet governments', and little more than an 'instrument of coercion' subject to Soviet 'control' and interests.[83] In consequence it was idle to pretend that the Soviet threat could be contained within an international system constituted on any basis other than armed deterrence. Not only was the Soviet Union 'founded upon [the] consuming international purpose' of imposing its political arrangements upon 'unwilling recipients, whether in its own domains or in the domains of clients and neighbours';[84] but insofar as its regime was 'purposive', it was inherently incapable of being 'governed by law in its dealings with its own subjects ... [or] in its dealings with other states'.[85]

It is unnecessary to dispute Scruton's claim that the objectives of western foreign policy are to be defined in terms of western interests – the claim was entirely defensible and entirely true. It is necessary, however, to insist that Scruton insinuated an un-

Oakeshottian association of the preservation of international peace with the enjoyment of certain constitutional arrangements by member states of the international order. The association was regrettable because of its ideological disingenuousness. It underestimated the exclusiveness of the particularist national interests of those states comprising the constitutionalist West. Scruton's disingenuousness was regrettable less because the inevitable pursuit of those interests was a matter of moralistic censure. It was regrettable, chiefly, because the ideological abstraction of which Scruton's disingenuousness was the rhetorical expression implied that the particularist interests of the communist east were to be understood in terms of ideological commitment and not of the economic and military necessities dictated by national interests.

Scruton's preference for the ideological style in the understanding and conduct of international relations together with his commitment to the ideology of liberal constitutionalism implicated him also in questionable historical assumptions which it is possible to challenge. His defence of the American alliance made assumptions about Russian intentions *vis-à-vis* western Europe, underestimating the extent to which Soviet aggression had a *defensive* rather than *expansionist* motivation in relation to China, Islam and central Europe. He underestimated also the degree to which the state of soviet military preparedness, the extent of soviet economic underdevelopment, together with the facts of soviet constitutional instability, soviet territorial heterogeneity and soviet failure to cultivate 'natural allies' were indications not of Russian *strength* but of Russian *weakness*. He assumed further that the destruction of soviet hegemony in eastern Europe and the consequent liberalisation of east European regimes would be *uncontestably* in the best interests of European peace. And he made a major assumption about the course of European history since 1941. He implied that the defeat of Germany in 1945 had not so much initated a durable settlement of longstanding territorial disputes regarding central Europe in favour of Russia rather than Germany, as confirmed what had been implicit in the development of European history since 1917: the ideological division of Europe between the communist east and the democratic west. This assumption, however, ignored the senses in which Russian diplomacy and war aims since 1917 have been concerned with Russian self-interest rather than with the ideological crusade of international communism. And it ignored the extent to which 1941 had marked the decline of European hegemony in global politics and the subordination of western Europe to American policy as much as the rise of Soviet hegemony in Eastern Europe.

These considerations should not suggest that the American alliance is not now essential to western Europe in the senses that Scruton has explained. But they do suggest that his defence of the alliance has lacked the dimension of historical relativism which his earlier Marxist sympathies might have been expected to introduce. They suggest further that in virtue of its postwar anti-colonialism, its failure to establish coherent objectives, its obsession with the relatively abstract principles of self-determination and democratic constitutionalism, and its reluctance to pursue western interests with sufficient ruthlessness or detente with sufficient longterm flexibility, American foreign policy since 1945 has *contributed* to the destabilisation of the international order, the threat to peace and the compromising of western interests. In fact, American policy has contributed to those states of affairs *through* its ideological commitment to the values of constitutionalism which Scruton admired, as surely as Russia contributed to them through its ideological adherence to the communism which Scruton denounced. Whether or not east-west detente is to be preferred to the stance of cold war belligerency that Scruton has adopted – which is questionable given that serious detente presupposes exactly the resolute rearmament he has advocated – it remains true that the detente about which Scruton has remained silent at least engages with truths about the international situation that he has not generally acknowledged: the extent to which the Soviet east and NATO powers have common interests defined in opposition to the emergence of nonaligned nationalism in the third world; and the extent to which the international anarchy created by that nationalism has been partly the result of an American foreign policy inspired by the very liberal and constitutionalist values whose preservation Scruton has regarded as inseparable from the pursuit of western interests.

With the issue of British socialism, Scruton displayed the historical subtlety lacking in his treatment of international relations. On occasions Scruton has implied that the British Labour party has represented a radical threat to constitutionalism and the rule of law. He has drawn parallels between Mussolini's fascism and Benn's corporatist socialism in polemical response to left-wing associations of Thatcherism with fascism.[86] And he has emphasised both the traditional antagonism of the Labour Party towards the House of Lords and its readiness to challenge 'judicial decisions whenever its legislative intentions are thwarted by the operations of natural justice'.[87] In general, however, Scruton has been clear that the socialist objectives of the Labour Party have been contained within the constitutionalist framework provided by the traditional British political establishment.

In one *Times* article[88] he acknowledged that the great political achievement of the Labour Party had been to provide genuine parliamentary representation for the British working class without undermining 'our national government . . . [or] our system of law'. Not only had the Labour movement acquired an establishmentarian identity by accepting 'the lineaments of parliamentary representation and . . . the trappings of monarchy and constitutional government'; it had achieved its success through rejection of the 'theories and practices of Leninism' and participation in a political dialectic with the Conservative opposition which 'by deflecting it from its revolutionary purpose . . . [had] forced the movement into the mould of parliamentary government'. The morals which Scruton drew from Labour acquiescence in the political establishment were, on the one hand, that the Labour Party had never been a *revolutionary* party; that it represented neither Leninism nor even radical state socialism but parliamentary – and ultimately bourgeois – radicalism; and that its traditional orthodoxies were parochial, intimately nationalistic and significantly remote from original Marxism. On the other hand, he drew the lesson that Labour policies were anachronistic and that they had failed and were continuing to fail to engage with the material aspirations of the working classes for whom post-war British socialism had been the vehicle. Scruton scorned the Labour Party's idolisation of the working class, asserting that the party remained 'wholly out of tune with the sentiments of emancipated labour'; ignored the party political implications of the economic truth that 'the modern worker is a property owner'; and continued to speak and act as though the legacy of Wilsonian socialism had involved the '"proletarianisation" of the middle classes, [not] the "embourgeoisement" of the worker'.[89] In saying that, Scruton was exposing the contradictions of British socialism. Nowhere was the exposure more powerful than in the critiques of those 'thinkers of the left' in *The Salisbury Review* whose doctrines reflected the predicament of socialism in the advanced industrial age which Scruton was most at pains to underline: the ideological estrangement of its intellectual leaders from the political and economic circumstances of the classes for whom they claimed to provide leadership.

On the one hand, Scruton demonstrated the implication of socialism in elitist intellectualism and middle class radicalism. He condemned the ultimate triviality of Foucault's 'anti-bourgeois' snobbery, attributing it more to the aristocratic disdain of the bohemians than to the inspiration of Marxist class analysis.[90] In response to the liberal theory of justice espoused by social democrats he offered an Oakeshottian analysis of Dworkin's jurisprudence.[91] He exposed the conflict between Dworkin's legal naturalism, which properly asserted the priority of rights to social requirements, and his ideological preference for egalitarian social policies which, in entailing that the 'preoccupation with individual rights should not obstruct the policies . . . [generating] greater equality', were as subversive of the natural law as Leninism. And he insisted that what differentiated Dworkinism from Leninism was not legal naturalism, but the fact that the latter represented revolutionary socialism in circumstances of serious class antagonism whereas the former represented little more than a 'radical chic' anti-authoritarian liberalism, propounded in an American context in which all classes, whether 'employer or employee', were engaged in 'scrambling up the ladder of success' provided by capitalism.

On the other hand, Scruton emphasised the distorting sentimentalisation of the working class which had made the contributions to British socialism of E. P. Thompson[92] and Raymond Williams[93] so remote from contemporary political reality. He made it clear that the intellectual and cultural traditions to which both belonged were not those of continental Marxism but the English traditions of Fabianism, nonconformity, anti-industrial utopianism and the literary and social criticism of Blake, Coleridge, Wordsworth, Morris and Ruskin. And he asserted that their repudiation of the coherence of Marxist analysis had involved them in the defence of a version of socialism which was little more than an ideological abstraction. Not only had Thompson's rejection of Marxism's 'materialism' and 'fixation with simple categories' in the explanation of working class consciousness not prevented him from according the working class the historical destiny assigned it in classical Marxism; Thompson's sense of that destiny was sustained by a sentimentalising 'abstract idealism' which distorted the nature of East European communism and ignored working class materialism and anti-internationalist chauvinism alike. As for Williams's ideal of a 'participatory democracy', insofar as it was defined in opposition to capitalism, consumerism, cultural elitism, class privilege and industrial exploitation and established upon the communitarian 'solidarity of a former labouring class', the ideal was fatally flawed in the respects in which British socialism itself was flawed. It assumed falsely that 'consumerism' was antipathetic to working class interests, whereas the economic truth was that 'consumerism' had been the economic concomitant of democracy in having extended the industrial worker's freedom of choice. And its plausibility was undermined by two entirely convincing historical claims: that the ideal of community solidarity providing the focus of Williams's nostalgic sentiment had been destroyed by 'the erosion of privilege, the loss of diverse classes and estates, [and] the destruction of hereditary entitlement' for which first liberalism and then socialism had been responsible; and that the democratisation of the civil life during the phase of industrial development had been the principal cause of the 'conditions of social impermanence' which Williams lamented as the inevitable 'consequence of privilege and power'.

Scruton's analysis of the predicament of British socialism was entirely persuasive. It must be understood as the utilisation of the Marxist assumption of materialism and the Marxist doctrine of ideology to demonstrate the gulf separating socialist ideology from the economic and political circumstances generating it and to confirm a profound historical truth concerning the British Labour movement: that so far from subverting the traditions of constitutionalist government, the political success of the Labour Party has testified to the flexibility of those traditions in their capacity to transform the revolutionary aspirations of socialism into the foundations of a consensus capable of commanding the consent of the containing political establishment. That truth is confirmed by any assessment of the Labour Party's contribution to the formation of the post-war consensus between 1940 and

1951. The Attlee government implemented enough of Beveridge to establish that a working commitment to the welfare state was a necessary qualification to govern for both parties. With the dismantlement of the Indian and far-eastern empire it confirmed the principal longterm implication for British power of British involvement in World War Two by making the conclusion of Britain's imperial phase a politically acceptable proposition to both the parties of the political establishment. And with the creation of NATO, the adoption of the nuclear deterrent and the cold-war polarisations of the immediate post-war period, the Labour government subordinated Britain to American policy and defined her national values in opposition to East European communism and her national interests in opposition to the extension of Soviet hegemony. After 1951 the defensive commitments assumed by Attlee's government have survived as Labour orthodoxies despite left-wing opposition to American involvement in Vietnam and the impact of CND. Moreover, notwithstanding the struggles over Clause Four, the party has remained embarrassingly committed to the mixed economy and widespread private ownership and generally reluctant to perpetuate the class struggle by assuming the role of subverter of capitalism. And finally it has upheld the rule of law, both preserving judicial independence and adhering, despite left-wing strictures about the will of the party conference, to the politically neutral and legally sovereign parliamentary establishment.

Given the strength of those commitments it is not clear why Scruton believed that the Labour Party needed to be resisted, especially since his analysis concluded that it posed no revolutionary threat to the social and political establishment. Nor was it clear on what basis resistance was to be conducted since, so far as adherence to constitutionalism, procedural natural justice and the rule of law was concerned, Scruton implied that there was not much differentiating Labour from Conservative Party practice. Further, it was not obvious that the ideological conservatism which Scruton prescribed departed *radically* from the lib-lab consensus he repudiated. There were certainly departures in tone and emphasis, although his ideological explicitness about the moral defensibility of conservative pieties previously rejected without argument conveyed greater hostility towards liberal radicalism than economic socialism. In the last resort, however, Scruton's defence of NATO and the American ascendancy made assumptions about defence harmonious with the working assumptions of the socialist consensus itself. And his silence about the desirability of the welfare state, the permissibility of the redistributive intentions of the fiscal policy financing it and the principle (if not the extent) of nationalisation served only to indicate the extent to which the socialist consensus had *succeeded* in establishing political commitments that British conservatism was virtually powerless to reverse. Perhaps the fact of that success explains the ultimate failure of *The Salisbury Review* to supplement its philosophical defence of conservatism with substantive political proposals capable of convincingly distinguishing the Conservative Party from either the socialist consensus or the stance of 'pragmatic adjustment' adopted by the party under Eden, Macmillan and Heath in resistance to socialism.

It is arguable that the failure of the *Review* in that respect was the most significant fact about it, sociologically speaking. In his analysis of British socialism Scruton was not explicit whether Labour implication in the political establishment was its triumph or tragedy. Certainly the betrayals of socialist aspirations during the phase of Wilsonian socialism demonstrated the tragic dimensions of the implication. On the one hand, the phase witnessed a victory for middle class meritocracy and 'permissive liberalism'. On the other, in its repudiation of incomes policies and the legal regulation of industrial relations between 1969 and 1974 in resistance to Heath, Wilsonian socialism abandoned socialist solutions to the widening social inequalities exacerbated by economic decline and embraced, instead, the role of guardian of trade union interests within a competitive capitalist system the fundamental structure of which remained unchallenged. Indeed, its lasting achievement was the creation of a political context in which those in employment had a stake in the preservation and success of consumer-oriented capitalism sufficient to make the economic alternative offered by the Conservative Party after 1979 an entirely reasonable and profitable political proposition for those who once formed an electorally indispensable component of the traditional socialist constituency. Although Scruton did not draw those conclusions publicly they were entailed by his diagnosis of the British left. Indeed they suggest a further conclusion: that just as the success of Thatcherism has depended in part upon the failure of Labour to make statism rather than moderate centrism essential to the post-war consensus, so *The*

Salisbury Review's failure to achieve doctrinal originality has reflected a great gulf separating the new ideological conservatism from the economic and political circumstances which have made its promulgation politically tenable and intellectually respectable.

vii

Throughout we have stressed that Casey and Scruton have much in common. Both were initially aestheticians. Both have moved from Wittgenstein to Hegel in the development of a *cultural* conservatism sustained by an aesthetic attitude towards the world. Both are implicated in the tradition of romantic liberalism. And both have made an unKantian assimilation of ethics to aesthetics; propounded a conservatism defined in opposition to the secular, liberal rationalism the Kantian antecedents of which it shares more by unargued aesthetic preference and moral prejudice than by doctrinal divergence; and both have left it unclear whether the authority of the state can *really* be morally justified on any grounds other than the utilitarian grounds which they have expressly rejected. Neither has had much that is positive to affirm about the libertarian whig legacy of the British political tradition. On the contrary, the line from Hobbes to Locke, through Hume and Bentham to Mill and down to contemporary heirs like Hart, Rawls and Nozick has represented the very political tradition which they have been most concerned to challenge – and it is that antagonism which has divided them from the liberal conservatism of Oakeshott and Mrs Letwin and the historically attested authoritarianism of Cowling alike. In one sense, the antagonism is explained because neither is an historian, least of all an historian of the British political tradition. In another sense, it is because the source of doctrine has been not English but German. Certainly there is a strong sense in which their Hegelianism offends against some very basic libertarian intuitions which derive as much from Locke, Bentham and Mill as Burke. And certainly it is doubtful whether their brand of Hegelian conservatism can be absorbed by an English national conservatism still inspired by the postwar ideology of anti-totalitarianism. That doubt is only confirmed by the sense that the untypical liberalism expressed by

Scruton in *The Salisbury Review* is — when examined closely — so politically conventional in its specific prescriptions.

Perhaps it is worth concluding that what is characteristic of both Casey and Scruton is *solemnity* rather than *pragmatism*. Each is ultimately a moralist for whom principle rather than possibility is fundamental, a truth which explains why neither has conveyed much realistic grasp of the political situation confronting him. With Casey the absence of realism was almost a deliberate intellectual strategy given that his conservatism of sentiment expressed a deeply personal hostility towards the modern world and insinuated a conception of state and culture as morally vast as it was politically disingenuous. With Scruton, who has been publicly direct about the political situation, the case is different. Throughout his writings Scruton has demonstrated formidable intellectual determination and enormous philosophical range, together with a powerful forensic strategy in the presentation of arguments. These remain great virtues, all the more admirable for being untypical of the Anglo-Saxon philosopher. They nevertheless conceal certain weaknesses. Particularly, there is about Scruton's writing a tone of doctrinal severity, a tone which has meant that his contributions to *The Times*, for instance, have been philosophically intimidating and undoubtedly the index of a distinguished mind yet, paradoxically, undistinguished *as journalism*. Perhaps it is the ultimate irony that a philosopher who has provided a sustained critique of the rationalist temper should remain an able and exemplary exponent of the virtues of rationalism itself.

4 Michael Oakeshott

i

Since the war Oakeshott has written on a wide range of subjects. Taken together these writings constitute the statement of a coherent conservative doctrine. The doctrine has not revealed any marked longterm party-political bias; nor have its implications been restricted to politics. In one sense 1945 is an arbitrary point of departure: all Oakeshott's post-war writings looked back to *Experience and its Modes*[1] and inherited its insistence upon the priority of practical experience. Nevertheless, there are three respects in which 1945 remains the appropriate starting-point for the purposes of this volume.

Firstly, politics was not central amongst Oakeshott's concerns during the pre-war phase dominated by *Experience and its Modes*. He made negative statements about the 'paralysing respectability' of Lockean liberalism in 'John Locke'[2] and about the *philosophe* mentality of Bentham and Mill in 'The New Bentham'[3] which served early notice of his contempt for the spirit of modern liberal rationalism. He also edited an anthology of political ideologies: *The Social and Political Doctrines of Contemporary Europe*.[4] However, *Experience and its Modes* made no statements supportive of political conservatism because it made no statements about politics whatsoever.

Secondly, the statements which *Experience and its Modes* did make – about science, history, religion and philosophy – carried virtually no positive implications for political conservatism. Where history was concerned, the book distinguished the historical past from the 'practical' past of the moralist or ideologue and from the 'past as it was'. It also asserted that 'historical explanation' demanded a coherent narrative of the 'unity or discontinuity' of historical events in terms of their contingent detail and that the historian was unavoidably responsible for the creative reconstruction of the past. The conclusions of *Experience and its*

Modes – which Collingwood considered the 'high-water mark of English thought upon history' – were confirmed in the philosophical idiom of the 1950s in 'The Activity of Being an Historian'[5] and in the philosophical idiom of the 1970s in *On Human Conduct*[6] and *On History*.[7] Inasmuch as they implied dissent from the neutrality of 'professional' history, the dogmatic causal assumptions of economic and sociological determinism and the deductive teleology of Hegelian historicism, the conclusions cohered with the general thrust of Oakeshott's post-war critique of rationalism. Nevertheless, Oakeshott's conclusions neither endorsed conservative judgements about politics nor sanctioned a distinctly conservative historiography. On the contrary, they undermined the claims to universality of all historical assumptions, whether liberal, Marxist, Christian or conservative, and insisted upon the invalidity of *any* subordination of the historical past to the moral and political preferences of the present.

About religion, Oakeshott espoused a nondogmatic, latitudinarian and not especially Anglican version of Christianity which had more to do with secular morality and aesthetic sentiment than theology, natural religion, politics and the ecclesiastical constitution. In addition to numerous book reviews there were two important articles on religion. 'Religion and the Moral Life'[8] expressed Kantian conclusions about the rational autonomy of 'personal assent' from the heteronomy of traditional Christian metaphysics and revealed law; and it made a Bradleyan identification of religion as the 'completion' of secular morality. 'The Importance of the Historical Element in Christianity'[9] denied that any determinate liturgical, doctrinal or ecclesiastical form which Christianity might have assumed in the history of Christian civilisation was to be identified *exclusively* with the 'whole original Christianity'. *Experience and its Modes* endorsed the underlying assumption of both essays that religion was a form of practical experience continuous with human morality. Not only was religion 'itself the conduct of life' – but the ideas of religion, 'of deity, of salvation and of immortality', were practical beliefs whose value did not depend upon a demonstration of their ultimate truth.

Since *Experience and its Modes* Oakeshott's work has retained powerful religious sentiments. They informed the Christian antiutopianism of 'On Being Conservative'[10] and the Nietzschean attack on pharisaical Christianity in 'The Tower of Babel'.[11] And they pervaded the literary religion of *On Human Conduct*[12] which, in yielding no place to original sin, grace or transcendent metaphysics and consigning theology to the realm of practical truth, confirmed the Bradleyan conclusions of *Experience and its Modes*. Above all, they were expressed through Oakeshott's sustained reflection upon the connections between religion, church and state. All that Oakeshott concluded in 'On Being Conservative' and *On Human Conduct* regarding those connections implied substantial agreement with the conclusions he attributed to Hobbes in the 1946 *Introduction to Leviathan*:[13] that the civil religion which it was the legitimate right of the state to institute and enforce was concerned 'not with belief but with practice' and directed 'not at undeniable truth but at peace'. The anti-liberal implications of those Hobbesian conclusions should not obscure the truths that Oakeshott's politics were entirely secular in orientation and that the 'civil association' which was their culmination combined an hostility towards the 'confessional' state with an assertion of the sovereignty of civil government over all subordinate ecclesiastical jurisdictions in such a way as to undermine any but formal ties between church and state.

It is doubtful whether the critical, Kantian perspective that Oakeshott adopted in *Experience and its Modes* did not implicate him in the secularising tendencies of Kantian liberalism and the pantheistic tendencies of Hegelian romanticism which were alike continuous with the Cartesian rationalism he later rejected. What cannot be doubted, however, is that *Experience and its Modes* had liberal rather than conservative implications for religion: it subverted the metaphysical claims of traditional Christianity and sanctioned the severance of religion from public education, social morality and the civil establishment of the state upon which Oakeshott subsequently insisted. Although the book preserved the rationality of religion from the attacks of history and science, it excluded both natural theology and revealed religion and concluded, in Kantian spirit, that religion could not rival philosophy in its concern with 'ultimate truth'.

About the claims of philosophy itself, Oakeshott has never really departed from the conclusion of *Experience and its Modes* that philosophical experience was 'experience without arrest, without presupposition or postulate' and 'critical throughout and unencumbered with the extraneous purposes which introduce partiality and abstractness into experience'.[14] That conclusion meant, firstly, that philosophy was a radically critical activity competent only to demonstrate the modal conditions of the various forms of experience with which it dealt. In the limited extent of its claims and in its rejection of transcendent metaphysics, Oakeshott's 'philosophy' thus inherited the standpoint of Kant's critical philosophy – far more, in fact, than it inherited the historicist perspective of Hegel's metaphysics, the dialectical and teleological assumptions of which *Experience and its Modes* explicitly rejected. Oakeshott's conclusion meant, secondly, that philosophical reflection possessed an autonomy from practical experience. In the sense that the perspective of 'philosophical disillusion' entitled the philosopher only to expose the fragility of all the partial assumptions upon which practical life inevitably rested, 'philosophy' afforded Oakeshott no standpoint from which to affirm a conservative politics or, indeed, any form of politics whatsoever. On the contrary, Oakeshott was clear that philosophy was not 'ideology'. He was clear also that much of what had passed for philosophy – theology, ethics and political philosophy – was merely 'pseudo-philosophical experience', that it had achieved no autonomy from practical assumptions and that it would effect no explanatory success unless it abandoned the normative enterprise of trying to 'decide what we shall do and how we shall live'.

It remains unclear upon what basis Oakeshott believed that the project of critical philosophy could be fulfilled with legitimate explanatory consequences for politics. 'The Concept of a Philosophical Jurisprudence'[15] went no way towards the ideal of a presuppositionless philosophy of law: it was so much concerned with establishing the philosophical character of jurisprudence in accordance with the requirements of *Experience and its Modes* that it made no substantial contribution to its subject. Oakeshott's post-war critique of rationalism no doubt inherited the mood of anti-intellectualism expressed in his earlier judgement as to the uselessness of philosophy to 'men of business and . . . men of pleasure'; and his Arnoldian defence of the autonomy of general culture certainly had roots in the distinction between philosophical experience and the practical attitude. But it remains the case that his anti-rationalism insisted upon the ideological status of philosophical reflection and that his post-war statements about ethics and politics were, from the perspective of *Experience and its Modes*, 'pseudo-philosophical' statements. So far from being free of presuppositions, they made very partial assumptions which undermined the universalist status that Oakeshott implicitly claimed for them. Whether the conclusiveness of Oakeshott's statements was jeopardised by the historicist perspective he adopted in challenging liberal rationalism is open to question. What is unquestionable is that his post-war doctrine failed to achieve the transparency about its assumptions which was the aspiration of *Experience and its Modes*.

The final reason for taking 1945 as the point of departure is that it coincided with the reforming Attlee administration. The polemical, pseudo-philosophical character of the stand which Oakeshott took up against the Labour government left little doubt that his conclusions about politics after 1945 had no self-evident foundation in his pre-war conclusions about philosophy. 'Contemporary British Politics',[16] for instance, provided a liberal conservative critique of the socialist project of a 'centrally planned economy'. The project had been inspired, Oakeshott argued, by the 'legends' of unemployment and war: the belief, on the one hand, that unemployment was an evil eradicable only under conditions of economic planning and the fact that wartime conditions had necessitated the statist mobilisation of all the resources of society on the other. The project was defective, Oakeshott concluded, because it rested upon a simplistic economic model and because the concentration of the previously diffused power of the private monopolies in the hands of government entailed the wholesale destruction of political rights and liberties. Under a centrally planned economy, Oakeshott predicted, the citizen would become the employee of the despotic state, whose stability would depend increasingly upon its 'monopolistic structure' and in which the 'slavery' of 'one-party' tyranny would be established.

Throughout the article Oakeshott made it clear that in its commitment to state socialism the Labour party was radically antagonistic towards the survival of traditional political liberties. He demanded that the Conservative party commit itself to 'preserve a diffusion of power', resist the concentration of political and economic power in the state, and instigate social and economic reforms only by the gradual application of all the legal principles constituting the 'recognised manner of adjustment in any civilised society'. In making these demands Oakeshott implied that political liberty depended upon both the preservation of economic arrangements which respected 'private property' and the maintenance of constitutional arrangements in which political power was diffused.

The defence of liberty in terms of its relation to particular economic and constitutional arrangements was extended in a subsequent essay which provided a virtual endorsement of *laissez-faire* economics: 'The Political Economy of Freedom'.[17] The essay asserted that political liberty depended, firstly, upon the 'coherence of mutually supporting liberties' and the 'absence from . . . society of overwhelming concentrations of power'; secondly, upon the right of 'voluntary association'; thirdly, upon the freedom to own and pass on property. Political freedom depended finally upon the existence of an economic order which excluded private and public monopolies upon the means of production and maintained 'effective competition' regulated by a legal order that did not as such organise the 'enterprise of getting a living and satisfying wants'. The greatest threat to political freedom, Oakeshott concluded, was posed by collectivism, whether in the form of communism, national socialism or the socialism espoused by the British Labour party. Not only was collectivism inherently incapable of tolerating a diversity of voluntary associations or legitimate political opposition to its objectives – it tended also to subvert the rule of law by an excessive use of executive power in the interests of economic policy.

It is probable that Oakeshott exaggerated the extent to which the practice of socialism in Britain would undermine the rule of law and destroy the plurality of voluntary associations. To the extent that it has acquiesced in the parliamentary constitution and implemented its policies through the exercise of legislative sovereignty, British socialism has, in fact, depended upon the rule of law rather more than Oakeshott predicted. In any event, the freedoms which the articles defended against the threat of socialism were not fundamental to Oakeshott's post-war doctrine. On the contrary, Oakeshott's post-war writings read less as the polemic of a conventional liberal conservative than as a comprehensive doctrine about politics and civilisation which did not formally entail any anti-socialist conclusions. The conservative position which the writings developed included statements about culture, education, democracy and morality. Above all, it combined a Hobbesian conception of law and civil government with an idiosyncratically Hegelian understanding of traditionalism and social ethics.

ii

In combining elements of Hobbes and Hegel the post-war writings looked back to two important pre-war statements about politics: 'The Authority of the State'[18] and 'Thomas Hobbes'.[19] 'The Authority of the State' provided a fully Hegelian definition of the state which rejected any ultimate separation of the constitution of state from civil society. The state could not, Oakeshott argued, be equated with a territory inhabited by merely 'legal', 'economic' or 'secular' persons, or identified with the 'political whole' of the legal arrangements constituted by civil government. On the contrary, civil government was concerned with 'no more than an aspect of life, never with the whole of it'. What it presupposed was 'the social whole': 'the totality in an actual community which satisfies the whole mind of the individuals who comprise it'. Most of the claims which Oakeshott made on behalf of the state in this early essay had little place in the post-war doctrine. The essay denied that the state was a relationship of 'legal persons', that its limits were described by the legal jurisdiction of its sovereign government and that its legal and constitutional order was distinguishable from 'society' and 'religion'. However, throughout the post-war period Oakeshott increasingly considered the state as the constituted association of 'legal persons' in terms exclusive of both 'society' and 'religion'. Indeed, so far from being an Hegelian in the respects common to Casey and Scruton, Oakeshott was strikingly unHegelian in the differentiation he made between the law and constitution which defined the state and the more extensive social and economic order of civil society.

Given the centrality of Oakeshott's differentiation between state and community, the *Scrutiny* essay on Hobbes was of greater consequence. Oakeshott attacked the orthodoxy that Hobbes was an anti-libertarian opponent of individualism and proponent of absolutism. On the contrary, the unconditional authority which Hobbes attributed to legal sovereignty within his system entailed neither absolutism nor 'despotism'. Moreover, Hobbes's authoritarianism was, Oakeshott concluded, a 'logical necessity' deriving from nominalist premises which made no 'ethical' assumption that human nature was inherently 'selfish'.

In its revisionist conclusions 'Thomas Hobbes' looked forward to the statements about Hobbes which Oakeshott made in the

1946 *Introduction* to *Leviathan*. The *Introduction* was important both because it spelled out the principles of civil government which were to underpin Oakeshott's entire conservative doctrine and to dominate the politics of *On Human Conduct* and because it demonstrated the extent of Oakeshott's problematic implication in the ethical and metaphysical assumptions governing the liberal tradition of 'natural right'. Oakeshott distinguished the tradition of 'will and artifice' of Augustine and Hobbes from the 'rational-natural tradition of political philosophy' initiated by Plato and Aristotle and culminating in the natural law doctrine of Aquinas. He insisted that in breaking with the rational–natural tradition Hobbes established the ruling ideas of the 'political philosophy of the last three hundred years'. Hobbes dissociated the authority of civil government from 'the superiority of reason'; rejected the Aristotelian association of law and government with 'nature', asserting instead their derivation from an artificial 'agreement of wills'; and substituted for the natural 'law and obligations' derived from reason, the fundamental principle of 'natural right' derived from the character of the individual will. The substitution of natural right for natural law presupposed, firstly, that the will was 'free from all law and obligation' and absolute in being 'not conditioned or limited by any standard, rule or rationality'. It presupposed, secondly, that all moral and political obligations arose from a 'voluntary act' and that the civil association which imposed them through 'known and authoritative rules of conduct' was 'artificial' in being created by the continuous consent of its subjects. In both respects, Oakeshott left little doubt that the fundamental *moral* idea governing the liberal tradition which Hobbes initiated was the voluntarist principle that there was "no obligation upon any man, which ariseth not from some act of his own".

The *Introduction* was significantly ambivalent about Hobbes's general relation to the liberal tradition. Oakeshott implied that Hobbes represented a more rigorous – and more libertarian – conception of liberalism than the subsequent tradition of liberal rationalism in virtue of his scepticism and authoritarianism. Not only was Hobbes 'not an absolutist precisely because he [was] an authoritarian', but Hobbes was distinguished from 'the rationalist dictators of his or any age' by reason of his 'scepticism about the power of reasoning'. Moreover, Oakeshott insisted that Hobbes's individualism was derived not from the moral principle of the 'value or sanctity of the individual man' affirmed by Kant and Mill, but from the philosophical postulates of late medieval nominalism: 'that the nature of a thing is its individuality', 'that both in God and man will is precedent to reason' and that 'the human being is first fully an individual ... in the activity of willing'.[20] Nevertheless, the principal elements of Hobbes's civil philosophy which Oakeshott endorsed were so much the staple of conventional liberalism as to make the ambivalence of the *Introduction* more a matter of tone and emphasis than principle. Hobbes's individualism rested ultimately, Oakeshott concluded, upon the distinction fundamental to liberalism between the civil structure of law and government and the social order. Not only was Hobbes's civil association not destructive of the individuality of 'natural man', but in excluding the coercive claims of community it represented the 'minimum conditions of any settled association amongst individuals'.[21] Since its unity lay exclusively in the 'single and sovereign authority' of its legal establishment, civil association presupposed 'no concord of wills, no common will, no common good' in either its generation or structure and conferred upon its subjects the 'freedom absent from law as custom or reason'. The Hobbesian dissociation of state from community – as fundamental to Oakeshott's conservatism as the voluntarist principle which it presupposed – tended, however, to implicate Oakeshott in the very illusions of liberalism which Casey and Scruton sought to expose: the illusion of the *instrumental* state, justified in terms of its regulatory function in securing the end of civil 'peace'; and the illusion of the *ethically indifferent* state, neutral between the diversity of objective values embodied in public culture and social morality. Moreover, the dissociation implicated Oakeshott in the dualisms which Casey and Scruton associated with the Cartesian assumptions of liberalism and rejected from the perspective provided by Aristotle, Hegel and Wittgenstein: the dualism between private belief and public practice, between the right of the sovereign to enforce the 'public cultus' on the grounds of convenience rather than truth and his powerlessness to 'dictate the beliefs of his subjects'; and the dualism between the restrictive legal obligations which defined citizenship and the 'true freedom' of the Hobbesian subject, his retention of those natural rights exercised in 'that area of the conduct of civil subjects which, on account of the silence of the laws, they [were] free to occupy on their own terms'.[22]

The difficulty about Hobbes was not the vulnerability of the liberal conclusions which Oakeshott persisted in drawing after 1946 to the Hegelian considerations advanced by Casey and Scruton. There was an obvious tension throughout the post-war writings between the Hegelian elements of Oakeshott's traditionalism and the Hobbesian claims he made in defence of civil association. The *Introduction* to *Leviathan* distinguished the principle of 'natural right' from the principle of the 'rational will' underpinning the 'cosmology' of 'the world seen on the analogy of human history' reflected in Hegel's *Philosophy of Right*. Although Oakeshott upheld the communitarian teleology of the *Philosophy of Right* in connection with the traditional social and political practices, he minimised its implications for the Hobbesian liberties integral to civil association which he identified more in terms of natural right than 'objective spirit'. Moreover, the universalist status which Oakeshott conferred upon the natural laws comprising the Hobbesian 'articles of peace' involved a capitulation to rationalism that was not warranted by the historicist assumptions of his traditionalism.

The real difficulty was, rather, one of ascertaining the nature of the principles upon which Oakeshott distinguished the libertarian model of Hobbesian civil association from those traditions like Marxism and utilitarianism whose ethical and political assumptions were equally derivative from Hobbes. Hobbes's identification of the will as the 'last desire in deliberating' and his assumption of the 'perpetual and restless desire for power' underlying all conduct and rational reflection were continuous with Marxist conclusions about materialism, ideology and power. Whereas Oakeshott implied substantial agreement with those conclusions in his Hobbesian exposure of liberal rationalism, he nonetheless obscured their implications for philosophy and culture, asserting the independence of both from the material world and denying their status as ideology. Oakeshott also ignored the explanatory power of Marxism in connection with the law and state. Particularly, he ignored the tendency of Marxist assumptions about power and the class struggle to discredit the formalism of civil association; to collapse the absolute distinction between the 'artificial person' in occupation of civil office and the 'natural person . . . moved only by his appetite to satisfy his own wants' upon which the legitimacy of civil rule depended; and to undermine the autonomy which Oakeshott claimed for the canons of procedural natural justice from the social and economic circumstances of their generation. Throughout the post-war period Oakeshott implied that Hobbesian liberalism yielded principles of political association which excluded utilitarian justifications of its authority. He thus developed the authoritarian and nominalist implications of Hobbes's identification of law with the 'command of the sovereign', affirming Hobbes's positivist conclusion that 'no valid law [could] be unjust' and invoking the command theory to establish that, contrary to the dogmatic rationalism of Benthamite utilitarianism, the authority of law was distinct from its utility or 'propensity to promote peace'. Nevertheless, it was the command theory deriving from Hobbes which provided the model of law for the tradition of legal positivism represented by Austin, Kelsen and Hart. And it was that tradition which conferred an instrumental character upon law, acknowledged merely *external* connections between law and morality, and made ultimately utilitarian assumptions about the justification of political action and the authority of the state.

It remains doubtful whether Oakeshott's civil association was intelligible in the absence of any utilitarian justifications of its authority and whether its excessive formalism was convincingly insulated from the reductive materialism of Marxist analysis. What remains certain is that the Hobbesian foundations of Oakeshott's conservatism warranted utilitarian and marxist conclusions as surely as they sanctioned the libertarian convictions underlying civil association.

iii

Whilst 'Political Education'[23] was a defence of traditionalism in politics, it did not celebrate the prescriptive authority of the great traditions in any Burkean sense. It insisted, rather, upon the circumstantial inevitability of the constraints which traditional continuities imposed upon political action. Oakeshott began by rejecting empirical politics as the product of a theoretical misconception which obscured the nature of reasoning itself. He also rejected the implicit claim of Laski's socialism that politics was a 'self-moved activity', consisting in the premeditated formulation of an 'abstract ideology' subsequently applied to the practical circumstances of political life. Ideological politics misrepresented the character of ideology itself. It treated as the result of disinterested reflection what was no more than an 'abstraction' of the political traditions of a given society. It also tended, Oakeshott argued, to obscure the dependence of all political activity upon the pre-existing context provided by a 'traditional manner of behaviour'.

'Political Education' proposed a much reduced conception of politics. Politics was simply the concern of a people united in terms of their recognition of a common means of attending to their arrangements, and the object of that concern was exclusively those political arrangements. Oakeshott did not deny that traditional political arrangements always intimated 'direction for change'. But he was clear that they excluded revolutionary discontinuities by definition and demanded a very acquiescent, contingent style of political practice. Being always the 'pursuit of intimations', political activity had no place for 'general principles' or indisputable moral and political standards like 'natural right' or 'ideal justice' abstracted from the contingencies of time and place. Moreover, since political argument was essentially deliberative rather than demonstrative, there was no 'mistake-proof' method of selecting the intimations of politics most deserving pursuit.

The character of political education itself, Oakeshott concluded, had to be understood in terms of the traditionalism developed in the essay. In its *practical* form, political education was not a specialised discipline but a form of practical knowledge 'acquired haphazard in finding our way about the natural –artificial world in which we are born'. And in its *academic* form, the principal purpose of the education provided by political history and philosophy was 'explanatory' rather than 'practical'. As Oakeshott concluded in the later essay, 'The Study of "Politics" in a University',[24] the study of politics was not a 'vocational' enterprise and was, indeed, corrupted by the intrusion of the idiom of 'participation': 'If there is a manner of thinking and speaking that can properly be called "political", the appropriate business of a university in respect of it is not to use it . . . but to explain it'.[25]

To the extent that Oakeshott took academic reflection upon politics to be insulated from current political preoccupations, he did not envisage a necessarily conservative relationship between philosophy and political practice. In fact, the potentially subversive relationship between theory and practice which the essay permitted was an indication of the radically sceptical character of Oakeshott's traditionalism. The ultimate appeal of the essay – and the basis of its conservatism – was probably its insistence that there were no universal guidelines in politics of unquestionable validity. In that respect its lesson for practical politics was simple and neutral: since the knowledge appropriate to politics was 'municipal' rather than 'universal', political wisdom was the art of making provisional judgements in some sense consonant with the customs of place and the requirements of the age.

'Political Education' expressed a Hobbesian hostility towards scientific politics. The grounds of Oakeshott's hostility were made clear in a later article: 'Political Laws and Captive Audiences'.[26]

Like 'Political Education', 'Political Laws and Captive Audiences' assumed both that the logic of political argument was deliberative rather than demonstrative and that its idiom of address was persuasive. It concluded further, however, that scientific politics had developed from a realisation of the danger arising from the persuasive character of political argument: the degeneration of politics into the art of persuasion practised with a view to acquiring and retaining power for its own sake. Oakeshott denied that scientific politics would succeed in eliminating persuasion from political deliberation. Rather, he insisted upon the pernicious consequences of the scientific idiom for the conduct of politics. The idiom would, Oakeshott predicted, permit politicians to persuade their audiences of the desirability of a policy by claiming that it followed from an 'inescapable' law of economic or social development. It would confer immense power upon any government capable of exploiting its subjects' belief that its policies were correct deductions from such laws and that its actions were unavoidable. And it would insulate the deliberations of politicians from the changing circumstances of political life by generating a 'closed real-imaginary world of political situations corresponding to itself'.

In asserting that the laws of scientific politics had reactionary rather than progressive consequences, Oakeshott was particularly acute about the relationship between political argument and the exercise of power. He recognised that arguments about 'correctness' and 'infallibility' merely obscured the underlying reality of political power and that scientific politics concealed the partiality of the moral, cultural and intellectual assumptions upon which political deliberation inevitably rested. Oakeshott's examples were taken from Eastern Europe and the object of attack was clearly soviet communism; but the morals which the article drew applied with equal force to liberal rationalism. In fact, they arguably applied with greater force to liberalism since the article made an assumption of the underlying materialism and egotism governing political practice that implied affinities between Oakeshott and Marx in addition to Machiavelli, Hobbes and Nietzsche. The assumption was a powerful weapon in Oakeshott's war against liberalism. It did not, however, prevent him from advancing a Hobbesian conception of law, state and government in which the subversive implications of Hobbes's materialism for the morality of political action were entirely neutralised.

'Political Education' said little about the law and constitution. The authority with which it dealt was the natural authority of political traditions rather than the form of authority vested in an entirely 'constituted' association. 'On Being Conservative', on the other hand, was an obviously Hobbesian essay which spelled out conditions of association that presupposed no participation in common traditions of political activity.

The essay defined the rights and duties of government in negative and legalistic terms. It was not the concern of government to impose common beliefs and activities upon its subjects or to lead, co-ordinate and galvanise their activities by an exclusion of 'the conditions of conflict'. Its 'office' was simply to rule, to 'preserve peace not by placing an interdict upon choice . . . nor by imposing substantive uniformity, but by enforcing general rules of procedure upon all subjects alike'. Those rules were embodied in the civil law. Not only could law not be used to arbitrate in a 'collision of interests', but it was obligatory because it was authoritative rather than 'wise' or 'correct' and inherently powerless to 'make men better' or dictate 'moral right and wrong'. Rulers possessed an absolute authority to revise law. Whatever restraints upon legislative discretion were suggested by 'Political Education', 'On Being Conservative' left little doubt that no merely prescriptive, traditional restraints should compromise the unconditionality of the legislative sovereignty integral to civil government.

The foundation of 'On Being Conservative' was a Hobbesian defence of civil liberty. Liberty hinged upon the freedom of thought and belief, which law was incapable of violating by definition, and the inalienable freedom of the agent to choose actions for himself, which his status as legal subject could not destroy by definition. The derivation of this liberty was not from any conviction that 'there is absolute value in the free play of human choice, that private property . . . is a natural right, that it is only in the enjoyment of diversity of opinion and activity that true belief and good conduct can be expected to disclose themselves'.[27] The derivation of civil liberty was much more fundamental: 'that we are not children *in statu pupillari* but adults who do not consider themselves under any obligation to justify their preference for making their own choices; and that it is beyond human experience to suppose that those who rule are endowed with a superior wisdom which discloses to them a better range of beliefs and activities'.[28] Oakeshott did not intend that this invocation of Hobbesian natural right should entail the principle that government derived its authority from the express consent of its subjects. Rather, it was intended to explain how the legal establishment of the state could acquire authority despite the ineliminable diversity and revocability of human choices. Oakeshott achieved this end by a Hobbesian demonstration of the minimal conditions under which the recognition of the state's authority could co-exist with the freedom of agency of its subjects. It was a measure of just how minimal those conditions really were that Oakeshott stripped from government every claim upon its subjects – including its assumption of 'superior wisdom' and its ambition to 'command for truth' – save that of its authority.

In its emphasis upon legislative sovereignty, 'On Being Conservative' had few obviously conservative implications. Its conservatism consisted rather in its affirmation of the superiority of the civilised goods of friendship and conversation over the narrowly civil relationship imposed by law and government. This affirmation did not, however, settle the question of the legitimacy of the compulsory association with which Oakeshott was concerned. The essay left it unclear how the authority of law and government was to be distinguished from the mere possession by the state of superior power. Oakeshott insisted that the rule of government was not an arbitrary 'tyranny' in the sense that government was subject to the rule of law. But he implied that the authority of political arrangements governed by the rule of law required no further justification and reflected no substantive ends and values other than the minimal utilitarian requirement of preserving the 'peace' of the association they constituted.

That conclusion was not qualified by a subsequent essay in which Oakeshott explored the connections between the moral law and the Hobbesian polity: 'The Moral Life in the Writings of Thomas Hobbes'.[29] The essay asserted the sovereignty of the positive law as presupposed by the Hobbesian position developed in 'On Being Conservative'. The only laws capable of imposing valid obligations were the civil laws; and their authority arose 'solely from the character of their maker and the manner in which they . . . [were] made, promulgated and interpreted'. Moreover, their moral obligatoriness did not derive from their reflection of a 'natural and universal obligation' prescribed by God. On the contrary, not only were there no 'natural' or 'uncovenanted' duties in the sense that all obligations arose from the voluntary acknowledgement of a 'known law-giver', but the laws of nature presupposed the existence of that which they were intended to legitimise: a structure of civil law and government capable of providing an authoritative promulgation and authentic interpretation of the natural law. Oakeshott thus confirmed the conclusion of 'On Being Conservative': that a civil association required no legitimising, higher law to supplement the positive obligations imposed by the civil law.

What sustained a civil association, Oakeshott concluded, was not a universal moral obligation underlying the diversity of determinate legal duties, but either 'self-interest instructed by reason' or 'acts of "nobility" which [made] no conditions'. Oakeshott emphasised that his invocation of the ethics of 'nobility' aligned Hobbes with the 'aristocratic' idiom of morality. He was nonetheless clear that the invocation did not presuppose the provision of an aristocratic constitution as an indispensable social correlative for aristocratic morality. On the contrary, 'nobility' was a matter of individual virtue or sentiment rather than a socio-political status or practice: the disposition to do justice inculcated by the 'moralisation of pride', and enhanced both by the qualities of 'generosity, courage, nobleness, magnanimity and endeavour for glory' and by the 'contempt of injustice' which provided the strongest incentive for fidelity to law. Moreoever, Oakeshott left no doubt that Hobbes's incorporation of the ethics of 'nobility' compromised neither his status as 'philosopher of the morality of individuality' nor his adherence to the tradition of natural right.

'The Moral Life in the Writings of Thomas Hobbes' was an important essay. It registered a distaste for the bourgeois morality of prudent self-interest that was Nietzschean rather than Aristotelian or Burkean. And it expressed anti-democratic and anti-Kantian sentiments about moral virtue whilst affirming principles of political association that were continuous with the ethical assumptions of Kantian liberalism. However, so far as the legitimacy and justification of civil government were concerned, the essay provided no resolution of the problems which 'On Being Conservative' left unanswered. It tended rather to confirm the disingenuous conclusions of the earlier essay: that the utility of civil government in securing peace was unproblematically consistent with the principles of natural right which Oakeshott treated as its foundation; and that certain activities of government were illegitimate in respects that its Hobbesian functions were not.

Those conclusions informed a subsequent essay which made it clear both that the democratisation of the constitution conferred no additional legitimacy upon political association – or additional authority upon its laws – and that democratisation had been generally antagonistic towards the liberties guaranteed under a settled legal order: 'The Masses in Representative Democracy'.[30] The essay distinguished the morality of individualism – the ethics of 'self-determinaton' expounded by Kant – from the egalitarian and communitarian ethics of the 'mass' man. The morality of individualism required a 'mode of association' in which civil government was sufficiently authoritative to insulate the individual subject from the communal pressures of family, church, guild and custom, and to enforce the legal order which embodied his positive rights. It was that 'mode of association', Oakeshott argued, which had been undermined by the ascendancy of popular democracy and the ethics of the 'mass' man. Not only had the representative of traditional 'parliamentary government' been transformed into the 'delegate' of 'popular government', but the rule of law had been subjected to the arbitrary majoritarian will of the community.

Oakeshott did not say how the moral authority of civil association was to be recovered in the light of the modern predominance of constitutional democracy. 'The Masses in Representative Democracy' certainly did not prescribe a reversion to the aristocratic constitution. On the contrary, the essay expressed its anti-democratic sentiments in the context of Oakeshott's underlying acceptance of political arrangements whose principles did not exclude ⌐ and arguably sanctioned –\the democratic practices being rejected. The anti-democratic sentiments were a powerful supplement to the aristocratic sentiments of the essay on Hobbes. But they should be understood primarily as an expression of Oakeshott's concern for the damage which the obsessive political activism of modern party democracy had done to the social goods and moral values embodied in the non-political practices.

Like Casey and Scruton, Oakeshott made the defence of the non-political values of culture and civilisation an integral part of his conservative doctrine. In 'The Claims of Politics'[31] he denied that political activity was the most effective expression of concern for the 'communal interests' of society. Political activity was, in fact, a 'highly specialised' endeavour, restricted to the 'protection and occasional modification of a recognised legal order'. Moreover, it was infected with 'spiritual callousness'. It was, Oakeshott concluded, because political activity was a morally trivial occupation that some members of society had a duty not to engage in it. This was especially true of poets, artists and philosophers, whose exile from the 'illusion of affairs' was the necessary condition of their continuing to 'recreate' civilisation.

'The Claims of Politics' expressed a very Arnoldian sentiment. It implied both the desirability of protecting cultural values from political control and the anti-materialist conclusion that social tensions were less the manifestation of underlying political conflict than the condition of a healthy, developing liberal civilisation. It also suggested that a conservative position could be made to include a defence of culture against the philistinism of modern politics.

After the war, the defence of culture implied in 'The Claims of Politics' led out in two directions. It resulted in an essay in expressionist aesthetics: 'The Voice of Poetry in the Conversation of Mankind'.[32] The essay stood squarely in the idealist tradition of Hegel, Croce and Collingwood. It concluded that artistic expression was a form of 'practical' knowledge distinguishable from science, history and philosophy, and that art, or 'poetry', demanded a mode of attention distinguishable from the 'practical attitude' appropriate to morality and politics. However, its concluding celebration of the triumph of 'poetry' over the 'illusory ends' of all practical activity left it unclear whether Oakeshott was a bohemian aesthete rather than a political conservative.

Of greater consequence was Oakeshott's defence of university education as the liberal custodianship of general culture. The senses in which university education was 'liberal' were spelled out in 'The Idea of a University'.[33] It was liberal, firstly, in being a form of humane learning distinguishable from both the antiquarian accumulation of 'information' and 'vocational' training. It was liberal, secondly, in tolerating a plurality of disciplines whose relationship was 'conversational' rather than 'competitive'. It was liberal, finally, in being insulated from the demands of practical life. Not only did university education provide the undergraduate with an entrancing 'break in the tyrannical course of irreparable events'; but it was not intended to fulfil any 'social purpose' dictated by extrinsic political considerations. These conclusions furnished the critical perspective for Oakeshott's review of Moberly's *The Crisis in the Universities*: 'The Universities'.[34] Oakeshott attacked Moberly for demanding that a university pursue a single 'self-conscious purpose' governed by 'an agreed ideology which embraced everything' and that its affairs be determined by the 'burning questions of the day'. On the contrary, the real crisis of the universities, Oakeshott argued, was their corruption by those utilitarians who, 'convinced only that "knowledge is power" ', treated them as 'the avenue to a good job'. Moreover, the 'crisis' represented by the 'fragmentation of disciplines' was not to be resolved by the provision of integrated 'general courses'. There was, Oakeshott insisted, no distinction between acquiring knowledge of a branch of learning and pursuing the general objects of education since the 'notion that you can think without thinking in some particular manner, without reference to some definitive universe of discourse, [was] a philosophical illusion'.[35]

Over the years Oakeshott has held to his faith in the values of university education. In 'Learning and Teaching'[36] he affirmed that education was concerned with the inculcation of discriminating judgement in the pupil rather than 'vocational' skills. And in 'A Place of Learning'[37] he reiterated previous statements about culture in the idiom of *On Human Conduct*: culture accommodated a limitless plurality of disciplines since it was neither a 'doctrine' nor a 'set of consistent teachings or conclusions' but a 'conversational encounter' in which each subject or 'language' possessed an exclusive autonomy and a determinate idiom.

In none of these essays did Oakeshott consider whether the increasing professionalisation of university education since the fifties posed a threat to the values of liberal education he prescribed. Although he affirmed that the 'justice' of academic institutions was 'internal' and shared Casey's insistence upon their autonomy from the prevailing doctrines of 'social justice', Oakeshott did not acknowledge that the quality of education might have to be sacrificed in the interests of its wider distribution. Yet, not only did the exclusion of all considerations of 'social purpose' leave it unclear in what terms the values which university education was intended to embody were themselves to be recommended; it tended also to deprive culture itself of all political significance. In fact, the autonomy of education from practice – together with the principle of the pluralism of academic disciplines – represented a commitment on Oakeshott's part to the liberal values of romantic culture. If the commitment meant that Oakeshott attributed an Hegelian significance to culture, it represented only a very liberalised Hegelianism which carried none of the political consequences emphasised by Casey and Scruton. On the contrary, the commitment tended to obscure the ideological status of the values of liberal culture and to minimise the extent of their derivation from the underlying social and political order. In these respects, Oakeshott's conclusions about education and culture conflicted with the insistence upon liberal disingenuousness about power and ideology which formed the principal message of his critique of rationalism.

Although 'rationalism' stood for an alien mentality in politics and an arbitrary conception of social morality, it stood chiefly for a defective theory of knowledge. The essay 'Rational Conduct'[38] was representative of what Oakeshott understood rationalism to mean and why he was convinced that it had to be challenged. The essay reiterated the conclusions of the earlier essay 'Rationalism in Politics':[39] that the Cartesian programme of reconstituting certain knowledge on the foundation of systematic and total doubt was flawed; that the natural scientific idiom had no superiority in rationality over the practical knowledge embodied in social custom and habit; and that there was no rigidly Cartesian opposition between belief and knowledge. Throughout the essay Oakeshott rejected not only the Cartesian method of enquiry but its epistemological legacy as well: the Cartesian ego, the self known through private and inward introspection.

It was the rejection of Cartesian presuppositions which provided the context for Oakeshott's distinction between *technical* and *practical* knowledge. Technical knowledge involved the formulation of propositions about an activity in abstraction from the circumstances of their application; and it presupposed that the knowledge required to implement the rules and propositions thus formulated was not as such a form of knowledge at all. Technical knowledge, Oakeshott concluded, dominated the modern conceptions of rationality to such an extent that it was assumed unquestioningly that all human action consisted of the dualism between the reflective consideration of 'ends' on the one hand and of the rules, means and procedures by which those ends were realised on the other. However, the rules of many activities and skills, Oakeshott insisted, were incapable of precise formulation. Moreover, technical knowledge, *as a conception of knowledge*, was inherently defective. Any rule required the exercise of judgement for its application in practice. Since the capacity to exercise such judgement was a form of knowledge which could be exercised correctly or incorrectly, the knowledge embodied in practical activity had always to extend beyond a propositional knowledge of the rules which governed it. The essay thus made Kantian and Wittgensteinian points to the effect that no rule carried the conditions for its application on its face and that the criteria for deciding whether the rules of a practice had been mastered were irreducibly 'public'. And in not excluding the possibility of a purely private practice of rule-following, the canons of technical knowledge obscured the relation of rules to practice in exactly the respects which Wittgenstein exposed throughout *Philosophical Investigations*.

About the illusions of Cartesian rationalism, Oakeshott was polemically explicit where Wittgenstein was tentatively suggestive. In 'Rationalism in Politics' he attributed rationalism to the three methodological principles of the intellectual doctrine prescribed by Bacon in the *Novum Organum* and by Descartes in the *Regulae* and the *Discours de la Methode*: 'a set of rules ... formulated as a precise set of directions'; 'a set of rules whose application is purely mechanical', requiring no 'knowledge or intelligence not given in the technique itself'; 'a set of rules of universal application' in the sense of being 'an instrument of inquiry indifferent to the subject-matter of the inquiry'.[40] Like Wittgenstein, Oakeshott implied that the Cartesian search for a method of universal applicability was self-defeating. All rules of method – whether of cooking, philosophy or carpentry – were *internal* to the practices they constituted. Moreover, all knowledge had an historical dimension which the Cartesian emphasis upon the universal authority of methodical inquiry ignored.

What distinguished Oakeshott from Wittgenstein was partly a difference of philosophical style. It was mainly, however, an explicit indebtedness on Oakeshott's part to the idealist tradition manifested in the obvious dependence of his anti-rationalist conclusions of the forties and fifties upon the doctrines of *Experience and its Modes*. Those conclusions drew principally upon the 'coherence' theory of truth enunciated in the earlier work. *Experience and its Modes* had demonstrated that the human judgements which actively constituted the world of experience were true or false in virtue of their coherent or incoherent relation to the containing system of judgements in which they were asserted, and not in virtue of their correspondence to a natural order fully independent of the ordering forms of human thought. Likewise, the subsequent anti-rationalist position presupposed that traditional continuities were constituted by a community of judgements about which there was implicit agreement at the public level of social practice, and which corresponded to no preconventional, natural or universal human order. The traditionalism which Oakeshott defended throughout his critique of rationalism was, in fact, an application to the social and political spheres of the 'coherence' theory of truth. As he insisted in 'Rational Conduct', all human actions were rational insofar as they succeeded in maintaining a 'place in . . . the coherence of activity, which composes a way of living'.[41] That principle applied to the activities of scientists as much as to those of carpenters or cooks. On the one hand, the coherence of the scientist's activity consisted not in his conformity to scientific rules and methods – which were, at best, abstract 'abridgements' of scientific activity – but in his 'faithfulness to the traditions of scientific inquiry'.[42] On the other, the irrational scientist was identified not only by his violation of scientific method but by 'his unfaithfulness to the whole tradition of scientific inquiry, by his ignorance of how to set about a scientific investigation'.[43]

Moreover, in its assertion of the priority of practical to technical knowledge, Oakeshott's critique of rationalism drew upon the doctrine of practical experience propounded in *Experience and its Modes*. In fact, it reflected a profoundly Hegelian conception of the nature of knowledge and activity. It presupposed that the self could know itself only through a direct knowledge of its own activity in and upon the public world. It concluded that the harmony reflected in the public world was established by 'the concrete mind . . . composed wholly of activities in search of harmony and throughout implicated in every achieved level of harmony'.[44] And it implied that the preference for technical knowledge within liberal rationalism obscured the point of Hegel's rejection of 'abstract idealism' in favour of 'objective spirit': that the agent's participation in the traditional continuities of social practice through acceptance of the inevitable restraints of education was the liberating condition of his self-knowledge.

The Hegelian character of Oakeshott's anti-rationalism was nowhere more apparent than in the essay which he devoted to social ethics: 'The Tower of Babel'. The conception of social morality which the essay defended drew out the full ethical implications of the doctrine of practical knowledge of *Experience and its Modes* and upheld the Hegelian elevation of *Sittlichkeit* over *Moralitat* fundamental to the structure of the *Philosophy of Right*. It did this by developing a contrast between two forms of the moral life and by making claims on behalf of communal morality equivalent to the claims which Bradley advanced on behalf of the sphere of 'My Station and its Duties' in *Ethical Studies*.

In one form, the moral life was a 'habit of affection and behaviour'. It required neither the self-conscious application of moral rules nor an intensive dedication to moral ideals. It required only that the individual should act in accordance with a 'certain habit of behaviour' through the 'unreflective following of a tradition of conduct'. So far from demanding the critical formulation of rules and ideas as a condition of moral sincerity, this form of the moral life demanded conduct which was 'nearly as possible without reflection'. And so far from depending upon the imposition of a moral code through a specialised training, the form of moral education which social morality required was 'coeval with conscious life', and less 'compulsory' than 'inevitable'. Oakeshott affirmed that the advantage of this form of moral life was its stability. It fostered the coherent integrity of individual character, 'the power to act appropriately and without hesitation'. And it promoted the stable coherence of communal life through which individual character was expressed by preserving social morality from 'the danger of moral criticism usurping the place of a habit of moral behaviour, or of moral speculation bringing disintegration to moral life'.[45] Implicitly, Oakeshott was asserting that the relatively stable traditions of social morality provided greater tolerance of individual divergence – because they imposed no abstract 'uniformity' upon conduct – than the more overtly liberal form of critical morality characteristic of rationalism.

Critical morality had developed, the essay argued, from that form of the moral life which rested upon the 'self-conscious pursuit of moral ideals' and the 'reflective observance of moral rules' translated into action. Although critical morality had acquired an anti-authoritarian veneer on account of its tendency to subject traditional social morality to the rigorous scrutiny of individual analysis and criticism, it had nonetheless had the anti-libertarian consequence of licensing the ruthless imposition of a 'vision of perfection' upon the individual. Moreover, so far from accepting the diversity of moral traditions, critical morality implied that any moral tradition which lacked 'an obvious universality' was 'inadequate for the needs of the society of its origins'.

To the extent that the increasing subjection of received moral authority had resulted in an excessive confidence about the power of moral reflection and a corresponding uncertainty about moral action, Oakeshott was clear that rationalist ethics had proved debilitating for both the personal morality of the individual and the integrity of communal morality. Not only had it become 'more important to have an intellectually defensible moral ideology than a ready habit of behaviour';[46] but the contemporary situation was one of a 'world dizzy with moral ideals' in which 'we know less about how to behave in public and private than ever before'.[47] Critical morality was defective not simply because it concealed hypocrisy. It was defective, mainly, because it embodied the philosophical illusion of dualism inherent in rationalism: it ignored the priority of practical knowledge and made it impossible to measure success and failure in moral conduct. What critical morality required – and what it was incapable of generating – was an authority provided by something other than the agent's sense of himself as having acted well, and that authority, Oakeshott implied, could be found only in the public standards embodied in communal morality. In implying this, Oakeshott expressed an Hegelian defensiveness about the embodied rationality of social custom and an Hegelian insistence that the moral integrity of the individual presupposed his coherent participation in social morality. And he wrote with an Hegelian contempt for the arbitrary subjectivism of ethical rationalism, which had made the mere possession of 'moral opinions' an adequate substitute for 'habits of moral behaviour'.

The mood of the 'The Tower of Babel' was consistent with the aristocratic ethics which Oakeshott was later to associate with Hobbes. It concluded that the individual's acquiescence in social morality was most effectively secured when 'the spring of his conduct [was] not an attachment to an ideal or a felt duty to obey a rule, but his self-esteem'.[48] The essay also implied affinities with Aristotle – in its emphasis upon practical reason and the social virtues – and with Nietzsche – in its dissociation of morality from the legalism of abstract rules and codes. In all those respects, it dissented from the spirit of Kantian ethics, particularly from Kant's democratising emphasis upon the conscientious good will. Nevertheless, the temperamental aversion to Kantian ethics which the essay registered should not obscure the fact that Oakeshott repudiated the dualistic and rationalistic implications of Kant's formalism and universalism alike from the securely post-Kantian perspective of Hegelian metaphysics. Indeed, the essay confirmed the secular orientation of Kantian ethics: it excluded any extra-human sanctions for morality, whether in the form of a natural or God-given law, and implied that human morality had no more substantial foundation than the anthropocentric integrity established by the historical continuities and traditions of moral practice reflected in the social world. Moreover, so far as Christianity was concerned, 'The Tower of Babel' was entirely negative. Oakeshott insisted that the tradition of ethical rationalism had been initiated at the point when the 'Christian habit of moral behaviour (which had sprung from the circumstances of Christian life) was swamped by a Christian moral ideology'. And he endorsed the spirit of Nietzsche's dissenting critique of Christianity as 'a morality of ideals which had never succeeded in becoming a morality of a habit of behaviour'.[49] Those negativities towards Christianity did not, however, undermine either Oakeshott's substantive conclusions about religion or his anti-naturalistic, Hobbesian conclusions about the secular generation of all social authority. Nor did they qualify his reservations about the phase of the Enlightenment that had, after all, accelerated the process of secularisation in which Oakeshott was implicated by challenging the authority of traditional Christianity.

'The Tower of Babel' should be read ultimately as a prophetic – and revisionist – statement about the 'predicament of western morals'. What it exposed was the 'corrupt consciousness' disclosed in the ethical and political traditions established during the Enlightenment. And what it concluded was that post-Enlightenment Europe had been 'dominated by the pursuit of moral ideals' and that the dominance had proved 'ruinous to a settled habit of behaviour'.[50] In their relation to the Enlightenment project of constituting a 'scientific morality' and the modernistic hunger for universality in morals and politics, the conclusions of the essay retain all the polemical power with which Oakeshott first invested them. The difficulty is in knowing whether the communitarian ethics which the essay prescribed were not radically incompatible with the morality of Hobbesian individualism that Oakeshott endorsed in connection with civil association; and whether the inspiration provided by Hobbesian voluntarism and the ethical assumptions of natural right to the post-Enlightenment tradition of Rousseau, Kant, Hegel, Marx and Nietzsche had not itself been ultimately responsible for the revolutionary fragmentation of the integrated ethical culture for the recovery of which the essay yearned. It was not clear from the essay whether Oakeshott believed that that ethical culture could be reconstituted in a post-Hobbesian context governed by ethical and political principles which celebrated its destruction; nor was it clear whether Oakeshott believed that such a culture had credible historical precedents. What was clear was that the tone of Oakeshott's denunciation of the post-Enlightenment tradition was discordant with the mood of agnosticism towards the plurality of moral traditions which the essay conveyed.

Although Oakeshott's anti-rationalist doctrine rested upon

firm philosophical foundations, it nonetheless had an obvious polemical motivation. It insinuated that the assumptions of liberal rationalism were culturally and historically relative, and that they were intimately related to exclusive traditions of social and political practice in historicist respects which the rationalist simply ignored. Moreover, through using the example of scientific inquiry, Oakeshott implied that all traditions of disinterested, rational inquiry exerted an arbitrary social coerciveness in senses which the liberal ideal of unconditional, critical freedom obscured. The mistake of the rationalist, Oakeshott was demonstrating, was to pretend that his methods of inquiry were value-free; whereas the truth was that they were shot through with ideological presuppositions the concealed partiality of which had to be exposed and contested.

Nowhere was the polemical motivation of Oakeshott's critique of rationalism more insistent than in the essay 'Rationalism in Politics' with its onslaught upon the predominance of rationalism in contemporary politics. Rationalism, Oakeshott complained, had become the 'stylistic criterion of all respectable politics'. It made the assumptions that politics was 'easy' and that scientism in politics was desirable. It implied that the apparatus of civil government was one of *administration* rather than *rule*. And it had promoted the 'ideological' mode of political participation in which even the resistance to rationalism represented by Hayek's *Road to Serfdom* was implicated in rationalism in having been 'converted into an ideology' as 'a plan to resist all planning'. Rationalist politics had developed, Oakeshott concluded, out of three forms of 'political inexperience': the inexperience of 'new rulers', for which the ideologies of Machiavelli, Locke, Bentham and Godwin were designed to compensate; the inexperience of the 'new ruling class' which had emerged during the period of democratisation; and the inexperience of the 'new political society'. Oakeshott asserted that, in the form which it had assumed in contemporary politics, rationalism had four manifestations. In its consecration of mere 'reason', it had challenged and largely destroyed the 'social, legal and institutional inheritance of . . . society'. It had rejected the prescriptive authority of settled political tradition in preference for 'an ideology, the formalised abridgment of the supposed substratum of rational truth contained in the tradition'.[51] It had inspired the facile utopianism of the 'politics of perfection'. And rationalism had tended to impose the anti-libertarian 'politics of uniformity'.

There was no doubting the strength of Oakshott's conviction that the growth of rationalist politics represented a corruption of the moral and intellectual traditions of European politics. In its denunciation of the ruthlessness of modern political pelagianism, 'Rationalism in Politics' had a polemical authority which rivalled the eloquence of 'The Tower of Babel'. Nevertheless, it was not obvious that Oakeshott's polemical conclusions stood in a necessary relation to the historicist perspective which provided the philosophical basis of his anti-rationalist doctrine. He did not explain upon what basis rationalism had developed its own traditional continuities of political practice, and why its undoubted success in developing such continuities was obviously regrettable given his insistence upon the transience and diversity of *all* human knowledge and practice. Nor was his hostile judgement upon the liberal constitutionalism of the United States – or, indeed, his criticisms of the actual politics of any society – easily squared with his rejection of all universal principles in politics and his exclusion of the idiom of 'participation' in favour of that of 'explanation'.

It is not necessary to complain at Oakeshott's polemical tendencies. 'Rationalism in Politics' and 'The Tower of Babel' belonged to their period; and they should be read, to some extent and in intention at least, as philosophically sophisticated variations on the theme of anti-socialism which Oakeshott had taken up during the years of the Attlee government. However, it is necessary to insist that his polemical conclusions incorporated unargued political preferences which were not guaranteed by the historicist premises of his anti-rationalist stance. In its emphases upon ideology, historical relativism and the priority of practice to theoretical understanding, Oakeshott's critique of liberal rationalism had powerful affinities with Marxism. Nevertheless, it was in virtue of the polemical conclusions which he drew from that critique that Oakeshott departed from Marxism and retreated into ideology at the same time as he denounced all ideological politics. The Hegelian character of his traditionalism not only associated him with the anti-materialism and anti-determinism which subsequently distinguished the Hegelian conservatism of Casey and Scruton – it also tended to involve him in a capitulation to the very idealism in politics which the anti-rationalist doctrine was intended to counteract. In part,

Oakeshott's anti-rationalism expressed a nostalgia for the aristocratic, pre-democratic traditions of European politics, most notably in the regrets which it entertained about the coming to power of the 'politically inexperienced' and the disappearance of 'the informality of English politics'. In part also, it expressed an aesthetic distaste for the aridity of the rationalist temper in general and the Benthamite, managerial tradition of government in particular. Lastly, it expressed a value judgement about the implications for public and personal morality of the ascendancy of liberal rationalism. However, whether as sentiment, nostalgia, moral idealism or aesthetic preference, the anti-rationalist doctrine not only failed to confront the full range of the circumstances of contemporary politics – it relapsed, as a consequence of that failure, into the very dualism between idealism and historical situation which had infected liberal rationalism and which the invocation of practical knowledge had been intended by Oakeshott to collapse.

The tensions between Oakeshott's appeal to historical relativism and his unHegelian implication in abstract idealism were not relieved in the very powerful book which appeared in 1975: *On Human Conduct*. In fact, the tensions were exacerbated inasmuch as the book promulgated a utopian politics, made universalist claims on behalf of an historically determinate tradition of civil government, and adopted the conceptual model underlying that tradition as a critical standard with which to question the moral validity of several tendencies of the post-Reformation, modern European state. Not only was the 'civil association' which the book explored the 'abridgement' of particular historical traditions; it was also a rationalist conception which tended to confer upon conservative 'resistance' the status of an 'ideology'.

iv

On Human Conduct was Oakeshott's most systematically philosophical work. Its first essay, 'On the Theoretical Understanding of Human Conduct', reiterated previous statements about philosophy, history and religion; and its doctrine of 'practices' gave philosophical transparency to the main ideas of the critique of rationalism. The centre-piece of the book, however, was the philosophical treatment of the state of the second essay, 'On the Civil Condition'. That essay provided the conceptual framework for the historical discussion of the European state in terms of the distinction between *societas* and *universitas* of the third and last essay of the book: 'On the Character of a Modern European State'.

Together with three essays which Oakeshott published after *On Human Conduct* – 'The Vocabulary of a Modern European State',[52] 'Talking Politics'[53] and 'The Rule of Law'[54] – the argument of 'The Civil Condition' represented the systematic restatement of the conservative doctrine developed in the post-war period. It confirmed the sceptical traditionalism of 'Political Education' and 'Political Laws and Captive Audiences'. It thus concluded that since political argument involved 'deliberative' rather than 'demonstrative' reasoning, it was neither 'infallible' nor 'value-free', and that in the absence of any universally authoritative guidelines the conclusions of that reasoning were culturally and historically relative. It rehearsed the principles of political association propounded in 'On Being Conservative', distinguishing 'ruling' from 'managing' and the relationships generated by friendship, 'enterprise' and customary authority from the civil relationship; and providing a narrowly legalistic definition of the state which asserted the 'positive' character of civil obligation and the 'unconditional' character of legislative sovereignty. 'The Civil Condition' also reiterated the anti-democratic implications of 'The Masses in Representative Democracy': that the provision of a democratic constitution conferred no additional legitimacy upon civil association. And 'The Vocabulary of a Modern European State' was even more explicit in its anti-democratic conclusions. It denied that the 'active participation' of the people in the exercise of civil rule enhanced the liberties intrinsic to citizenship; and it insisted that the connections advanced by Mill between democracy and 'the welfare of the community', 'the interests of the majority' and 'the greatest happiness of the greatest number' had been detrimental to the legal morality inherent in civil association.

The 'civil association' described in the second essay embodied the principles of Hobbes's civil philosophy that Oakeshott had been expounding since the thirties. Firstly, the derivation of civil association from the postulates of human conduct explored in the first essay – 'free agency', 'deliberation' and 'persuasion' –

established that its fundamental ethical principle was harmonious with the spirit of Hobbes's voluntarism and his assumption of the priority of natural right: the inalienable and morally indefeasible right of human beings to make choices for themselves.

Secondly, the rights and powers vested in civil association corresponded to the principal attributes of Hobbes's *civitas* which Oakeshott had detailed in the *Introduction* to *Leviathan*. Thus, civil association exercised the sovereign right to make laws, vested in the legislative office; the 'right to interpret them, to administer them and to punish those who [did] not observe them', vested in the judicial and executive offices; and the more problematic powers concerned with the conduct of foreign policy, including the rights 'to negotiate, make war, conclude peace, levy taxes ... and raise an army of volunteers'.[55] Moreover, Oakeshott wrote in the Hobbesian recognition that civil association required no more extensive rights of civil rule, the association embodying the minimum conditions of settled political association and the necessary conditions for the rule of law. In fact, in exploring civil association exclusively in terms of law and the constitutional offices of legislation, adjudication and executive rule, 'The Civil Condition' preserved the distinction between the legal establishment of the state and the social order which had represented Oakeshott's principal Hobbesian departure from the Hegelianism of 'The Authority of the State'. Not only was the authority of civil association distinct from the natural authority exerted through the family and from the rights of 'lordship'; but its skeletal unity was so defined as not to require the participation of its subjects in common political, cultural, moral or national traditions. Indeed, Oakeshott implied that all the social bonds capable of generating *allegiance* to civil association – upon which Aristotle and Hegel placed such emphasis – were insulated from the compulsory obligations imposed by law.

Lastly, the Hobbesian principles of the voluntarist nature of civil obligation and of the sovereign character of the civil authority generated by the social contract underpinned the distinction between 'enterprise association' and civil association upon which the argument of 'The Civil Condition' was constructed. An enterprise association – a church, a public corporation or a political party, for instance – was identified by the 'common purpose' or 'common interest' which constituted it. Such an association could be 'managed', and its managers could prescribe rules whose authority derived from their instrumental relation to the purpose or interest they promoted. What was crucial about an enterprise association, however, was that continuing membership of it presupposed a voluntary and revocable choice to pursue the common purpose which constituted it; and that it was a necessary condition of the member retaining his rational autonomy that he be free to dissociate himself by 'a choice of his own'.

On Human Conduct betrayed no hostility towards enterprise association as such. It betrayed hostility only when enterprise association was confused with – or permitted to corrupt – the containing association which it presupposed: civil association. Enterprise association had to be distinguished from civil association, however, for three reasons.

Firstly, the model of enterprise association failed to make clear the authority peculiar to the state, the liberties peculiar to its subjects and the precise character of their obligations. It failed in these regards because of a fundamental distinction between itself and civil association: the noncompulsory and purposive nature of enterprise association, and the compulsory and nonpurposive nature of civil association. Since an enterprise association was constituted by the choice of its members to be and remain associated in the pursuit of its defining purpose, their freedom to revoke that choice at will, and thus release themselves from the jurisdiction of its rules, was the condition of the association preserving the 'link between belief and conduct which constitutes moral agency'.[56] The freedom unique to civil association, however, consisted in its exclusion of any constituting common purpose and the consequent irrelevance of any choice on the part of its members to be and remain associated: 'There is, then, nothing in civil association to threaten the link between belief and conduct which constitutes "free" agency, and in acknowledging civil authority *cives* have given no hostages to a future in which, their approvals and choices no longer being what they were, they can remain free only in an act of dissociation'.[57] It was in that sense that Oakeshott prescribed civil association as the only form of political association consistent with the ethical requirements of the voluntarism which he inherited from Hobbes.

Secondly, the managerial government of an enterprise association lacked by definition the quality of unconditionality which Oakeshott treated as the essential feature of the office of rule most fundamental to civil association: a sovereign office of legislation, bound neither by the approval of its subjects, the sanction of a superior legal authority nor by any antecedent conditions or articles of association. It was, in fact, the absence of any constituting purpose within civil association – together with the consequent absence of any 'indisputable and ready-made criterion' for assessing the desirability of legislative proposals – which conferred upon the office of legislation the *nonretractable* rights of sovereignty that Oakeshott regarded as essential to the modern European state.

Thirdly, since an enterprise association existed to serve some end or purpose *external to itself*, it lacked both the moral quality and the moral authority intrinsic to civil association. In particular, it was not essential to the character of an enterprise association that it should adhere to the canons of procedural natural justice which Oakeshott asserted were 'inherent in the notion, not of a just law, but of law itself'.[58] It was these canons of legal morality which Oakeshott took as representing the essential requisites of the rule of law itself, as yielding the indispensable principle of legitimacy governing the actions of civil association, and as conferring a uniquely moral character upon the civil law and the administration of justice. What they reflected were the 'attributes intrinsic to association in terms of non-prudential rules': 'the quality of legal subjects; rules not arbitrary, secret, retroactive, or awards to interests; the independence of judicial proceedings (i.e. all claimants or prosecutors, like defendants, are litigants); no so-called "public" or "quasi-public" enterprise or corporation exempt from common liability for wrong; no offence without specific prescription; no penalty without specific offence; no disability or refusal of recognition without established inadequacy of subscription; no outlawery'.[59] Oakeshott did not insist that an enterprise association was inherently incapable of respecting legal morality in the administration of its constituting purpose. His implication, however, was obvious. The more a civil association assumed the purposive character appropriate to enterprise association, the more justifiable would become the violation of legal morality in the interests of furthering its purpose; and the more precarious would become the legal rights of its subjects enshrined in procedural natural justice – to the point where, and Oakeshott was unambiguous, a government would be *justified* in permitting the judicial condemnation and extermination of its innocent subjects should their mere continuing existence prove 'irredeemably prejudicial to the pursuit of its purpose'.[60]

Oakeshott's invocation of the canons of procedural natural justice was fundamental to the revisionist intentions of *On Human Conduct*. It represented an attempt to reestablish the internal connections between law and morality which ethical utilitarianism excluded by definition, and which had been neglected in the tradition of legal positivism of Austin, Kelsen and Hart. And it implied that the foundations of modern liberal constitutionalism consisted not in the principles of constitutional democracy or welfare socialism, but in the subjection of government to the 'internal morality' of the rule of law together with the judicial independence which that necessitated. To that extent, Oakeshott was prescribing a doctrine of natural law: the requirements of legal morality were understood to impose restraints upon the state in the exercise of its sovereign will which were not, as such, generated by positive law; and to bind the subjects of the state irrespective of their voluntary consent. Nevertheless, the exact status of the canons of legal morality remained ambiguous; and it was unclear whether the ethical and political principles of the association they governed supported the weight which Oakeshott placed upon them.

At one point, Oakeshott suggested that the Aristotelian *polis* exemplified the features of civil association in the respect that it was a 'self-complete' moral association in having 'no extrinsic substantive purpose' and in being a 'constituted' association of 'equals'.[61] Yet it is crucial to understand that Aristotle's *polis* was radically unlike Oakeshott's civil association. This was so not simply because Oakeshott dissociated citizenship from the exercise of the social and political virtues, and defined it instead as a legal status carrying specific obligations imposed by a civil jurisdiction. It was so chiefly because Oakeshott's indebtedness to Hobbes involved fundamental departures from Aristotle regarding both the generation of civil association and the kind of considerations relevant to the justification of its authority. Oakeshott excluded the naturalistic sanction for civil association essential to Aristotle in favour of the voluntarist principles derived from Hobbes. Moreover, he represented civil association as an 'artificial' association generated by the consent of its subjects, and rejected explicitly the teleological justifications of its authority which had guaranteed the legitimacy of Aristotle's *polis*. In fact, Oakeshott prescribed the canons of procedural natural justice within the framework of a political association governed by Hobbesian assumptions radically subversive of the naturalistic ethical foundations upon which Aristotle and Aquinas had constructed the traditional natural law. Not only did Oakeshott's civil association exclude a substantive natural law established by rational reflection upon the human good; but it presupposed no substantive theory of human nature by reference to which even the ends of procedural legal morality could be justified.

In 'The Rule of Law' Oakeshott acknowledged that Hobbes had regarded the laws of nature as summarising, in one of their aspects, 'the formal principles inherent in the character of *lex*'.[62] But that acknowledgement did not, so far as civil association was concerned, qualify what Oakeshott concluded in the *Introduction* to *Leviathan*: that the laws of nature with which Hobbes dealt were rational 'theorems' or psychological laws regarding 'the optimum satisfaction of human wants';[63] that they imposed no authoritative moral obligations, but merely licensed the unconditional exercise of natural right; and that they acquired a moral character only after their incorporation within a system of conventional, positive law created by human will and sustained by human consent. Moreover, the priority of natural right to law within Hobbes's civil philosophy associated him with the tradition of Hume, Kant, Mill, Nietzsche and Sartre which asserted the autonomy of morality from nature and rejected the teleological derivation of ends and values from any determinate conception of human nature. In these respects, Hobbes provided Oakeshott with no metaphysical sanction for prescribing the kinds of ends and values embodied in the traditional natural law of Aristotle and Aquinas to supplement the ends of legal morality.

It was problematic whether Oakeshott's conclusions about Hobbes did not compromise the claims which he made on behalf of the procedural morality of law. The principles of Hobbesian civil association were historically continuous with the utilitarian, democratic and totalitarian traditions which Oakeshott regarded as antagonistic towards legal morality. They were also continuous with the post-Reformation secularisation of political association which deprived the procedural residue of natural law of its metaphysical connection with theistic religion and its traditional dependence upon organised Christianity. Moreover, the naturalistic status which Oakeshott attributed to procedural legal morality conflicted with his Hobbesian affirmation of the dependence of all law and morality upon will and convention; just as the universalist claims which he advanced on behalf of the association it governed conflicted with his anti-rationalist emphasis upon the derivation of all constitutional principles from determinate historical practices and traditions.

Oakeshott did not conclude that the procedural natural law legitimised the legal enforcement of substantive morality. He implied rather that it functioned within civil association as an essential precondition of the fundamental Oakeshottian distinction between state and community. Whereas such an enforcement was consistent with the teleological conclusions which Casey and Scruton drew from Aristotle, Aquinas and Hegel, it was plainly problematic for Oakeshott given the voluntarist principles which he derived from Hobbes. At any rate, Oakeshott was clear that the civil establishment required to generate the rule of law was no more extensive than the skeletal constitution of the Hobbesian *civitas*. However, the minimal extent of that establishment did not make it any easier to accept Oakeshott's conclusion that its compulsory character required no more substantial justification than its conformity to the internal morality of law.

What the rule of law required, firstly, was a system of law - *lex*. Not only did civil association define the requirements of 'justice' by providing authoritative rules, but, Oakeshott concluded, 'justice' was entirely conventional in being a matter of civil law. This was so in the Hobbesian senses that 'authentic *lex* [could not] be *injus*';[64] and that the rule of law presupposed a distinction between '*lex* (a rule understood in terms of its authenticity) and *jus* (a rule understood in terms of the "rightness" or "justice" of what it prescribes)' in which the validity of law was to be ascertained in terms of law itself, and not in terms of its intrinsic 'rationality', 'desirability' or 'justice'.[65] Moreover, since membership of the association which it constituted was neither chosen by its subjects nor revocable at will, the civil law had to comprise a 'self-sufficient system' and identify and impose its own jurisdiction according to the truism that ' "law regulates its own creation" '.[66]

What the rule of law required, secondly, was a legislative

office; thirdly, an office of adjudication; and, fourthly, agencies of executive rule (a police force, army and bureaucracy) authorised to enforce and administer the law. All these offices of civil rule were constituted in laws identifying their jurisdiction and the conditions for their legitimate occupation, and were subject to the morality inherent in the rule of law. Thus, the power exerted through offices was neither 'unconditional' nor 'tyrannical'. So far from being an 'unpurged residuum of violence', legitimate power was restricted to the enforcement of penalties for the breach of existing law in accordance with legal and judicial procedure. And so far from enjoying exemption from law, rulers were bound in their 'private' capacity by the rules which their 'public' office authorised them to enforce. Moreover, courts were bound by law and its jurisdiction in the exercise of their adjudicative function. They were not empowered to usurp the legislative office and prescribe retroactively binding legal obligations. They had no authority over disputes falling outside their jurisdiction. And the legitimacy of a judicial conclusion depended entirely upon its being a justifiable interpretation of existing law. Furthermore, the exercise of adjudication had to conform to the requirements of procedural natural justice. This meant, firstly, that the procedure of the court was 'litigious and not inquisitorial' and that its conclusions were 'judicial' and not 'managerial' decisions. It meant, secondly, that judicial proceedings were 'independent' in the sense that courts were authorised to enforce the law against the state and its officers. It meant, thirdly, the exclusion from judicial reasoning of all appeal to 'general moral considerations', ' "subjective" opinion about good or bad conduct', a 'separable equitable jurisdiction' not validated in law, or to a 'social policy' or 'common interest' not expressed in positive law. And it meant, fourthly, that the defendant had the right to be heard in his own cause and the corresponding obligation to demonstrate nothing 'save that the case against him [was] insufficiently established'.[67] In all those respects, the nature of judicial procedure and reasoning was designed to safeguard the individual subject from the arbitrary power of customary morality and consensual opinion.

As we have seen, the moral authority which Oakeshott attributed to civil association – and which he denied to a compulsory enterprise association – derived from his voluntarist premises. In this respect, civil association represented Oakeshott's resolution of the internal contradictions between the three principles of moral obligation governing Hobbes's voluntarism: 'that no natural man can have the authority to impose obligations on another, that no man may choose his own obligations, and that no man can become obligated save by a choice of his own'.[68] Oakeshott insisted that the generation and persistence of civil association required the continuous consent of its members. He did not adopt the idiom of social contract favoured by Hobbes, Locke and Kant. But he was clear that the idiom was appropriate to civil association providing that the social contract was understood to represent 'acknowledging the authority of an office' rather than ' "finding good" ' what the office prescribed;[69] and providing that the acknowledgement was understood to be an 'intelligent' act not in virtue of the subjects's participation in a 'definitive act of endowment' but because the authority of the state existed only through their 'continuous recognition' that it had it.[70] Moreover, he insisted that the mere power exerted by civil association was neither irresistible nor absolute, and that it was incapable of sustaining the association in the absence of consent: 'In the total absence of the recognition of authority, power was never enough to create and maintain an association of human beings'.[71] Not only was the 'will' of rulers expressed through the prescription of legally binding obligations rather than as arbitrary power, but compliance with obligations necessarily involved more than 'obedience' to superior force since 'to fulfil an obligation [was] always to make a choice'.[72] And lastly, Oakeshott was emphatic that the primary business of civil rule was not the exercise of executive power but legislation and adjudication. On the one hand, it had been the mistake of Hobbes and Bodin to associate sovereign authority with an 'absolute will'. On the other, the office of rule could be identified as the custodian of the *legitimate* apparatus of power only if the obligations it enforced derived their authority not from that office but from 'God' or 'nature'; and only in the Lockean sense – alien to the Hobbesian character of civil association – in which governments secured rights they had no authority to prescribe and 'where the "consent" of subjects [could] legitimise nothing more than the apparatus of power . . . necessary . . . to provide that security'.[73]

The difficulty remained that despite its voluntarist presuppositions, civil association was a compulsory association, that the sovereign rights generated by the consent of its subjects were nonretractable, and that it claimed a monopoly upon the exercise of all legitimate power within its jurisdiction. Oakeshott emphasised that power was necessary to civil association in the sense that the rights which law created required a civil establishment capable of enforcing them: to that extent, civil association was unavoidably the agent of violence. He also insisted that all power was circumscribed by the rule of law, and that the authority of the legal order through which it was exercised was determined 'in terms of the resources for decision which *lex* itself provides'.[74] Nevertheless, the legally 'self-authenticating' character of civil association in no sense explained the legitimacy of its legal and coercive structure considered as a whole. On the contrary, it tended to collapse the distinction between arbitrary power and legal authority upon which the moral legitimacy of civil association depended; and to leave unjustified the inevitable restraints upon individual rational autonomy the preservation of which was the moral end of civil association and the point of its differentiation from enterprise association.

That conclusion was confirmed, firstly, by Oakeshott's rejection of any legitimising principle which conferred a justifying purpose upon civil association. He denied that the authority of civil association was conditional upon its embodiment of 'a common good or general interest'; upon the approval of its subjects or their consensual agreement regarding the desirability of its rules; or upon the virtue, wisdom or other natural attributes of its rulers. Nor, Oakeshott insisted, did its authority derive from its correspondence with a preferred principle of distributive justice, or with an 'inherently just "higher" or "fundamental" law, a law of nature or of God' or 'a set of "fundamental values"'.[75] The consequence of these exclusions was to divest civil association of any purposive justification whatsoever – including whatever purposes were served by the very existence of a legal order in the first instance.

The conclusion was confirmed, secondly, by Oakeshott's excessively formalistic conclusions about the degree of political liberty necessary to preserve moral autonomy within civil association. He denied that the liberty essential to civil association depended upon 'unconditional' exemptions from legal obligations; the legal recognition of Mill's distinction in *On Liberty* between the self- and other-regarding actions; the preservation of a *laissez-faire* or free-enterprise 'capitalist' economy;[76] the provision of democratic rights of participation in the exercise of civil rule; the constitutional 'declaration of inalienable "rights" ' or a 'Bill of Rights representing a Basic or Fundamental Law';[77] or upon human rights secured through the conferment by government of substantive benefits like free education or health and employment. On the contrary, Oakeshott affirmed that civil liberty was entirely conventional inasmuch as it depended upon the exercise of rights which *presupposed* the legal order: the right of the civil subject to have enforced in his favour the general obligations imposed by the civil law; the right to act without legal restraint in contexts covered by 'the circumstantial silence of the law'; and the rights of judicial representation and legal personality guaranteed by the canons of procedural natural justice. Otherwise, the only pre-conventional liberties which Oakeshott recognised were the inalienable freedoms emphasised by Hobbes: the integrity of private thoughts and beliefs regarding which no civil obligation *could* be authoritative; and the inherent powerlessness of civil association to destroy the freedom of its subjects, in the minimal sense that their subjection to civil obligations did not relieve them of 'the necessity, or . . . the opportunity, of choosing what to do or say'.[78]

Oakeshott's conception of the liberty peculiar to civil association was not only excessively legalistic; more strongly, it involved the illusion of an entirely formalistic freedom, divorced from both objective values and real powers. The coherence of the conception depended too much upon the tenability of the dualisms which Oakeshott associated with Hobbes, and upon an implicit rejection of the full range of the implications for politics of Hobbesian materialism. The conception ignored the intimate dependence of political freedom upon the active participation of the civil subject in the objective social order which law presupposed. It minimised the extent to which the civil establishment conferred legitimacy upon the underlying social order; and the extent to which the conventional rights and liberties upheld in the civil law reflected the diversity of material interests and the substantial inequalities generated by that order. Above all, the conception implied that the moral autonomy which was the precondition of civil association was prior to all other moral values except the ends of legal morality; and that the free exercise of the sovereign rights generated by that autonomy was subject to no restraints save those of legal procedure. It was the conditionlessness of the passage from the priority of formal moral autonomy to the legitimacy of the virtually unrestrained exercise of sovereign rights which tended to impose an arbitrary character upon the power exerted by civil association. It tended also to collapse the distinction between civil association and enterprise association which Oakeshott needed to make morally absolute. This was so not just because Oakeshott admitted – problematically – that a civil association necessarily pursued the collective purpose of ensuring its own survival through the conduct of a foreign policy – 'the care for the interests of a state in relation to other states'.[79] Nor was it so just because a civil association by definition lacked any constituting articles of association to prevent its sovereign legislative office from imposing the character of 'enterprise' upon it through valid legislative enactment in accordance with authorised procedure. It was so because Oakeshott's affirmation of the permissibility of qualifying moral autonomy through the compulsory imposition of the rule of law left it unclear why other qualifications – whether Aristotelian, Thomist, Rousseauesque, Hegelian, utilitarian, Leninist, collectivist or socialist – which civil association expressly excluded were uncontroversially unjustifiable; or why their imposition was of a different moral order from the imposition of the ends of legal morality. In that respect, the strategy of 'The Civil Condition' inherited the principal ambiguity of Hobbes's civil philosophy, which the *Introduction* to *Leviathan* had confronted but left unresolved: the emptiness – and self-contradiction – of the contrast between the self-evident legitimacy of the exercise of nonretractable sovereign rights by the state in the interests of the 'peace and security of subjects', *despite* its inevitable violation of the foundational moral principle of natural right, on the one hand; and the self-evident illegitimacy of their exercise in pursuit of more extensive ends like those of 'lordship', *because* of the state's consequent violation of the natural rights of its subjects, on the other. Whether that ambiguity was resolved by the respects in which the distinction between enterprise association and civil association was tautological is not clear: certainly Oakeshott's admission that the conduct of foreign policy was a purposive enterprise was fatal to the internal consistency of the distinction. What is clear is that the last essay of *On Human Conduct* made statements which left no doubt that

Oakeshott believed that the distinction was historically substantiated and morally decisive.

v

'On the Character of a Modern European State' sketched the emergence of the modern European state from the medieval period. Its principal historical claim – that the crucial phase in the development of the modern state fell during the sixteenth century – implied that the model of civil association of the second essay was an 'abridgement' of the post-Reformation polity which had replaced the feudal constitution. Thus, the defining features of the modern state, Oakeshott insisted, were its acquisition of a ' "free" or "sovereign" ' character on the one hand, and the status of its ruler as a 'single inalienable authority without superior, partner, or competitor' on the other. And its emergence had involved, firstly, the 'transformation of feudal and personal relationships' into 'an association in terms of legal relationship'. It had involved, secondly, the transformation of 'a grand seigneur' or 'the lordly proprietor of a domain' into a civil ruler whose 'public' office was concerned exclusively to uphold 'a "law of the land" prescribing the rights and obligations which identified subjects, . . . a judicial system, [and] authoritative procedures for making and amending this law and for raising public revenue'.[80] It had involved, thirdly, the incorporation by the state of all subordinate jurisdictions together with the repudiation of the *potestas jurisdictionis* of the Pope and the external authority vested in the Imperial constitution. And it had involved, lastly, the acquisition by the state of the legislative sovereignty necessary 'to emancipate itself continuously from its legal past' and to establish 'the supremacy of the legislative act over ancient law and custom'.

'On the Character of a Modern European State' also made a polemical assertion and a revisionist claim. It asserted that the antinomies reflected in the vocabulary of modern European politics between liberal and conservative, left and right, liberty and authority, and so on were fundamentally confused. And it claimed that the confusion would be eradicated only by attention to the tension between the state understood as a *societas* and the state understood as a *universitas* which went back to the adoption by medieval jurists of the terminology of the Roman private law in the designation of legal associations.

The idea of a *societas* corresponded to the model of civil association in three respects. Firstly, it denoted 'a formal relationship in terms of rules' rather than an association constituted 'to pursue a common substantive purpose'. Secondly, in the absence of any constituting purpose, what was essential to the membership of a *societas* was not a 'choice to be related' but simply 'the recognition of understood terms of relationship'.[81] Thirdly, the laws and offices governing a *societas* constituted a 'nomocracy' in the sense that they served no end external to themselves.

The idea of a *universitas*, by contrast, had been adopted by medieval jurists to characterise public corporations like boroughs, universities, Imperial cities and collegiate churches. It was in virtue of its corporate character that a *universitas* provided a precedent for Oakeshott's model of enterprise association. A *universitas* was constituted in 'the pursuit of some acknowledged substantive end'. It was created by an 'act of authority', subject to 'inspection by the authority which created it', and liable to dissolution for any 'manifest divergence from its acknowledged purpose'. The membership of a *universitas* was both entirely voluntary and revocable by choice or expulsion. Finally, the rules and offices of a *universitas* constituted a 'teleocracy'in the sense that they promoted the realisation of some end or purpose external to the association they governed. What the idea of a *universitas* had inspired, Oakeshott asserted, was the conception of the managerial state constituted in the pursuit of a 'purposive concern', whose office of government was teleocratic, whose rules were 'instrumental', and whose 'land and natural resources' were subject to administration and distribution as 'corporate property'. However, Oakeshott concluded, the idea had proved inappropriate to the character of the modern European state in two respects. Firstly, in being entirely subject to the jurisdiction of the superior legal authority that created it, a *universitas* lacked the legally sovereign character essential to the post-Reformation state, which existed, Oakeshott insisted, only in virtue of the 'denial of any such subjection'. Secondly, since a *universitas* was *by definition* 'a voluntary association', it lacked both the compulsory character of the modern state and the irreversibility of the authority which it exercised.

Throughout 'On the Character of a Modern European State', Oakeshott extended the tradition reflecting the idea of *societas* to comprehend virtually any theorist who celebrated 'the "freedom" inherent in agency'. The tradition embraced Pico della Mirandola, Rabelais, Luther, Cervantes, Montaigne, Charron, Pascal, Hobbes, Hume, Kant, Blake, Kierkegaard and Nietzsche. And its ruling ideas were exemplified in the work of Machiavelli, Locke's *Treatises* on civil government, Montesquieu's *De L'Esprit des Lois*, the American Declaration of Independence and the authors of the Federalist Papers, the *Declaration de Droits de l'Homme et du Citoyen*, and in the moral and political thought of Mill. Those latter inclusions represented a remarkable reversal on Oakeshott's part of the anti-Enlightenment position which he had adopted throughout the critique of liberal rationalism in the forties and fifties. They were significant in demonstrating the extent to which Oakeshott's allegiance to the tradition of *societas* was an allegiance to the broadly conceived tradition of European liberalism; and the extent to which civil association was a distillation of the tradition of natural right stretching from Bodin and Hobbes, through Spinoza, Kant and Fichte, and culminating with Hegel.

In connection with Bodin's *Les Six Livres de la Republique*, Oakeshott recapitulated those features of the modern European state which he had earlier attributed to Hobbes in the *Introduction to Leviathan*, and which formed the basis of civil association. Firstly, Bodin's *Republique* was 'a relationship in terms of law' which had the liberal inclusiveness of civil association in comprehending 'persons and groups of divergent affections, interests, ambitions and beliefs'. Secondly, it had a 'civil' constitution whose authority derived not from 'a divine endowment', an 'antecedent proprietary right' or a 'notional or historic act of endowment', but from the 'continuous recognition' of its subjects. Lastly, the *puissance souveraine* and *puissance absolue* attaching to the legislative office of *Republique* represented the very attribute of legislative sovereignty which Oakeshott regarded as the defining feature of the modern state: 'the sole and unconditional authority to make, to amend, or to repeal any law' without being 'subject to a superior authority' or having to negotiate with a 'non-authoritative partner'.[82] Although Hegel's *Philosophy of Right* was included as the culmination of the tradition initiated by Bodin and Hobbes, the inclusion did not represent a return on Oakeshott's part to the Hegelianism of 'The Authority of the State'. On the contrary, Oakeshott was clear that the conditions of *das Recht* embodied in Hegel's state were 'civil' in constituting 'a system of known, positive, self-authenticating, non-instrumental rules of law (*Gesetze*) enacted by human beings according to a procedure authorised in the system of law; capable of being considered in terms of their desirability and deliberately altered; related to the contingent conduct of persons within their jurisdiction in a judicial procedure which is further empowered to penalise inadequate subscription to the conditions they prescribe; and enforced in administrative procedures similarly authorised.'[83] Where Hegel diverged from Hobbes, Oakeshott implied, was in his emphasis upon the historical character of the human will whose exercise generated the state. Thus, so far from corresponding to 'a law of "nature" or of God' which possessed a nonhuman sanction or preconventional status, the conditions of *das Recht* were irreducibly 'the contingent products of the achieved self-understanding of historic finite intelligence'. Oakeshott did not discuss whether the implications of Hegel's historicist divergence discredited the naturalistic status which he tended to confer upon the procedural morality of civil association; or whether Hegel's association of natural right with the illusions of 'abstract right', and his critique of the ethical and political implications of the model of the social contract favoured by Hobbes, discredited the excessive formalism of civil association. Nevertheless, it was clear that Oakeshott's legalistic reading of the *Philosophy of Right* did not carry the anti-liberal conclusions which Casey and Scruton drew from Hegelian historicism. Not only was *der Staat* exclusively 'a relationship in terms of *das Gesetz*' which 'neither [enjoined] nor [forbad] any other mode of association'; but Oakeshott was emphatic that the politicisation of culture and morality sanctioned by Hegel's identification of state with civil society was an aspiration of the tradition of *universitas*.

There was no doubt as to the strength of Oakeshott's faith in the uniquely *moral* authority vested in the tradition of *societas*. There was equally no doubt as to the vulnerability of that tradition to the teleocratic tendencies inherent in the post-Reformation state upon which he laid emphasis in 'On the Character of a Modern European State'. In fact, the essay affirmed the prevalence of the traditions associated with the idea of the state as a *universitas* in modern – and particularly post-industrial – European history. The tradition of *universitas* had become entrenched through the continuing extension by governments since the sixteenth century of the administrative and executive apparatus of civil rule. It had been reflected in the efforts of rulers to 'generate a sentiment of solidarity' uniting their subjects in terms, like those of national self-consciousness or religious confession, other than of a common law and civil administration. Thus, the Lutheran prince had sought 'to define a "confession" for his subjects . . . [and] to insist upon uncompromising uniformity' in religious observance; and in Calvinist Geneva, Soviet Russia and Nazi Germany the enforcement of 'religious and cultural homogeneity' had represented an entire 'corporate purpose' imposed and regulated by the state. Moreover, the tradition of *universitas* had persisted in the tendency of the modern state – particularly in the post-Napoleonic period – to impose a 'compelling corporate purpose' in deference to the necessities of 'war and military preparation'; and to acquire a teleocratic character 'in proportion to the magnitude of the claims it makes upon the attention, the energies and the resources of subjects'.[84]

Above all, Oakeshott affirmed that the increasing assumption by modern government of political responsibility for 'the problem of the poor' had involved commitments to the idea of the state as a *universitas* which had proved fundamentally antagonistic towards the values of civil association. In asserting the implication in teleocracy of the governmental and legal practices associated with modern socialism, Oakeshott was reiterating the polemically anti-socialist statements which he had first made immediately after the war. What was new was the exploration of the foundations of modern post-industrial socialism in the survival of the elements of the seigneurial arrangements of medieval feudalism in the post-Reformation period. The exploration of those foundations provided the basis for the most important of Oakeshott's revisionist conclusions in *On Human Conduct*: that the rights of 'lordship', which Bodin and Hobbes had systematically denied to civil government, had been repeatedly reasserted by modern governments to the detriment of the integrity of the civil association prescribed in the tradition of natural right. The true precedent for modern socialism, Oakeshott was saying, was not the authoritarian or allegedly absolutist government of the Hobbesian civil association. Rather, it was the survival of the lordship 'concerned with the ownership . . . of an estate, with the exploitation of its resources and with the lives of the agents of exploitation'. And the conception of the state underlying modern collectivism, Oakeshott was asserting, was that of the 'seigneurial domain', 'understood as an enterprise of a certain sort, its territory as an "estate", its laws as instrumental to the success of the enterprise, the office of its government as estate-management, and "subjects" as role-performers in an undertaking'.[85] It was that conception which had informed Bacon's understanding of the modern state as a 'corporation aggregate . . . recognised to be, and not merely to have, an economy'.[86] It had provided the models of settlement and administration for the British, Spanish and French colonisations of the Americas as private 'extensions of a royal domain'; and for the government of British India by the employees of a licensed public corporation, the East India Company, who exercised rule 'in the interests of their enterprise'.[87] It had inspired the 'lordly engagements' of the enlightened despots of the eighteenth century in increasing the extent and efficiency of the apparatus of state administration and bureaucracy in the interests of the 'managerial' government appropriate to the 'Baconian vision of a state as a technological enterprise'.[88] It had survived the association of socialism with popular democracy, despite the teleocratic confusion that 'where "the people" is lord, there is no lordship'. It had promoted the socialism of Saint-Simon, Fourier, Owen, Louis Blanc, the Webbs and Lenin; and fostered the association of civil government with the administration of a 'corporate productive enterprise' in accordance with a ' "scientifically" deliberated plan', and the identification of legal justice with the fair distribution of the resulting 'corporate income'. And it had culminated in the 'Servile State' of modern statism. Whether in the form of German national socialism, communism, welfare socialism or state socialism, the 'Servile State' had transformed taxation into the 'means of acquiring direct control over a large part of a "national income" to be expended in favoured projects or distributed . . . [as] notionally tied income'; witnessed the recession of civil law 'before instrumental rules and adjudication of civil disputes before the administration of instrumental rules and orders';[89] and reduced parliaments to 'markets where private interests clamour for awards from patron governments'.[90]

'On the Character of a Modern European State' did not say how the tradition of *societas* was to be reconstituted in the modern industrial age. On the contrary, Oakeshott concluded that the 'teleocratic drift' of European governments during and after the two world wars had served to strengthen the teleocratic apparatus of statist administration appropriate to the understanding of the state as a *universitas*. That conclusion made it all the harder to understand upon what practical basis Oakeshott really believed that the predominantly teleocratic tendencies of the modern European state were to be resisted and reversed. In fact, Oakeshott's silence about the kinds of social and economic policies, and the kinds of constitutional reform, that would be necessary to fulfil the aspirations of *societas* in the contemporary world was deafening. The unargued preferences for the superior morality of a certain *style* of politics which the essay implied did not make it any easier to accept Oakeshott's silence concerning those questions.

The reticence of 'On the Character of a Modern European State' did not, however, detract from the polemical power of Oakeshott's negativities about the state of modern politics and the condition of contemporary morals. Although it betrayed none of the romantic nostalgia for the medieval age characteristic of Burkean conservatism, the essay certainly betrayed a tone of sentimental nostalgia for the pre-industrial age in which the ideals of *societas* were understood to have had social and political correlatives in some objective form of life. It is difficult to be certain about the reality – or the formal historical status – of the 'past' which Oakeshott reconstructed in his testament to the tradition of *societas*. Although Oakeshott was educated as an historian, and although he has written importantly on the philosophy of history, 'On the Character of a Modern European State' remains his single substantial essay in historical reconstruction. Nevertheless, for all its brilliance, the essay collapsed the methodological distinction between the 'historical' and 'practical' pasts which Oakeshott had first prescribed in *Experience and its Modes* and which he was still asserting in *On History*. In fact, the past which the essay reconstructed was a 'practical' past, subordinated to the preoccupations of contemporary politics and designed to substantiate the prescriptive conclusions of a moralist or ideologue. Whether the essay's procedures were invalidated by Oakeshott's conclusions about historical methodology, or whether, as is more probable, they merely underlined the unreality of his exclusion of all practical considerations from historical understanding, is neither clear nor very important. The essay so obviously reconstructed a moralist's past, and the preferences and negativities which it expressed were so unmistakably polemical, as to make an *historical* evaluation of its claims inappropriate. Indeed, Oakeshott's indictment of the traditions of *universitas* and his celebration of those of *societas* were so resounding as to make the virtual absence of any *historical* explanation of the causes of the development of modern teleocracy – or of the material needs and moral aspirations it satisfied – of little consequence for their prescriptive authority.

What cannot be denied is that the anti-teleocratic conclusions of 'On the Character of a Modern European State' represented departures from the Hegelian and Hobbesian positions which Oakeshott adopted in the forties and fifties in the direction of the very 'abstract idealism' which his anti-rationalism explicitly rejected. Those conclusions derived their authority from their relation to the abstract 'abridgement' of civil association, and the abstract principles of legitimacy essential to it. As such, they failed to engage with the historical circumstances of contemporary politics or to provide any *practical* indication as to how the ideals of civil association were to be realised in the teleocratic conditions of the modern world. In fact, the anti-ideological strictures of 'Political Education', together with the relativism demanded by the essay's historicist perspective, suggested an unOakeshottian conclusion about modern teleocracy: that political wisdom in the contemporary world required the acquiescent 'pursuit of intimations' in practical deference to containing traditional continuities in which the conventions of modern teleocracy were firmly entrenched. And the Hobbesian position developed in 'On Being Conservative' permitted a further unOakeshottian conclusion: that the teleocratic arrangements of modern government were circumstantially legitimate insofar as they had succeeded in maintaining the civil peace and retaining the consent of their subjects. Neither essay – nor, for that matter, the argument of 'The Civil Condition' – supported the polemical conclusions of the last essay of *On Human Conduct*: that the teleocratic authority claimed by modern governments was illegitimate; and that their teleocratic engagements had diminished the freedom of their subjects. So far as legitimacy was concerned, Oakeshott denied the universality of *all* abstract principles of legitimacy and demanded only that government should satisfy the formal requirements of the rule of law: and, in the last resort, those were formal requirements which did not preclude the exercise of legitimate power by sovereign governments in the interests of policies more appropriate to a state understood as a *universitas*. And so far as freedom was concerned, Oakeshott made essential to civil association only those Hobbesian liberties which were inalienable *by definition*; and of which the civil subject could not *formally* be deprived, however extensive – or teleocratic – were the arrangements and engagements of the state constraining him.

Nevertheless, throughout *On Human Conduct*, Oakeshott wrote in the clear conviction that, from the voluntarist premises of Hobbesian liberalism, the teleocratic subversion of civil association was a moral outrage of the first order. That is a fact about the book which no commentary can ignore altogether. In this respect, *On Human Conduct* may be interpreted as a reversion to the anti-socialist position which Oakeshott took up in 1945 in opposition to the Attlee government. This interpretation is confirmed by the Swiftian demolition of the follies of modern collectivism – 'The Tower of Babel'[91] – which appeared as a coda to 'The Rule of Law' in 1983. Whether or not Oakeshott intended that its moral should supplement the jurisprudential conclusions of the essay on law, the message of 'The Tower of Babel' lent itself all too easily to the cause of liberal conservatism in the struggle against statism and socialism. Nevertheless, the anti-socialist interpretation of *On Human Conduct* diminishes the status of the book as a modern philosophical classic to be ranked with the more celebrated but ultimately less compelling classics of Hart, Rawls and Nozick. It also tends to obscure the respects in which Oakeshott's anti-socialist intuitions were not warranted by the foundational principles of the conservative doctrine which he enunciated in the forties and fifties; and the respects in which his more fearful anti-socialist predictions were not vindicated by post-war events, given the extent to which British socialism has been absorbed by the traditional constitutional arrangements of British politics and the extent to which its objectives have been realised in deference to the rule of law.

Above all, the anti-socialist interpretation obscures the senses in which the *moral* persuasiveness of Oakeshott's anti-teleocratic conclusions was compromised by the problematic status of civil association itself. Those conclusions did not escape the tendency of 'The Civil Condition' to universalise an 'abridgement' of the constitutional principles governing the post-Reformation polity, in defiance of the historicism presupposed throughout the critique of liberal rationalism. They also inherited its tendency to attribute a naturalistic status to the canons of procedural legal morality in the absence of any substantive theory of human nature capable of explaining the human ends they were intended to serve, and capable of providing them with some ground of ahistorical validity in accordance with the naturalistic requirements of the traditional natural law. Moreover, the conclusions were shot through with the unclarity of the moral principle by which Oakeshott assumed that the compulsory imposition of the rule of law was permissible without further justification, whereas the compulsory imposition of the more extensive arrangements of teleocracy was not. Much of their moral status depended, in fact, upon ignoring the legerdemain by which Oakeshott established that the arbitrary external restraints upon moral and rational autonomy were justifiable when imposed by a civil association, but not when imposed by a nonvoluntary enterprise association. And their historical authority was undermined by the extent of the dependence of the argument of 'The Civil Condition' upon the principles of Hobbesian politics which, in their emphases upon materialism, will and sovereignty, were continuous with the democratic, utilitarian, distributivist, Rousseauesque, Marxist and Leninist traditions that Oakeshott deplored.

The reservations which this chapter has entertained regarding the internal coherence of civil association are important because they establish a context for the discussion of the two thinkers which forms the basis of the next chapter: Maurice Cowling, who rejected Oakeshott's dissociation of civil association from ideology and the social order and disputed the romantic and secular orientation of Oakeshottian liberalism, whilst retaining Hobbesian intuitions about political action and endorsing the burden of Oakeshott's attack upon liberal rationalism; and Shirley Robin Letwin, who wrote in general as a convinced Oakeshottian, yet whose association of the sceptical conservatism of Hume with the core of Oakeshott's liberal conservatism involved problematic capitulations to the very utilitarianism which civil association was designed to exclude.

5 Two Oakeshottians: Maurice Cowling and Shirley Robin Letwin

I

Like Oakeshott, Maurice Cowling has written in dissenting opposition to secular improving liberalism in general and the elitism of its professional priesthood in particular. In this connection Cowling has adopted the principal insights of Oakeshott's anti-rationalism: that all of human conduct, and political activity specifically, is a manifestation of practical experience, that it rests upon very partial assumptions and that it cannot be abridged into an ideology without retreat into abstraction. Nevertheless, there remain significant discontinuities between Oakeshott and Cowling. What this chapter will establish is that Cowling's mature historical work represents a recession from Oakeshottianism after the phase of doctrinal acquiescence which produced *The Nature and Limits of Political Science*[1] and *Mill and Liberalism*.[2] It will imply that in his understanding of the connections between morality, culture and politics he is closer to Casey and Scruton than Oakeshott. And it will claim that he is remote from Casey and Scruton because the Anglican recognitions conveyed in his most recent work – *Religion and Public Doctrine*[3] – have identified romanticism in both its Arnoldian literary and Hegelian historicist forms as ultimately subversive of historic Christianity; and because he has written with an historical sense of the exposed political position of conservative values within nineteenth and twentieth century British democracy.

i

The Nature and Limits of Political Science was a polemically Oakeshottian book. It adopted the procedures of *Experience and its Modes* and spelled out the principles of government in terms familiar from *Rationalism in Politics*.

The book's third section was a critical examination of the different intellectual disciplines in the light of Oakeshott's doctrine about philosophy. Like Oakeshott, Cowling asserted that philosophy was a radically subversive procedure of critical enquiry which licensed the philosopher to undermine all the 'pragmatic certainties' upon which practical activity depends. Philosophy was 'thought without arrest or limitation; explanation with as few assumptions as possible'. Like Oakeshott again, Cowling implied the desirability of the philosopher accepting his limitations in relation to political activity. The philosopher had particularly to be cured of the delusion that 'articulate doctrine' and 'self-conscious premeditation' were necessary features of good government, that 'political freedom consists ... in pursuing a premeditated course unequivocally knowable to the literate, educated or enlightened leaders of society'.[4] Associated with that delusion, Cowling concluded, was the prevalent assumption that the only defensible philosophical style was anti-metaphysical and positivist, whereas the truth was that no single style of philosophical enquiry had a 'perennial, incontrovertible certainty' and that every philosopher, whether Newman or Ayer, made 'metaphysical assumptions'.

About the particular disciplines which philosophy was competent to examine, Cowling concluded what Oakeshott concluded before him. Theology, for instance, was merely the articulate formulation of the moral assumptions of a religion and had, as a form of *practical* truth, to be distinguished from the 'philosophy of religion'. And with history, Cowling reiterated the received orthodoxies of Oakeshott's philosophy of history: the distinction between the 'past as it was' and the past reconstructed by the historian; the intimate relation of history to 'the character, intelligence and shape of mind of the historian himself'; and the impropriety of the philosopher of history imposing a 'divine or necessary purpose' upon the details of the past narrated by the historian. All this recapitulation of *Experience and its Modes* was in polemical service to the Oakeshottian conclusion that history provided no lessons capable of guiding contemporary political action and that no historian possessed a normative authority in relation to practice in virtue of his explanatory competence as an historian.

If the third section of *The Nature and Limits of Political Science* was summary *Experience and Its Modes*, its fourth section, dealing with politics and government, was summary *Rationalism in Politics*. Cowling was clear both that government had to be understood in terms of its circumstantial authority, to the exclusion of all universalist principles of legitimation; and that the element of arbitrary authoritarianism upon which effective government depended was as essential to liberal democracy as to monarchy or aristocracy. Where political action was concerned, Cowling implied agreement with the traditionalist message of 'Political Education'. He thus expressed Oakeshottian reservations regarding 'unconditional freedom of action' given men's bondage to political 'conditions over which they . . . exert little control';[5] and Oakeshottian doubts about the efficacies of abstract principles in politics, once it was recognised that principles emerged from the continuities provided by habit, education and custom rather than from 'preaching or reflection or exhortation on every occasion in advance of action'.[6] And like Oakeshott, Cowling concluded that the confusions generated by contemporary political philosophy had arisen from the ascendancy of rationalist politics. Some of those confusions concerned the study of politics itself, and were to be avoided by understanding that the history of political thought had no special priority in the explanation of political activity and that study of 'the structure of government' provided no special illumination of the functioning of British politics. Other confusions betrayed a blindness towards ideological partiality for which Oakeshottian traditionalism was prescribed as an antidote. Thus, it was improper, Cowling asserted, to use slogans like 'freedom' and 'national interest' as though they possessed a 'self-evident moral content apart from the situations to which they might be applied', since political slogans had primarily an ideological function in legitimising the arbitrary exercise of political power. And it was equally improper to attach a special political significance to the explanatory authority of the theorist, since the truth was that political philosophers commanded less influence in political activity than 'those who have responsibility for action'.[7]

The strategy of *The Nature and Limits of Political Science* was polemical and dissenting. Its aspiration to subject politics and political science to the scrutiny of an 'ethically indifferent philosophy' need not be taken at face value. Cowling was so obviously *prescribing* the anti-theoretical style of politics in opposition to the 'powerfully organised squadron' of the liberal democratic tradition that the book came nowhere near the realisation of that Oakeshottian ideal. In any event, the book was followed by an essay in intellectual history which made it clear that 'ethically indifferent philosophy' was a liberal illusion.

Mill and Liberalism developed the insights of *The Nature and Limits of Political Science* in two directions. It emphasised the ideological character of Mill's liberalism, exposing the contestability of Mill's liberal rhetoric of 'impartiality, rationality and unquestionable self-evidence'. And it provided an Oakeshottian critique of Mill's exaltation of General Sociology, implying that general sociology was ideology rather than philosophy, and that its conclusions were practical preferences rather than demonstrable certainties.

Cowling's revisionist objective in *Mill and Liberalism* was to overthrow the orthodoxy that Mill was a 'libertarian'. On the contrary, Mill was a 'moral totalitarian' whose emphasis upon 'social cohesion' and 'moral consensus' excluded 'variegated human development' rather more than his libertarian reputation suggested. Not only was Mill an admirer of the medieval church as custodian of civilisation and embodiment of universal moral authority; but he was, Cowling stressed, determined that the consensus of liberal culture should provide a commanding ethical doctrine capable of reviving the spirit of communal participation which the fragmentation of medieval Christendom had destroyed. In these respects, Cowling concluded, Mill was essentially a moralist, whose liberalism was a competing doctrine propounded with an intolerance and intellectual jealousy comparable to Marxism and Christianity. And what Cowling demanded was that Mill's liberalism be recognised as a doctrine intended to undermine historic Christianity in favour of a brand of liberal rationalism – the 'Religion of Humanity' – which was as ethically exclusive as the dogmatic and ecclesiastical religion it was designed to supplant.

Cowling's critique of Mill was developed in the contexts of Mill's ethics and his sociology.

About Mill's ethics, Cowling insisted that *On Liberty* did not defend individual freedom unequivocally. Rather, it prescribed social and political safeguards for the elitist clerisy against the 'collective mediocrity' of the moral majority. Indeed, Mill's great principle of individuality presupposed substantial restraints upon the exercise of liberty since it was an ethical ideal which included 'less than all the ends to which men might want to move'.[8] Moreover, the distinction between the self- and other-regarding actions was ultimately subordinate to the utilitarian principle of maximising the 'greatest amount of happiness altogether', with the consequence that the individual had a prima facie duty to demur to the social good. In these respects, Cowling was claiming that the assaults of *On Liberty* upon the conventional consensus imposed by the tyranny of custom disguised Mill's underlying preference for the imposition of the consensus of cultivated opinion upon the diversity of customary morality. To the same conclusion, Cowling claimed that *Utilitarianism* was not an unambiguous statement of ethical utilitarianism. What Mill's principle of utility licensed was not the pursuit of any form of pleasure, but the cultivation of the 'higher sentiments'. In that sense, the problematic ethical distinction between the higher and lower pleasures demonstrated the extent of Mill's elitist tendencies since it implied that the hedonistic diversity of the lower pleasures was to be explained in terms of 'unreasoning prejudice and the despotism of custom'. What was thus objectionable about *Utilitarianism*, Cowling concluded, was Mill's importation of ethical assumptions whilst pretending that he made none, and his consequent failure to acknowledge explicitly the values in the name of which the coercive power of the liberal consensus was to be exercised.

Cowling challenged the General Sociology developed in Mill's *System of Logic* on the Marxist ground that it involved a radical misunderstanding of the relationship between theory and practice. In the last chapter of *Mill and Liberalism*, 'The Authority of the Clerisy', Cowling attacked Mill's attribution of normative political authority to the clerisy by appeal to the Oakeshottian principle that all political reasoning was the calculation of possibilities inherent in contingent circumstances. The principles of Mill's General Sociology were empty tautologies which carried no self-evident or uncontestable applicability to specific political circumstances. Cowling did not claim that the clerisy exerted no influence upon the conduct of politics, only that its political authority was unrelated to the exercise of its explanatory function of summarising the empirical laws of general sociology. Indeed, the deference of the statesman to the clerisy depended less upon his confidence in the explanatory authority of its injunctions than upon his 'confidence in the judgement of the person, or group . . . giving the explanation, and his judgement of the desirability of appearing to favour that group in those circumstances at that time'.[9] In this respect, Cowling's conclusion was clear: Mill's liberalism did not escape the brutal truths that any political order – whether its leadership was based on 'social superiority' or 'intellectual superiority' – was ultimately coercive, and that its authority rested upon *force* and ungrounded *consent* as much as *reason*.

Mill and Liberalism was generally harmonious with the spirit of Oakeshott's critique of liberal rationalism. However, Cowling's subsequent work reflected substantial departures from those principles of Oakeshottianism which most obviously involved capitulations to liberalism. Since *Mill and Liberalism* Cowling has endorsed neither Oakeshott's Arnoldian disjunction between academic reflection and practical commitment nor the liberal vision of university education to which it led. In the context of historiography, he has rejected Oakeshott's insistence upon the absolute discontinuity between the practical and historical understandings of the past, concluding that the historian unavoidably contributes to general culture and that historical literature is accordingly continuous with practical understanding. And in the context of religion, he has dissented from both Oakeshott's association of religion with secular morality and his separation of its ecclesiastical embodiment from the civil establishment of the state. In each context, Cowling has been clear that academic reflection, religion and historical literature all possess an ideological character. In connection with politics, Cowling has shared neither Oakeshott's concern with the procedural morality of civil association, nor his Hobbesian emphasis upon legal sovereignty as the defining feature of the modern European state. So far from celebrating the post-Reformation polity that Oakeshott associated with Hobbes, Cowling has regarded it as a decisive phase in the problematic secularisation of political association. And so far from affirming the liberty peculiar to civil association as the supreme moral and political value in Oakeshott's sense, Cowling has insisted that all civil law enforced by the state necessarily curtails freedom by preserving the unequal distribution of powers, privileges and material interests embodied in the underlying social structure.

In his emphases upon ideology and social structure, Cowling has written with an unOakeshottian respect for Marxism. His historical work has certainly implied the inadequacy of the Marxist assumptions of crude mono-causal determinism and of the priority of collective agents in the explanation of political change. But it has taken entirely seriously the Marxist recognition that the central political problem remains the class struggle; made materialist assumptions concerning the ultimate motivation of professional politicians in the context of modern liberal democracy harmonious with the materialist assumptions of classical Marxism; and emphasised the explanatory power of the Marxist dogmas of ideology and praxis in the understanding of political action. Indeed, in its affinities with Marxism, Cowling's historical work has demonstrated the main limitations of the formalism of Oakeshott's civil association as a conception of political practice. This is one reason why it is discussed at length in this chapter.

ii

Cowling's historical work resulted in three books: an account of the passing of the 1867 Reform Act – *1867, Disraeli, Gladstone and Revolution*;[10] an account of the fall of Lloyd George's coalition in 1922 – *The Impact of Labour 1920–24*;[11] and an account of British foreign policy from 1933 to 1940 – *The Impact of Hitler*.[12] Each book was an historical demonstration of how democratic politics should be understood. Cowling had previously spelled out the assumptions of that understanding in the third section of *The Nature and Limits of Political Science* where he challenged the claims of democratic politics on a broadly Oakeshottian front. Like Oakeshott, he implied that democratic constitutions had no greater authority than others and that it was naive to defend them on the ground that they maximised their subjects's opportunity to participate actively in the exercise of political rule. For all its advantages, a democratic polity was merely one instrument with which power was exercised. What sustained a democratic polity was not the surface ideology of abstract constitutional principle but its underlying social and political structure as established 'through the arbitrary exercise of power and . . . arbitrary conjunction of circumstances'. And what perpetuated the structure was not the popular will but the deployment of rhetoric by democratic politicians to gain the measure of popular consent necessary to ensure the continuing existence of the regime.

In defining the foundation of political association, Cowling, like Oakeshott, invoked a doctrine about the limits of human practical reason. The principal implication of that doctrine was that the exercise of political reason in general – and by the political actor in particular – was necessarily an exercise of individual, rather than collective, practical reason, concerned with the calculation of the consequences of actions in the light of partially understood circumstances. What was denied the political actor was the *certainty* that any course of action was demonstrably correct. All that rescued political action from the contingency and arbitrariness arising from the 'luck, chance and accident' that everywhere qualified human conduct was the system of 'professional conventions' observed mutually by politicians. Moreover, their subscription to those conventions had to be understood chiefly as a 'combination of calculation and thoughtlessness, scheming and simplicity, competence and blundering, avarice, ambition and altruism, stupidity, sense and sanctimoniousness'.[13] What this combination of Machiavellian pragmatism, Hobbesian nominalism, Marxist praxis and Oakeshottian anti-rationalism provided for Cowling was a methodological principle for the reconstruction of three pivotal episodes in the history of British democracy. In the process of its application, Cowling arrived at radically unOakeshottian conclusions about the nature of both political action and the political problem, rejecting Oakeshott's association of politics with deliberation about law and affirming instead that politics 'decides not what is to be done . . . but which party or group shall command sufficient support to make the decision'.[14]

1867, Disraeli, Gladstone and Revolution was an 'essay in political sociology' which reconstructed the 'logic of conservative resistance' by treating the Reform Act as 'an incident in the history of party' and liberalism as the ideology of a political party. It provided a solution to an historical paradox: why the Conservative administration of Derby and Disraeli passed a reform bill in 1867 extending the franchise more widely than Russell's abortive bill of 1866 which the Conservatives had defeated in alliance with the Liberal Adullamites. In providing a solution, the book emphasised the importance of the public espousal and parliamentary implementation of electoral reform to a Conservative cause which had been on the defensive since the fall of Peel in 1846. And it demonstrated that the 1867 measure had electoral advantages for the Conservative party which the 1866 bill lacked since its provisions for county redistribution resulted in compensating gains for the Conservatives to offset the anticipated Liberal gains under the more generous franchise provisions.

Throughout the book Cowling drew subversive conclusions about the complacent liberal orthodoxies concerning the 1867 Act. He dissented from those historians like Morley and Trevelyan who assumed that the Liberal party was unambiguously progressive in relation to the redistribution of political power; and from those historians like Royden Harrison who interpreted the Conservative volte-face as a capitulation by the traditional parties to the working class pressure exerted through the public agitation of the Reform League. Those interpretations were defective firstly in ignoring the extent to which the political parties were responding to the parliamentary situation confronting them rather than the force of extra-parliamentary opinion; secondly, because they obscured the conservative character of parliamentary politics. Not only was the 1867 measure enacted by a parliament inherently resistant to any form of democratisation likely to undermine the integrity of its rule, but the disagreements of party politicians about the extent and merits of reform presupposed their fundamental agreement about 'the importance of electoral arrangements in maintaining the social and economic structure ... and the overriding need to maintain it'.

With those conclusions Cowling was vindicating the capacity of a conservative constitutional establishment to contain revolutionary upheavals by tactical adjustment. He was demonstrating that in the understanding of democratic politics, the ambitions of politicians – whether Disraeli and Derby or Bright and Gladstone – to create and control party alignments within the parliamentary context were central. And he was illustrating the principle that their historical reconstruction required a detailed narration of events in which participant politicians played a dramatic rather than emblematic role. In all these respects *1867, Disraeli, Gladstone and Revolution* looked forward to a book which examined the acquiescent participation of the Labour party in the pragmatic, consensual politics it treated as the norm of parliamentary government.

The Impact of Labour was a narrative of the 'high politics' of the period from 1920 to 1924. It dealt with the transformation of the Labour party from a subversive electoral force in 1920 into the main party of progressive opposition after 1924; the destruction of Lloyd George's coalition in 1922; the elimination of the Liberal party as a party capable of commanding the moderate centre; and the emergence of Baldwin's Conservative party in 1924 as principal 'defender of the social order' in 'resistance to socialism'. The book established that the beneficiary of the high political conflicts of the period was the Conservative party. It traced the disengagement of the party from the Lloyd George coalition after the rebellion of the die-hard and moderate backbench factions mobilised by Salisbury; the failure of Bonar Law to safeguard the party from the threat of a reconstituted centre coalition by incorporating the Chamberlainite coalitionists; the subsequent failure of Baldwin to adopt protection as the basis of a progressive policy enabling the Conservative party to rebut the charge of reactionary die-hardism and differentiate itself from the socialist solutions prescribed by Labour; and it concluded with Baldwin's rejection of protection and ultimate triumph with the programme of 'undoctrinaire resistance from which, once planted in mid-1924, the Conservative party has never really moved'. The point being established was that Baldwin recaptured for the Conservative party the centre ground previously held by Lloyd George, which Birkenhead, Churchill and Salisbury had wanted occupied by a centre party excluding the Conservative Right and including the Asquithian Liberals, and which others had associated with the projected leadership of Grey, Lloyd George or Austen Chamberlain. In these respects Baldwin's consensus registered divergences from the past. Nevertheless, Cowling's conclusion was that the divergences were not radical. Not only was Baldwin's broad-based administration continuous with the coalition it displaced in commanding 'all the forces that Lloyd George had tried to lead from 1920 onwards' – it was harmonious with the consensus which had created it: the 'overwhelming agreement amongst all non-socialist leaders that the major problem of the future was to provide leadership and create conditions in which the existing social order could be preserved'.[15]

The continuities Cowling described dictated the need he felt to explain the transformations of the period in terms of a context which excluded the collective agents of the class struggle. The context he provided was the conservative and self-perpetuating world of 'high politics'. It was a world inhabited by professional politicians who shared only a common adherence to the conventions governing the conduct of 'high politics'. Those conventions were designed to exclude the active participation of the electorate in the institutional establishment they governed, and to neutralise political conflicts by confining them to the realm of 'high politics' they constituted. Moreover, the conflicts resolved through 'high politics' were less about ultimate objectives than the 'rhetoric and manoeuvre' necessary to find 'new landmarks for the electorate . . . [and] to ensure that the right people provided the rhetoric'. And they hinged upon personality as much as principle, since within 'high politics' the 'antipathy, self-interest and mutual contempt' of individual politicians provided the chief motives for political action.

The concept of 'high politics' was a methodological principle which crystallised the insights expressed in *The Nature and Limits of Political Science*. It was central to Cowling's doctrinal concerns in *The Impact of Labour* for four reasons.

First, the concept was particularly appropriate to the politics of the period under consideration. Politicians had to make unguaranteed calculations about the putative intentions of the new electorate created in 1918. And that electorate was confronted with a Labour party, two Liberal parties and the possibility of a divided Conservative party. These factors, Cowling claimed, explained the five year delay in constructing the party of resistance which all non-socialist politicians desired, the role of the mutual antipathies of politicians in delaying it, and the exaggerated precariousness of the calculations made in constructing it.

Second, it complemented Cowling's Oakeshottian insistence upon the contingent character of the political action narrated. The lesson was that the finality of Baldwin's triumph did not alter the fact that between 1920 and 1924 there had been 'equality of opportunity for all the groups concerned'. Thus Cowling denied that the destruction of the Liberal party had been inevitable, affirming that in 1923 the Liberals had had an opportunity to replace the Conservative party which they might have taken had Asquith and not MacDonald taken office in 1924. And he insisted that had MacDonald avoided a General Election in 1924 he might have prevented the Baldwin landslide and created an electoral situation advantageous to the Liberal and Labour parties.

Third, the concept confirmed the anti-democratic implications of *1867, Disraeli, Gladstone and Revolution*. Cowling emphasised that the enlarged electorate of 1918 and the advent of working-class politics did not compromise the shared commitment of all the political parties – which transcended their rivalries – to uphold the exclusiveness of the parliamentary establishment. That commitment not only presupposed the consensual defence of a social order in which inequalities would continue to exist – it involved no belief in the desirability of the participation of the electorate in a fully democratised constitution. Cowling did not deny that the emergence of Labour had implications for the class struggle the reality of which all politicians understood. But he insisted that the party realignments effected through the high politics of the period were intended to emasculate the class conflict, and that all parties 'found in parliament a terminal point beyond which conflict would not ride'.

Last, the concept of 'high politics' demonstrated a truth about the function of the Labour party. The objective of the party had been to establish itself not as a 'party of revolution', but as a 'parliamentary success' acting in deference to the constitution and the rule of law. So far from intending a programme of revolutionary socialism, its leaders assumed 'that the political and social system could not be overturned and that it was impossible to establish a hegemony of the poor over the rich'. And they committed themselves to the conventions of 'high politics' in realising their objective, thus ensuring that the impact of Labour would not be subversive of the consensual continuities of parliamentary government stretching back through 1918, 1884 and 1867 to 1832. In Cowling's analysis the Labour party's success was a consequence of its leaders's willing involvement in 'high politics': in fact, it had been MacDonald's exploitation of the tactical situation in 1924 created by Asquith's miscalculation and Baldwin's decision to destroy the Liberal party which offered Labour the opportunity to demonstrate that in office 'socialism meant men of business pursuing the half-measures constitutive of radical progress as England knew it'.

Although a brilliantly complex book, the message of *The Impact of Labour* was simple. Through its acquiescence in the containing consensus of Baldwinian conservatism, the Labour party had posed no radical threat to the Constitution and social order. Whether the acquiescence was a triumph for Labour or its ultimate tragedy, whether the party's status as 'true heir to radical liberalism' did not entail betrayals of socialism, and whether the containing consensus implied retreats from Conservative positions, Cowling did not say. In dealing with the events which destroyed the consensus Labour had helped create these questions acquired point and urgency.

The Impact of Hitler advanced a methodological principle. Affirming that foreign policy had a centrality in British politics in the thirties comparable to Protection in 1846 or Ireland in 1886, it insisted that the conduct and discussion of foreign policy had to be understood through party political considerations. This explained why Cowling concluded that the foreign policy conflicts provoked by the impact of Hitler were a continuation of the party conflicts initiated in the early twenties; that the prevention of a possible Labour General Election victory in 1940 was a dominant factor in the foreign policy assessments of Halifax and Chamberlain; and that the failure of their policy together with the 'international-conflict programme' adopted by Eden, Churchill and Sinclair provided Labour with opportunities for recovery and ultimate ascendancy not implicit in the party political situation of 1931.

Cowling did not deny the ideological character of history in *The Impact of Hitler*. Rather, he insisted upon it, spelling out that the book was a revisionist exercise intended to subvert the acts of 'self-congratulation' by which historians had transformed the post-war consensus into an historiographical orthodoxy commanding moral and political authority. The consensus complacencies which needed challenging were the assumption of the longterm reliability of the regime which had defeated Hitler, the uncontested premise that the welfare politics of the Attlee years and the subsequent phase of Butskellism constituted the only respectable politics, and the moral superiority acquired by the Labour party over the Conservative consensus discredited by Munich.

Cowling attacked the consensus on several fronts. He attacked its self-deceiving avoidance of the truth that 1945 represented British defeat and Russo-American victory. He attacked the negativity towards Chamberlain inspired by Churchill's differentiation of the wartime coalition from the period of appeasement. Above all, he challenged the legend of Churchill by reducing his posture as heroic defender of civilisation after the decadent regime of Baldwin and Chamberlain and insisting that his status as political actor was no different from Chamberlain's or Halifax's. Ultimately, in May 1940 Churchill was an 'opportunist' who stood only for 'the prosecution of a war which was not to be prosecuted and the preservation of an Empire which was not to be preserved'; whose coalition was merely an 'arrangement of convenience'; and whose chance to offer himself as 'saviour of the nation' arose only when, contrary to everyone's expectations including his own, France fell 'six weeks later'.

In diminishing Churchill, Cowling stressed that his coalition had had paradoxical consequences at odds with Churchill's long-term political objectives. This was so in relation to the socialism which he had resisted after 1919 given that his coalition depended upon the involvement of Labour as 'a major element in a centre government'. And it was so in relation to the Empire, given that the Anglo-American relationship which he emphasised operated contrary to imperial interests and, when coupled with the pre-war failure to develop a financial and military structure for its defence, made its liquidation inevitable.

If the book had a negative aim in demolishing Churchillian complacencies, it had the positive aim of recovering the 'coherence' of Conservative foreign policy after the phase of post-war denigration. Cowling was clear that the rehabilitation of Chamberlain did not involve demonstrating that appeasement was designed to postpone an unavoidable and anticipated confrontation with Hitler, or that Chamberlain was right to declare war over Poland when he had not done so over Austria and Czechoslovakia. Rather, what had to be established was the defensibility of Chamberlain's policy commitments to imperial security, detachment from Russia, the defence of the low countries and the maintenance of economic stability. And what had to be assumed was that Chamberlain was as rational as Eden or Churchill; that military confrontation with the dictators was not inevitable; that it was 'neither depravity which determined policy up to September 1939 nor a reign of virtue that began in May

1940'; and, overridingly, that it was neither 'morally obligatory' nor 'prudentially self-evident' that Hitler be obstructed in Eastern and Central Europe. The last assumption was crucial and it rested upon the recognition that Eastern and Central Europe were not vital areas of British concern and that German expansionist ambitions in respect of them were not intrinsically antagonistic towards British imperial interests as defined by 'the thin line of oil and trade through the Mediterranean, Red Sea and Persian Gulf to India, Malaya, Hong Kong and Australasia'. Chamberlain's dilemma was that, however desirable, British detachment from European involvement was impossible, and had been recognised as such since the pre-1914 association of imperial security with the end of British isolation from Europe. He was thus confronted with a situation in which the defensive interests of Britain and France coincided in the common need to maintain defensive frontiers on the Rhine and Britain was hence committed to an ally who identified the integrity of those frontiers with preserving an encircling second front against Germany.

Given his dilemma, Chamberlain's mistaken assumption was not that Hitler would be reliable after Munich, but that Hitler would be unable to inflict a knock-out victory upon France. Unlike the question of Hitler's reliability, Cowling insisted, the impossibility of French collapse was an assumption Chamberlain shared with his critics. In fact, Chamberlain's policy involved no substantial disagreement with his critics since 'except at Munich, [it was] so much the same as theirs that their criticisms were about . . . the names of the game he should be playing . . . to find words to prevent war'. Apart from the assumption about France, Cowling concluded, Chamberlain's policy from Munich to May 1940 was entirely consistent with his objective of preserving detachment by preserving peace. In pursuing it, Chamberlain was not constrained by 'defensive deficiencies' or 'logistical impossibility', since he did not comprehend a longterm war and made the reasonable assumptions of naval superiority, French impregnability and British capacity to withstand air attack. He was justified in his ambivalence towards American involvement given both its likelihood to accelerate dependence upon a commercial rival and his recognition that 'American half-commitments might produce an Anglo-Japanese war at the same time as Britain went to war with

Germany'. And with regard to Russia, so far from being a diplomatic disaster the Anglo-German pact represented the very abandonment by Hitler of the anti-comintern policy which Chamberlain had desired since 1937. Cowling insisted that although it was designed to preserve detachment, the Munich agreement was crucial because its failure forced Chamberlain to bow to domestic political pressure and adopt a policy of involvement culminating in the Polish guarantee after the occupation of Prague which he had intended avoiding. That pressure did not prevent Chamberlain from pursuing detachment under the cover of involvement, however, since the British commitments of 1939 were made 'so that the threat of war would prevent war being declared just as the declaration of war would make it unnecessary to fight it'.

Cowling emphasised how, in bowing to pressure, Chamberlain was responding to the party political situation. The pressure exerted by Halifax after Prague to secure a Russian alliance was prompted by the recognition that appeasement was costing the Conservative party its moral authority *vis-à-vis* its opponents and the conclusion that an interventionist policy would have to be pursued irrespective of the destructive consequences for the social and imperial structure the party was committed to preserve. That the consequences were destructive Cowling was clear, since he concluded that the deposition of Chamberlain on grounds of foreign policy failures was significant chiefly in marking the destruction of the Conservative party and the creation of post-war socialism as 'Attlee, Bevin and Morrison took on post-war reconstruction . . . in 1940.'

In some respects Cowling's negative conclusions about 1940 were exaggerated: *The Impact of Hitler* reiterated the consoling lesson of *The Impact of Labour* that Labour was fully committed to the consensual politics of the parliamentary establishment. Cowling did not declare whether 1940 was, as he said, a 'lib–lab trap for Conservatives or a Conservative trap in which Attlee was the victim'. He certainly implied that it was a 'lib–lab trap' insofar as 1940 upset the conservative structure and necessitated the espousal of an egalitarian 'Tory Socialism' by the 'new range of leaders' including Butler, Eden, Macmillan and Heath. But he insisted also that the intentions of 'Tory Socialism' were identical with the intentions of the National Government in seeking 'to contain class warfare by enveloping it' and preserve the 'social structure . . . by talking about something else'. Given the post-war success of a politically responsive 'Tory Socialism', Cowling's insistence may be interpreted as implying that 1940 was, in the longest run, a Conservative victory. He implied that 1940 was a 'Conservative trap' by stressing Attlee's continuity with the regime he replaced as much as his consensual authority for the future. So far from being revolutionary, the emphases upon nationalisation, increased taxation and Indian independence merely confirmed processes initiated by 'the India bill, the Statute of Westminster, by state activity in the first war and the public corporations since' and by rearmament, conscription and the level of wartime taxation. And Attlee's legacy was a consensus in which socialism was transformed into 'elitist radicalism' and 'Labour, Liberal and Conservative opinion' was led by 'safe hands' towards 'democratic radicalism'.

Cowling did not ask what distinguishing role the Conservative party had to play in the post-war consensus. Nor did he ask how the party was to differentiate itself from the consensual orthodoxies enshrined in 1940. Nevertheless, the introduction to *Conservative Essays* which Cowling wrote in 1978 implied that differentiation was possible and necessary.

'The Present Position'[16] was written before the Conservative victory of 1979 and conveyed no confident anticipations of the triumphant endorsement of 1983. Cowling acknowledged that differentiation had taken place. Mrs Thatcher had inherited the legacy of Powell's critique of Butskellism and succeeded, in the aftermath of Heath's failure to act upon it resolutely, in imposing its 'necessary truths upon the Conservative party at the point at which [Powell] had left it' in 1974. The expression she had given to the sentiments of those Conservatives who regarded Macmillanite, Butskellite and Churchillian conservatism as a 'capitulation to socialism', together with her espousal of a strident economic liberalism, had marked a final point of departure from the consensual conservatism of the fifties and sixties. And she had established the principle that in the seventies and eighties conservatism had to involve giving 'political form to the idea of "rolling back the frontiers of the state" '. Nevertheless, Cowling insisted that differentiation had been difficult and was not assured of success. On the one hand, so far from representing 'capitulation to socialism', Butler's liberal conservatism had been indispensable to the party's survival during the phase of left-liberal ascendancy – and it was not obvious that the party would survive its total abandonment. On the other, the 'acquiescent conservatism in relation to prevailing interests and practices' characteristic of Callaghan's socialism reflected the entrenched authority of the 'governing experience' stretching from Churchill through Attlee and Macmillan to Wilson. And it embodied the 'genuine bond of sympathy' which had once existed between Conservative politicians and the public and which was not necessarily to be reconstituted by Mrs Thatcher's tone of 'enthusiastic conservatism'. What Cowling was saying was that the tone of Thatcher's conservatism reflected relapses into liberal illusion and ideological abstraction which had to be avoided if the Conservative party was to discharge its function with any chance of longterm electoral success.

Cowling's objections were based partly on tactical considerations. There were, for instance, built-in dangers in staking the party's electoral reputation upon the promise of increased material prosperity under monetarist policies: there was no guarantee that the policies would accelerate economic growth, especially since it was understood to depend upon factors beyond government control, and some reason to suppose that economic disappointments would discredit a Conservative party claiming to have policies for avoiding them.

Cowling's principal objection, however, was that the liberalism obscured the nature of the political problem and, insofar as it was taken at face value and proclaimed as ideology, stood to hinder the Conservative party in the discharge of its function. About the political problem – the neutralisation of the class war within the framework of constitutional democracy and the defence of national interests within the restraints imposed by the international balance of power – Cowling wrote with brutal directness, conveying the sentiments articulated by Casey and Scruton and recognising the parallels between Marxism and conservatism. Thus he insisted that Smithian economics possessed no self-evidently conservative orientation and were pernicious in diverting attention from Marxism which, with its emphases upon ideology, practical assumptions and historical relativism, was an invaluable ally to conservatism in its battles with liberalism. About the function of the party, Cowling's directness was qualified only by his insistence upon the need for its articulate spokesmen to misrepresent it with political self-knowledge. Its function was not to promote the unconditional 'freedom' celebrated in liberal ideology. So far from being an ultimate moral value or the end of political action, freedom was an 'abstraction'; and so far from being universal or unconditional, it existed only in the form of the particular liberties – like the right to own, accumulate and dispose of property – conferred by the legal order. Freedom was a *value* only inasmuch as it provided the legitimation of the ultimate end of conservative action: the preservation of a stratified social structure shot through with ineliminable inequalities and necessarily exclusive privileges: '[It] is not freedom that Conservatives want; what they want is the sort of freedom that will maintain existing inequalities, or restore lost ones, so far as political action can do this. . . . [It] is a way of not saying what they want, a way of . . . attributing principle to a social structure they wish to conserve or restore'.[17]

Cowling did not deny the political advantages of the party's penchant for tactical disingenuousness. And he recognised that the rhetoric of 'freedom' had been beneficial in detaching liberal opinion from the socialist consensus. But that did not alter the stark truth that the function of the Conservative party was to protect the class interests of those who derived benefit from the inequalities embodied in the social and economic order.

In several respects 'The Present Position' was a fundamental essay. It underlined Cowling's recession from his initially Oakeshottian positions and extended the analysis of 'high politics' to the contemporary political predicament. And in its emphasis upon the priority of the social structure, it was a testimonial to the conservative Hegelian positions adopted by Casey and Scruton in the late seventies. In those respects it reflected the profound dissatisfaction with conventional liberal assumptions which, whether from the perspective of Hegel, Hobbes, Salisbury or Wittgenstein, was the common characteristic of all the thinkers discussed in this volume. Cowling left little doubt that the association of conservatism with the anti-totalitarian stance adopted by Hayek, Talmon, Popper and Berlin in the phase of post-war resistance to Labour constituted the problem to which the thinkers were responding: the anti-totalitarianism had merely aligned conservatism with ideologies ultimately liberal in orientation and consequently subversive of the intellectual and moral values of traditional conservatism. He left little doubt also that, to the extent that it challenged the alignment, the work of thinkers like Casey and Scruton had immense prospective importance. Indeed, their work vindicated the principal conclusion of the essay: that the late seventies provided the best opportunity since 1940 to undermine the ascendancy of the left-liberal consensus by claiming unfamiliar intellectual territory for conservatism.

With the benefit of hindsight, Cowling was probably wrong to stress the danger of promising material prosperity as the consequence of Conservative rule in circumstances of economic recession. Despite low economic growth and high unemployment, the government has presided over conditions in which the prosperity of those in work has created a secure electoral base for its ascendancy. Cowling was probably wrong to stress the openness of the intellectual situation in the late seventies. And he was certainly wrong to exaggerate the extent to which 1979 would mark a radical departure from the previous consensus. In fact, Cowling had been ambiguous about what the departure would involve. He emphasised the necessity of not taking economic liberalism too seriously; yet he conveyed agreement with the aspiration of 'rolling back the frontiers of the state' as the principle of conservative action. Nevertheless, about the substantive policies which the principle was to entail Cowling was unspecific. He insisted that it should entail a reduction in the level of taxation such as to create 'control by individuals and families over a larger proportion of their earnings'. The insistence was problematic given that public commitment to reduction would tend to diminish the longterm consensual authority of conservatism during the phase of economic retrenchment as much as, in short-term electoral respects, it stood to establish it. But so far as the extent of 'governmental sprawl' was concerned, Cowling had been comparatively restrained. Like Scruton, he said nothing to challenge the commitment to the apparatus of the welfare state or the principle of nationalisation. Given that events since 1979 have reflected little abatement in that fundamental commitment, Cowling's restraint seems to have been justified. In fact, the substantive departures – about local government and the extent of nationalisation – have to be understood in the context of increasing public expenditure to maintain very extensive 'frontiers' of state control.

A retrospective gloss upon 'The Present Position' tends to endorse the applicability of the principal lesson of Cowling's historical work to the analysis of the Conservative ascendancy which the essay anticipated: that consensual continuities and underlying social and economic processes are little affected by the ideological polarisations reflected in the rhetoric, actions and realignments of functioning politicians.

In part, the lesson established the appropriateness of high political analysis to the explanation of the ascendancy. It is certainly possible to raise questions about the relation of the initial success of 1979 to the high politics of the early seventies – particularly the abandonment of incomes policies by Labour and its failure to regularise industrial relations in circumstances of low unemployment – and to Callaghan's high political miscalculation in 1978 in postponing an election. It is equally possible to raise high political considerations about the victory of 1983, emphasising the Falklands war, the self-destruction of a split and depressed Labour party, and the impact of the Alliance in marginal Labour constituencies as central factors in creating a parliamentary landslide in the context of a slight fall in popular Conservative support. These considerations tend to confirm that Conservative success was more contingent than its ideological apologists have suggested and was, in some respects, the resolution of high political conflicts within the consensus that it is alleged to have destroyed.

Cowling's historical work is instructive, chiefly, because of its argument about the Left in Britain. Cowling has not shared the dogmatic anti-communism of *The Salisbury Review* – understandably so given the anti-ideological conception of foreign policy proposed in *The Impact of Hitler*. 'The Present Position' adopted a conciliatory stance towards Marxism, implying both that it shared the realism of intelligent conservatism in its perception of the political problem and that British socialist was neither Marxist in doctrine nor Leninist in practice. It thus confirmed the persuasive conclusions of *The Impact of Labour* and *The Impact of Hitler*: that the Labour party was not dedicated to the revolutionary overthrow of the constitution and social order; that it was committed to moderate egalitarianism and moderate corporatism within a containing constitutional and capitalist structure which it had no will to destroy; and that Attlee's success after 1940 had been to confer a *conservative* character upon the consensual assumptions which he had helped generate, Wilson's socialism had entrenched, and from which Callaghan's socialism had gained. Cowling's conclusions had – and have – immense negative power. They established a point of contact between Conservative assaults upon Labour hypocrisy and Marxist analysis of a vulnerably bourgeoisified Labour party. After the implication of Wilson's socialism in consumerism, working-class materialism and middle-class ambition, and its associations with the permissive liberalism of educated radicalism, the conclusions sanctioned a characteristically astute Cowlingite intuition: that the Labour party's betrayal of socialism was a factor operating in the longterm political interests of the Conservative party. But it was not obvious from Cowling's conclusions how the Conservative party was to pass from 'undoctrinaire resistance' to the establishment of a consensus in which conservative *values* would be significant since, as he asserted, Labour's consensual politics posed no radical threat to their survival and since, as he implied, Labour's consensual involvements represented a major Conservative electoral asset. Indeed, it is doubtful whether the party has, since 1979, distinguished itself from the consensual assumptions to which Labour capitulated in office. And it is arguable that its greatest success has been about not economic recovery so much as the exploitation of the party political situation to the effect that the Conservative party should possess ascendancy during the next phase of 'undoctrinaire resistance' to Labour.

Given the nature of its success, it is uncertain what causal connections exist between the New Conservatism which *Conservative Essays* celebrated and the Conservative ascendancy. What is certain is that the various futures to which the book looked forward have been thwarted by the very conditions and features of Conservative success in office. As it has unfolded, the future has not been Thomist (Casey), Arnoldian (Casey and Scruton) or Hegelian (Casey and Scruton), but consumerist, industrial and market economic. It has not been aristocratic (Casey, Oakeshott and Mrs Letwin), but meritocratic and technocratic. It has not been 'civil' (Oakeshott), but moderately corporatist within the context of a deflated commitment to state planning and an inflated commitment to free enterprise at the level of rhetoric. It has not been about the reassertion of national identity (Casey and Scruton), so much as about the renewed, ideological commitment to the American alliance first necessitated by the international transformations effected in 1940. Nor, apropos Cowling himself, has the future been Christian, but secular, pluralist and materialist. In this last respect, events since 1979 can hardly be said to have confounded Cowling's expectations. 'The Present Position' concluded that the Conservative party would have to pursue 'undoctrinaire resistance' by mobilising 'that large body of opinion which, while being conservative about social and political questions, is indifferent towards religion' on the assumption that despite 'a Christian monarchy and an established Church, England is not a Christian country'. That pessimistic conclusion served to indicate that, for Cowling at least, the problem about conservatism was no longer party political but a problem about Christianity concerning which Thatcherism was virtually irrelevant.

iii

Religion and Public Doctrine in Modern England marked a return on Cowling's part to the preoccupations of *Mill and Liberalism*. Religion was central because all doctrine had a religious character in virtue of its resting upon assumptions which concealed the kind of practical commitments appropriate to religion. In fact, the secularisation of learning after 1840, 'so far from involving liberation from religion has involved merely liberation from christianity and the establishment in its place of a modern religion whose advocates so much assume its truth that they do not understand that it is a religion to which they are committed'.[18] That misunderstanding easily convicted the advocates of secularisation of disingenuousness or calculated deception, but what was unarguably true, Cowling insisted, was that they were inevitably contributing to public doctrine. Liberal disingenuousness was regrettable because it refused to engage with ultimate ends and values, and because it had resulted in the trivialising 'professionalisation' of learning. Cowling's assaults upon 'professionalisation' were important in two contexts: history and philosophy.

About history Cowling recanted the Oakeshottian conclusions of *The Nature and Limits of Political Science* by affirming that professional history was an 'illusion' and all history an ideological instrument of public doctrine. Accordingly, he insisted upon the ideological orientation of the Christian histories of Walter Ullmann, Owen Chadwick and Edward Norman, and expressed dissent from the rationalist assumption rendered explicit in Plumb's *The Death of the Past* that practical commitment was incidental to the historical enterprise. And he drew attention to the discrepancies within Butterfield's corpus between *The Whig Interpretation of History*, with its distinction between the practical and historical pasts; *The Englishman and his History*, with its vindication of the ideological efforts of the Whig historians; and *Christianity and History*, with its insistence that all historical literature was written from practical assumptions the partiality of which it was the duty of the historian to expose.

What Cowling conveyed about history held universally for all academic reflection. Thus he was clear that the Oakeshottian appeal to 'philosophy' as a value-free form of explanation was as illusory as the procedures of liberal rationalism which Oakeshott had subverted. Ultimately, all philosophy was a contribution to public doctrine, and all academic reflection expressed unargued ideological commitment. To that extent Cowling was as much committed to one principle of Marxism as Casey and Scruton, whose anti-deterministic resistance to Marxist reductivism he generally shared: that doctrine is in harness to the exercise of power in the political world. This principle supported his view of religion as embracing 'not only belief and liturgy but also a structure of public action' and provided a critical standpoint for his review of the contributors to public doctrine.

The application of that principle explained Cowling's conclusion that Edward Norman had failed to establish a relationship between 'inward spirituality' and the public action of the visible church and remained unacceptably reluctant to allow Anglicans to 'identify their own teaching with permanent truth'. It explained his doubts about Butterfield's emphasis upon the 'internal nature' of Christian observance given Butterfield's insistence that Christianity could not regain its former ecclesiastical monopoly upon the exercise of political authority within the modern state and his preference, in *The Englishman and his History*, for the gradualist, liberal polity of Whig England in which the civil privileges of ecclesiastical religion had been eroded. It explained his treatment of Oakeshott, who was interpreted as the propounder of a non-doctrinal and not especially Anglican brand of Latitudinarian Christianity, which required neither belief in dogmatic truth, liturgical precision nor incorporation by the state through a church establishment. And it explained his conviction that Oakeshott and Butterfield represented a recession from the Anglicanism of Charles Smyth, Kenneth Pickthorn and

Edward Welbourne, who had all, Cowling argued, rejected 'natural religion' in favour of the institutional integrity of the Church of England and the supernatural object of Christian faith.

It is doubtful whether Cowling conveyed adequately the importance which Oakeshott attached to the distinction between civil and enterprise association in establishing that the church was a radically distinct form of association from the modern European state. What cannot be doubted is that Cowling's strictures upon Oakeshott's severance of state and religion implied a general objection to Oakeshottian liberalism that was entirely justified: that Oakeshott's civil association was a utopian conception that failed to confront the brutal fact of the irreversible power exercised by the modern state; failed to insist upon the necessity of articulate commitment to ends more substantial than those reflected in the legal culture of respublica; and implicated Oakeshott in liberal illusion, in virtue of his implicit denial that 'moral, legal and social norms' are both 'objective' and sustained by an ineliminable element of 'compulsion and arbitrariness'.[19]

What Cowling was saying was that Oakeshott was a Whig and that his Whiggishness obscured the truth that the 'central problem in the English polity in the three centuries that followed the Reformation had not been liberty but the Church of England ... and the powers and privileges of landowners'.[20] The interrelation of those institutions explained why *Religion and Public Doctrine* was primarily a book about politics; and it explained Cowling's assessment of the two politicians discussed in the book: Churchill and Salisbury.

With Churchill, there was a recapitulation of the revisionist interpretation of his career after 1940 provided in *The Impact of Hitler*. What was new was the emphasis upon Churchill's indifference to the Church of England together with his tendency, in the early writings, to celebrate a 'secular and pagan heroism' that was anti-clerical and anti-theological. The Cowlingite inferences from this were entirely subversive of Conservative complacencies concerning the Churchillian legacy. The place of organised Christianity and the integrity of social morality had not been assured within the Churchillian consensus. Rather, the consensus of 1940, together with the Butskellism which it presaged, was continuous with the secularised 'Tory Democracy' Churchill had been preaching since the 1900s. And the wartime rhetorical polarisations between German 'scientific barbarism' and the 'Christian civilisation' reflected in Britain's democratic traditions and her imperial mission had established assumptions ultimately destructive of the appropriate connections between morality, religion, politics and international relations. In all these respects Cowling intended that Churchillian Whiggery should contrast unfavourably with the doctrinal subtlety of Salisbury.

Salisbury was important for four reasons. First, he provided a searching diagnosis of liberalism, resisting Bright and Gladstone for their espousal of 'eclectic, free-thinking democracy', attacking French and American democratic practice, upholding instead the 'Vienna settlement as the foundation of European peace' and demolishing the illusions which had produced 'Manchester Isolationism', 'Quaker Pacifism' and 'the liberal admiration for nationalism' in Eastern Europe.

Second, Salisbury insisted upon the necessity of ecclesiastical Christianity and its consequent character as a 'political religion'. Not only had he recognised that the Anglicanism and anti-democratic interests of the landed classes were essential to, and the enfranchisement of the working classes subversive of, the civilisation represented by private property and the established church. He had recognised further that unless the Church asserted its established character and preserved its dogmatic integrity as the 'exponent of revealed truth', then Christian morality would be dissipated by a 'latitudinarian revolution' and traditional Christianity destroyed in the aftermath of democratisation.

Third, Salisbury identified the German ideology of Goethe, Hegel, Schelling, Schlegel, Strauss and Feuerbach as infidelity, and associated German romanticism with liberal democracy and nonconformity as the enemy of historic Christianity and the Church of England.

Fourth, Salisbury perceived the central political problem – the challenge to a social structure founded upon 'an inequality of property' posed by working-class enfranchisement and liberal radicalism – in class terms and created a viable Conservative consensus capable of resolving it. He had done this, before 1867, by recognising that the 'satisfied classes', whether Whig, liberal or Conservative, had a sufficiently strong common interest in the preservation of a 'socially secure upper-class parliament' to make the Conservative party an effective instrument of broad-based resistance. He had done it, after 1886, by absorbing moderate Liberals within an expanded Unionist party and establishing that radical socialism was an elitist position unrepresentative of working-class interests.

Cowling stressed that Salisbury's consensus had been politically successful. His earlier treatments of Labour and Hitler confirmed that verdict since they implied that consensual conservatism had survived the democratising forces which Salisbury had first identified and then contained. However, they implied also that its survival had been at the expense of the ecclesiastical and moral authority of Christianity which Salisbury had regarded as its legitimate *end*. Cowling admitted that the 'Unionist party of property, education and respectability' had not achieved a longterm victory for church-state Anglicanism – rather, he stressed that it had accommodated itself to 'the gradual elimination of Anglican teaching from schools . . . , the secularisation of Oxford and Cambridge and the proliferation of secular universities and the creeping advance of the intellectual fashions that Salisbury detested'. The fact of that accommodation raised the question of the appropriateness of Salisbury to 'the present position' – a question to which Cowling delivered the negative answers that Salisbury himself had not expected Anglicanism to survive in a confessional state and had failed during his ascendancy between 1880 and 1902 to act 'the part he had rehearsed between 1857 and 1866'.

The accommodation raised the wider question of the future form in which the anti-liberal position propounded in *Religion and Public Doctrine* could acquire a political correlative. Cowling did not conceal his pessimism concerning the answer. He concluded the book by asserting that the reconstruction of a 'dominating Christian intelligence' was little more than a vain hope and that Christian conservatism was most likely to survive only as Oakeshottian self-enactment – that is, as a religion of sentiment rehearsed in the context of an irretrievably secularised state and society. This conclusion implied a greatly reduced role for conservatism in the context of a modernity of which the Conservative retreats after 1940 were one manifestation and the contraction of European values after Hitler's defeat another. In fact, it implied that the conservative attitude was either an intellectual strategy – a 'conviction that the modern mind is corrupt' – or a moral sentiment – a dissenting 'Jacobitism of the mind' – allied to an acceptance that conservative coherence was not to be recovered. In respect of the isolation the attitude imposed, Cowling was close to Casey, except that he appreciated that recovery was impossible because Whiggism was integral to the British political consciousness, libertarianism an aspect of the conservative mind, and German romanticism and classical paganism an element of the problem and not its solution. In respect of the toughminded realism it conferred, Cowling was at least clear that Oakeshottianism was not to be taken at face value. In that respect he diverged from both Scruton and Oakeshott's authentic disciple: Shirley Robin Letwin.

II

Of all the thinkers discussed in this book, Mrs Letwin is most obviously the propounder of a liberal doctrine. She is an admirer of Hayek and in her tribute to his work – 'The Achievement of Friedrich A. Hayek'[21] – she implied powerful affinities between Oakeshottian conservatism and Hayekian liberalism. As an Hayekian, it is probable that she envisages a far stronger connection between liberal individualism and the economic arrangements of the free market than Oakeshott and regards Oakeshottianism as providing the theoretical basis for an Hayekian resistance to socialist collectivism. And she probably associates Oakeshottianism with the post-war anti-totalitarianism of Hayek, Popper, Talmon and Berlin, assigning, within her much reduced politics, little place for 'positive liberty' in either its Rousseauesque, Burkean or Hegelian forms. In consequence, she shares none of the Hegelian concern of Casey and Scruton to identify state with community, endorse the claims of high culture and celebrate citizenship as the culmination of ethical life. She certainly associates doctrinal resistance to Cartesian rationalism more with the sceptical tradition of Montaigne, Pascal and Hume than the post-Kantian tradition of Hegel and Wittgenstein. It is not, perhaps, that she excludes the realm of 'objective spirit' upon which Casey and Scruton placed such emphasis. It is rather that she writes with an Oakeshottian recognition that 'objective spirit' manifests itself through a multiplicity of institutional and communal forms, all of which should ideally be accommodated within the common legal order that the state imposes. Since she acknowledges the existence of many cultures, there is a strong sense in which the politicisation of high culture prescribed by Casey and Scruton must represent to her as alien an intrusion of elitism into the civil life as that of the Millian liberalism she has explicitly decried.

It is significant that Mrs Letwin should not share the hostility of Casey and Scruton towards the contractarian tradition. Not only are Hobbes – a contractarian – and Hume – a utilitarian – her touchstones rather than Kant, Hegel and Wittgenstein; but her work, especially her major work, *The Pursuit of Certainty*,[22] was an Oakeshottian testament to the liberal and empiricist British political tradition. In fact, the book implied powerful negativities towards the tradition of German romanticism which Casey and Scruton associated with political and cultural conservatism, and which Mrs Letwin associated with the cultural liberalism of Mill she was committed to combatting. Despite a reticence about Hegel, the book was explicit about Burke. It differentiated Burke, whose rationalism aligned him with the natural law tradition of Plato and Aristotle, from Hume, whose allegiance was to the anti-rationalist tradition of Augustine and Hobbes in which political arrangements were generated by 'will, artifice and imagination'.[23] It attacked Burke for making 'government responsible for the highest morality' by an association of the state with the social and cultural life of its members. And it asserted that Burke had prefigured the totalitarian theorists of the state in transforming civil society into 'the temple of God, and the state, along with the church . . . [into] its guardian'.

In attacking Burke in those anti-romanticist terms, *The Pursuit of Certainty* also conveyed negativities towards the aspirations of ethical naturalism and the natural law tradition – negativities from which Mrs Letwin has not moved since and which do most to distinguish her from Casey and Scruton. Indeed, so far from prescribing ethical naturalism, her preference for Hume associated her with the anti-naturalistic distinction between facts and values central to Hume's ethics and the Kantian doctrine of the autonomy of morality from nature which the distinction anticipated. And so far from reviving the natural law, Mrs Letwin upheld the principal implications of the natural right tradition of Hobbes, Spinoza and Kant. Thus she conveyed agreement with Hobbes's *nominalism*, inasmuch as she assumed that all law and morality was grounded upon will and choice rather than nature, and that the state was the product of 'consent'; with his *voluntarism*, inasmuch as she implied that all law was positive, that the obligation it imposed arose with the agreement of its subject, and that the 'justice' which it defined was created by the will of the sovereign legislator; and with his *authoritarianism*, inasmuch as she concluded that the legitimacy of law depended upon the authority of its source, rather than its rationality or connection with the human good. In all these respects, she was implicated in the ethical assumptions of Kantian liberalism, particularly its assertion of the priority of the right to the good, its dissociation of rights from values and its repudiation of the teleological justification of the state characteristic of the natural law doctrine of Aristotle and Aquinas.

In rejecting natural law, Mrs Letwin tended to undermine the objectivity of the moral law. This was so even when, as in 'Morality and Law',[24] she denied any absolute separation of state and communal morality and defended the legal enforcement of substantive moral values. The rejection of natural law meant that communal morality possessed only the kind of anthropocentric integrity conferred upon it, most notably, by Hegelian historicism. It left it unclear in what sense the legal arrangements of Oakeshott's civil association were *morally* defensible in fundamental respects that the more extensive arrangements of state socialism were not. And it left it unclear in what senses the power exercised through those arrangements was justifiable on any save utilitarian grounds. Given her association of Oakeshottianism with Hume, Mrs Letwin's implication in utilitarianism was inevitable. But the fact remains that Humean utilitarianism consorted ill with the procedural natural justice integral to the Oakeshottian brand of liberal individualism. And Mrs Letwin's preference for it suggested strongly that the grounds of her Oakeshottian dissent from utilitarianism, and the redistributive and corporatist socialism to which, she alleged, it had led, were grounds of aesthetic sentiment as much as principle.

In her recognition that conservatism was not to be identified with romanticism, Mrs Letwin was close to Cowling. Like *Religion and Public Doctrine*, *The Pursuit of Certainty* attacked secular, liberal rationalism on a broad front. And in its scepticism about the claims of modern democracy the book confirmed the lesson of Cowling's historical work: that the democratisation of the constitution had resulted less in its increasing responsiveness to the popular will than in its subordination to the will of an elitist, middle-class intelligentsia.

Nevertheless, Mrs Letwin did not share Cowling's positive conclusions about the authoritarian social structure which he derived from Salisbury; and she lacked his sense of the provisional status of individual freedom in relation to the social order upheld by the legal establishment of the state. Above all, she did not share his positive conclusions about religion. *The Pursuit of Certainty* certainly expressed intimations of a Christian dimension in its determination to undermine the assumption of secular liberalism that the 'City of Man' was the 'Heavenly City itself'. However, the book provided neither endorsement of ecclesiastical religion nor emphasis upon liturgy, dogma and law, resisted the association of organised religion with the establishment of state, and was, in consequence, vulnerable to the considerations which Cowling advanced against Oakeshott.

The vulnerability was increased by the later Oakeshottian defence of religion as the culmination of ordinary, human morality in *The Gentleman in Trollope*.[25] Ultimately, religious faith embodied an intensive moral attitude which provided 'a warning against presumption, a ground for resignation, an injunction to keep our expectations modest'.[26] On the one hand, the attitude had to be evaluated as much in aesthetic as in doctrinal, ecclesiastical or ethical terms. On the other, it had to be understood as a form of practical knowledge yielding no theoretical knowledge of God or the universe, in a Kantian sense. Not only was there no 'certain knowledge of God's will', but the 'relation between man and God [was] a mystery mitigated solely by the will to believe'.[27] Moreover, the book denied the Augustinian gulf between God and human nature bridgeable only by the mediation of God's Grace. On the contrary, human sinfulness arose not from the 'inborn evil' of Original Sin but from the 'conditions attached to a human condition'; and human beings were excluded from perfection not by the inherent corruption of their nature, but by 'their mortal rationality, their capacity to interpret and respond from different standpoints without being able to see or do everything at once'.[28] In fact, there was nothing about Christian doctrine to undermine the autonomy of reason upon which Kant had insisted – not only did scriptural authority not provide 'access to non-human guarantees of human conclusions', but it failed to 'destroy the gap between the revealed word of God and human interpretations of it'.[29]

It is open to question whether Mrs Letwin's defence of religion undermined the metaphysical claims of traditional Christian dogma and exposed religion to the secularising tendencies of romantic culture which, in its pantheistic aspect, she was disposed to reject. What is unquestionable is that the defence had no conservative implications where Christianity itself was concerned. It did not compromise her penchant for the pagan ethics of Hume. She made Nietzschean points about the inadequacy of pharisaical Christianity, insisting upon the circumstantial appropriateness of 'breaking the rules made by God-fearing and judicious men' in the interests of a 'complicated moral understanding' of which mere rules were the 'abridgement'.[30] And she dissociated the Christianity of the gentleman from the 'stern devotion to duty' and 'abhorrence of anything pleasant' characteristic of the puritan conscience. Nor did the defence of religion compromise the secular foundations of her politics. Far from asserting the desirability of a confessional state, she was explicitly antagonistic towards the puritan, evangelical obsession with 'securing uniformity in outward action'; and she insisted that amongst the plurality of denominations, doctrines and public ceremonies, there was no necessity 'either to eliminate the variety or to insist upon the universal superiority of any set of observances'.[31] She did not deny that the gentleman might conform to the ecclesiastical arrangements of a public religion in the Hobbesian sense of 'agreeing to regard a communal interpretation of God's will as authoritative'. But the identity of a church was sustained by the continuous consent of its members to its 'authority' and not by reason of its embodiment of 'indisputable knowledge of God's will' – and the authority of a church was grounded not upon supernatural sanction, but upon the traditional continuities of the human community itself. The conclusion was that not only was Christianity not to be identified exclusively with any determinate form it assumed in history, but that 'nothing [followed] about the character of a man's faith from the church that he [attended]'.[32] The implications of that conclusion for Christianity were latitudinarian, and for church-state relations, anti-establishmentarian and liberal. In consequence, they diverged from the conclusions upon which Cowling insisted: that a religion must be concerned with truth as well as convenience, that its credal and institutional determinacy remains a fully political matter and that it is necessarily in competition with other faiths and denominations to exercise power within the visible world.

i

The early essay 'Rationalism, Principles and Politics'[33] was a summary review of the contemporary critiques of rationalism provided by Hayek, Popper and Oakeshott and a qualified defence of 'principle' in politics. It was not an Oakeshottian essay. Oakeshott was, indeed, important only as the representative of a critical fashion. The essay criticised the Oakeshott of 'Rationalism in Politics' for having implied both 'the extreme position that prudential principles are the only valid ones' and that the priority of 'practical' to 'technical' knowledge entailed the exclusion of all principles from political activity. Doctrinal inspiration for the review was provided not by Oakeshott but by Burke, whose writings confirmed the conclusion which contemporary anti-rationalists like Oakeshott had ignored through their overreaction to rationalism: that avoidance of the errors of rationalism did not make it necessary to 'renounce all principles or condemn all reason in politics'.[34]

'Rationalism, Principles and Politics' was an exploratory essay. It remains noteworthy because it registered an aversion to the rationalist temper that was to inform the conservative doctrine Mrs Letwin was to develop subsequently, and because it recorded a preference for Burkean conservatism which was to disappear as that doctrine reached its maturity under the influence of Oakeshott in the sixties and seventies. Of greater significance was an essay which appeared two years later in 1954.

'Representation without Democracy'[35] was an analysis of the elitist and anti-democratic implications of the Webbs's *Constitution for a Socialist Commonwealth* which conveyed much of the spirit of Oakeshott's critique of the scientific idiom in politics of the forties and fifties. Mrs Letwin denied that the Webbs adhered to the ideals of popular democracy; stressed that they had been jealous of aristocratic privilege and that there was a parallel between their socialist constitution and the ancient constitution defended by Burke; and demonstrated that the Webbs had proposed a 'representative, benevolent but despotic government' which accommodated democracy not as 'a model of determining public policy' but as 'a technique for securing general consent to a predetermined public policy'.[36] The polemical exposure of socialist disingenuousness was less important than the explanation of its cause: the Webbs's recognition that mass democratisation militated against the efficiency of any government required, as in the industrial age, to assume responsibility for economic and social planning. In saying that, Mrs Letwin was dissenting from the complacent assumption of a necessary harmony between socialist corporatism and popular democracy. She was also looking forward to the book to which 'Representation without Democracy' was the overture.

The Pursuit of Certainty was an exercise in intellectual history comparable in its scope with Oakeshott's essay 'The Character of a Modern European State'. The book amplified the 1954 analysis of the Webbs's *Constitution*: it provided a class analysis of the Webbs's bureaucratic social scientism which treated it as elitist ideology rather than science, emphasised the coercive structure of governmental power which it presupposed and drew attention to the tendency of its managerial elite to acquire a particularist corporate interest distinguishable from that of the citizenry at large. And the book extended the analysis of the Webbs by tracing an historical development from Hume through Bentham and Mill to their state socialism in highly revisionist terms. Thus it challenged the categorisations of progressives as collectivists or socialists and reactionaries as 'individualists or defenders of capitalism or . . . laissez-faire' which had become the staple of modern democratic political vocabulary. And it insisted that the erosion of the old liberalism represented by Hume had resulted from the politicisation of the 'problem of poverty'. Together with the increased administrative power of government it necessitated and the currency of egalitarian ideology, the politicisation had established the redistribution of wealth as a central policy of state to which the individual rights formerly guaranteed under the old liberalism had been sacrificed.

In those respects Mrs Letwin was endorsing the substance of Oakeshott's critique of democratic politics: that the preoccupation with policy within democratic politics had progressively undermined the liberties enjoyed under the rule of law; and that the procedural considerations of legal justice traditionally guaranteeing those liberties had been superseded by a political concern with principles of justice, especially of distributive justice, extrinsic to the legal process itself. Since she treated Bentham's attack upon the Common Law as the decisive phase in the process it was obvious that the real enemy was utilitarianism, as it had been for Oakeshott. If it was consequently puzzling that Hume was her point of reference, that puzzlement should not obscure the fact that the book argued for a differentiation of Hume's libertarian politics from the liberal rationalism of Mill and Beatrice Webb, whose achievement represented less a development of Hume's libertarianism than a recession from it.

Mrs Letwin's critique of Bentham reiterated Oakeshott's early conclusion that Bentham's work represented the intrusion of the alien 'philosophe' mentality into the British political tradition. She did not deny that Bentham's 'modest sort of utopianism' upheld the cause of liberal individualism in matters affecting liberty of taste, conscience and opinion and the relation of state to society. Indeed, to the extent that the *Introduction to the Principles of Morals and Legislation* was founded upon the *ethical* principle of self-determination rather than the prudential principle of utility, his politics did not differ substantially from Hume's. What distinguished Bentham from Hume, she claimed, was the rationalism of his intellectual temper. Although Bentham adopted the arguments of Hume's rejection of natural law and the original contract throughout the *Fragment on Government*, he did not share Hume's sense of the contingency of politics. In fact, Mrs Letwin implied, Hume's conception of politics corresponded more closely to the English law defended in Blackstone's *Commentaries*, with its rival jurisdictions of Equity and Common Law and dependence upon historical precedent rather than statute law, than it corresponded to the mono-principled utilitarian politics with which Bentham sought to replace it.

The Pursuit of Certainty conveyed the recognition that the consequences of Bentham's rationalism had been pernicious. Firstly, it had led to the increasing predominance of the scientific method in politics, with its prescription of an 'impersonal, foolproof system' to resolve the practical problems of politics and to rationalise the civil law by deriving a 'perfect system of legislation' from the single 'grand principle of utility'. Secondly, Bentham's rationalism had imposed a separation of law from morality potentially destructive of justice itself. The pursuit of efficiency in the administration of justice that Bentham's reforming utilitarianism demanded had tended to undermine the liberties which the proceduralism of the Common Law had guaranteed. Mrs Letwin stressed that Bentham's proposals for reform – particularly, the removal of restrictions on the rules of evidence and subordination of judicial representation and judicial independence to the interests of the executive branch – represented massive increases in the power of the state *vis-à-vis* the private citizen. She insisted, against Bentham himself, that statute law was no different from Common Law in requiring the exercise of a judicial discretion by lawyers and judges in its application to particular cases. And she implied agreement with Blackstone's defence of the Common Law, implying that the inconveniences inherent in its procedures of justice provided the firmest guarantee of individual liberty. Her subsequent defence of the procedural natural law against utilitarian encroachments derived much of its inspiration from the historical thesis that the Common Law which embodied it had been under attack since Bentham's association of statute law with the policy of state.

With Mill, Mrs Letwin reiterated the conclusions of Cowling's *Mill and Liberalism*. So far from harnessing Bentham's ethically neutral utilitarianism to the defence of liberal individualism, Mill's *Utilitarianism* prescribed a preferred form of human development. And so far from questioning the desirability of an ethically commanding doctrine such as traditional Christianity had once provided, Mill admired both the cohesiveness of medieval Christendom and the 'German religion' of Kant, Fichte, Goethe and Schiller. What Mill questioned, Mrs Letwin insisted, was that traditional Christianity, as distinct from the undogmatic religion of culture expressed in the ethical and aesthetic doctrines of Coleridge, Sterling and Maurice, could provide a commanding ethical doctrine compatible with the 'spirit of the age'.

Like Cowling, Mrs Letwin concluded that Mill's liberalism was compromised in an internal sense, that *On Liberty* conveyed only a partial affirmation of libertarianism and that *Representative Government* expressed only a conditional commitment to democratic principles. With each book Mill's progressive liberalism was everywhere subordinate to his ethical commitment to the preferred form of human development. Thus, *On Liberty* was designed both to protect the independence of the exceptional man from the tyranny of the consensus and to establish that his freedom promoted the moral and intellectual progress of society. And it prescribed, as its ethical ideal, the life of the 'ideal individual' of complete rational freedom 'self-consciously [choosing] for himself how he will live' and '[surveying] all the alternatives before him and [choosing] with a clear perception of the reasons for his choice'.[37] Just as *Utilitarianism* insisted upon the normative implications of the distinction between the 'higher and lower pleasures', so *On Liberty* insisted upon the supremacy of the 'higher over the lower morality'. Both books, Mrs Letwin claimed, had the *authoritarian* consequence of providing the enlightened liberal with a moral justification 'for withholding personal liberty from any claimant unable to demonstrate that he was pursuing the "right" ideal and was possessed of sufficient will power to pursue it steadily and energetically'.[38] Moreover, Mill's commitment to democracy did not escape that authoritarian consequence since, according to Mrs Letwin, *Representative Government* presupposed the context of Mill's ethical aspiration 'to see men climbing together, their ranks ever tightening as they moved upward to the topmost peak, where each and everyone . . . could bask in perfect unity, knowledge and goodness'.[39] That context established that the book endorsed democracy not because democracy safeguarded the liberty of the citizen or promoted his active participation in government, but because democratisation was understood to create greater social cohesion and to confer the additional authority of rational consensus upon liberal government.

The negative critiques of Bentham and Mill were developed in the light of an affirmation of the Oakeshottian spirit of Hume's politics. Thus the first part of the book – 'David Hume: Pagan Virtues and Profane Politics' – recovered his politics in terms close to the tenets of Oakeshott's conservatism by emphasising Hume's reduced and legalistic conception of the office of government. Politics was concerned with neither 'absolute truth' nor 'fixed goals' and all political action was deprived of 'demonstrable certainty'. The concern of politics was simply 'to mediate collisions of interest . . . and generally to protect members of society while they [engaged] in their private activities', and its objective was simply to preserve 'liberty and peace' through 'the activity of enforcing stable rules of conduct'. Since the liberty of the subject depended upon his protection from 'illegal violence', the most important feature of the office of government was the integrity of its legal status under the rule of law rather than the extent or effectiveness of its power.

As for the legitimacy of government and its constitutional form, Mrs Letwin stressed Hume's indifference to the claims which Mill and Bentham were to advance on behalf of democracy and his conclusion that no constitutional form had an unconditional or timeless validity. The truth was that Hume had recognised neither an unconditional 'right of resistance' of the Lockean variety, nor the Toryism which appealed to ancient precedent as the legitimising principle of current political arrangements. On the contrary, Hume's message was that government was not founded upon any unconditional principles of legitimacy, but upon a highly complex 'combination of force, habit and rational assent', and that there was no absolutely binding rule about how government secured that combination. In all this, Hume was conveying a central maxim of Oakeshottian conservatism: that with regard to the legitimacy of government, all that could be said with certainty was that there were no indisputable guidelines of unambiguous application to the diverse circumstances of time and place.

The final impression which *The Pursuit of Certainty* created was that conservatism had no necessary connection with either natural law, prescription, divine right, Christianity or market economics. In the Humean form which Mrs Letwin defended, conservatism was ultimately a matter of a particular *style* of political activity, inspired by a Humean scepticism about the limits of human reason and complemented by Hume's antipuritanical ideal of the virtuous life.

In connection with the political style, Mrs Letwin emphasised the association of political knowledge with the mastery of circumstantial detail which Hume had adopted as a working principle throughout his *History of Great Britain*. On her reading of it, Hume's *History* was a fulfilment of Oakeshott's requirements concerning historical literature. Hume avoided the grand, retroactive moral judgements of liberal historiography, recognising instead the role of accidental contingencies in thwarting the efforts of all participant politicians to exercise rational control over events. And so far from being the inevitable outcome of the conflict between progress and tyranny, the Civil War for Hume had been simply an 'occasion when certain ambiguities and contradictions in the constitution could no longer be tolerated, and an unfortunate congruence of events and passions had produced a catastrophe instead of the peaceful adjustment that might have been'.[40] The implication of Mrs Letwin's reading of Hume was clear: the prescription of a particular style of historical understanding was inseparable from the prescription of a particular style of political activity. It was a style in which the 'integrity' of the individual statesman ranked as the supreme political virtue. She emphasised Hume's defence of the Stuart kings for their respect for established legal precedent, and his condemnation of the Commonwealth men for their persistent violation of established legal procedure. And in doing so she implied that the relationship between integrity and law represented the kind of moral commitment which Oakeshott associated with the Hobbesian virtue of 'justice': '[the] basic disposition to remain true to standards and pledges regardless of immediate advantage, and an antipathy to deceit'.[41]

About Hume's scepticism, Mrs Letwin brought out the centrality of the arguments of the first book of *The Treatise of Human Nature* to Hume's conservative conclusions. By reducing causal necessity to a belief arising from habit and custom, Hume had implied that the conclusions of reason – even in matters of scientific induction – were saved from arbitrariness only by the stability of communal belief and social convention. And about the virtuous life, she stressed that Hume's ethics were derived from natural inclination and presupposed only an approval of the virtues in terms of their 'usefulness' to mankind; and so far from postulating any non-secular sanction, they 'required no struggle with sin, no repression, no divine intervention, nothing but what would come naturally to human beings'.[42] Moreover, by affirming the core of the sentimentalist ethics of motive of Shaftesbury and Hutcheson, Hume had avoided entirely the puritan association of virtue with 'conscience' and the Calvinist insistence upon natural depravity. What Hume's emphasis upon motive excluded was rationalist ethics, as surely as his scepticism excluded rationalist epistemology. Whether he was attacking the Cambridge Platonists or rationalists like Wollaston and Clarke, the implications of Hume's ethics were clear: there was no moral code to be deduced from absolutely certain and demonstrable principles; and there were no universal rules of morality which transcended the diversity of moral allegiances inspired by education, personality, law and custom.

ii

The Pursuit of Certainty represented an attempt to recover a tradition of liberal politics distinguishable from the tradition of liberal utilitarianism which tended to associate liberalism with the implementation of favoured social policies rather than with the maintenance of stable and politically neutral procedures. As such it must be read as providing a substantial historical foundation for the explicitly Oakeshottian positions which Mrs Letwin adopted in the seventies concerning rationalism, individualism, law and ethics.

'Nature, History and Morality'[43] was a defence of traditionalism. It was not, however, a Burkean defence. On the contrary, it expressed a sceptical doctrine in which philosophy was left subverting the more cosmic, transcendental pretensions of the great traditions, Mrs Letwin left celebrating their diversity and traditional continuities left exerting a very commonplace, everyday kind of authority.

The point of the essay was to effect an Oakeshottian compromise between the extremes of classical naturalism and the formalism of Kantian freedom reflected in the work of existentialists like Sartre. In this respect the essay was a defence of *objectivity* in knowledge and morality which both paralleled the defence Oakeshott conducted in *On Human Conduct* and *Rationalism in Politics* and assumed the principal tenets of his anti-rationalist doctrine: that objective standards exist nowhere save in the human conventions constituting a civilisation and are, in consequence, irreducibly historical in character. It was the absence of any objective, naturalistic foundation for the multiplicity of human conventions which explained Mrs Letwin's rejection of the model of classical naturalism developed by Plato and Aristotle. The model had established both that the human world reflected the 'eternal design' of nature and that the natural order intimated a uniform standard of rational conduct divergence from which was a mark of irrationality. Those claims were implicit in Plato's transcendentalism, in which all truth was 'knowledge of [a] rational cosmic order' possessing 'one logical pattern' and all 'inconsistency in our knowledge [was] necessarily an imperfectly grasped truth'. And they were implicit in the Aristotelian entelechy, in which man possessed an 'essence' derived from his participation in 'the ordering principle of the universe' which was entirely distinguishable from the individuating 'properties or appearances' marking him out as an inhabitant of 'the contingent world'. With both cases the conclusion was identical: classical naturalism was a rationalistic philosophy which ignored the immanence of reason in history and the diversity of the forms through which that immanence was manifested.

Although it criticised the abstraction of Sartrean freedom, the essay shared Sartre's rejection of all explanatory theories which made the assumption of determinism. It implied that, like classical naturalism, deterministic theories imposed a uniform pattern upon the diversity of human conduct which served only to subvert historical comprehension. Thus, the essay rejected the 'evolutionary' historicism of Comte and Marx in which events in the human world were understood as 'phases of a mechanical process which determines rather than reflects human behaviour'. And it rejected the structuralism of Levi-Strauss for its assumption that the 'historical world is a chaos asking to be understood in terms of a fixed unconscious reality'. These rejections signalled a recognition on Mrs Letwin's part not only that human autonomy had to be safeguarded from scientific reductivism but that crudely causal theories embodied the rationalist disposition to curtail the terms upon which conduct should be understood.

The rejections did not, however, lead Mrs Letwin to embrace the Sartrean alternative without qualification. However admirable its emphasis upon Kantian autonomy, Sartre's radical subjectivism was an illusion. Although he preserved the idea of moral choice, Sartre nonetheless neglected the objective context provided by the social conventions of the historical world through which choice was exercised. So far from implicating men in Sartrean 'bad faith' participation in the public conventions of moral practices was a precondition of moral choice itself. Moreover, however compelling in the deep sense conveyed by Sartre's notion of *engagement* moral choices were neither arbitrary nor irrational; they were entirely rational because made 'within the context of a moral practice . . . [providing] objective grounds for understanding and choosing alternatives'.[44]

In characterising the objectivity provided by the moral practices, Mrs Letwin confirmed what Oakeshott had concluded about traditional continuities. Moral practices were 'historical' yet 'contingent' in the sense of having neither 'cosmic sanction' nor 'rational necessity'. They were authoritative because they provided the stable background without which change was unintelligible, in much the way that language itself exerted an inevitable authority by providing the irreducible context for all significant utterance: 'men cannot alter or question their language without speaking it'. Nevertheless, the fact that moral practices had to be appropriated by learning meant that their authority was not external to conduct in any way that compromised rational autonomy.

That 'Nature, History and Morality' conveyed an anti-rationalist position was everywhere apparent. It was apparent particularly in its reduction of the pretensions of scientific understanding. The mere fact that their principles could be formulated explicitly did not provide scientific or mathematical inquiry with any monopoly upon rationality; nor, indeed, were they 'superior forms of knowledge'. Not only did they depend upon the exercise of a rational judgement which could not be guaranteed by the principles themselves, but each was a tradition of inquiry whose stability depended upon an authoritative system of education in a manner no different from the arts: 'Science and poetry, logic and painting, are all stable manners of making coherent connections and they are familiar and comprehensible to those who have been educated in their patterns'.[45] The qualifications of science reflected the anti-Cartesian thrust of the essay. Ultimately there was no limit to the 'number or variety' of the diverse 'languages' and 'objectivities'. That diversity was irreducible since there was 'no single structure to knowledge and no unity of truth'. And the only real truth, Mrs Letwin concluded, was that 'no man can be master of all knowledge and no method can be a universal key to truth' in the sense intended by Descartes.

The essay was anti-Cartesian in the further respect that it insisted upon the priority of the practical to the theoretical and of belief to knowledge. Human self-knowledge was inseparable from the practical commitment to civilisation itself, and that commitment rested upon a bedrock of assumptions and presuppositions which had to be 'taken on faith'. This was true of the language of science in which 'we cannot ultimately justify our views about the uselessness of rolling stones for getting rain other than by declaring a commitment to a particular manner of explaining such phenomena'.[46] And it was true of religion which, in yielding no theoretical knowledge of a supernatural order, was unable 'to provide . . . a rational justification for our commitments'. The conclusion was that science and religion enjoyed a parity in rationality such that neither could impugn the rationality of the other. And the lesson was that there was no unconditional, Cartesian point of departure from which all social, historical and practical assumptions could be expunged and from which men could 'survey everything from a non-human standpoint beyond history'.[47] The only available standpoint was philosophy, understood in the Oakeshottian sense that it left practical commitments untouched once it had completed its radically subversive work of demonstrating that men must 'stand firmly on certainties . . . they know to be fragile'. But even in that regard philosophy possessed no reforming function in the Cartesian sense; its business was not 'to displace historical objectivities, but to explain their presuppositions and character'.

'Nature, History and Morality' was a highly suggestive essay. Even if it had no place for his historical teleology and diminished rather than elevated the function of philosophy in relation to practice, the essay suggested the Hegel of *Sittlichkeit* and 'objective spirit' in its emphasis upon the intimate connection between human self-knowledge and participation in the public traditions of human society. If there was little about Kant, Sartre's existentialism did full duty for Kantian formalism as an object of quasi-Hegelian attack upon the vacuity of 'subjective freedom'. The essay suggested the later Wittgenstein in its emphasis upon the priority of a public, linguistic context to human thought and action. And it suggested Hume in its emphasis upon the practical commitment in knowledge and its rejection of any presocial contractarianism in the explanation of communal practice. That the historicism which the essay defended was compatible with the core of Hume's philosophy was clear from a further essay: 'Hume: Inventor of a New Task for Philosophy'.[48] And that its Hegelian conclusions about communal life could be harmonised with Hobbesian conclusions about government and the state was clear from a later essay: 'On Conservative Individualism'.[49]

'On Conservative Individualism' should be read as a restatement of the version of Hobbesian liberalism conveyed in Oakeshott's 'civil association'. As such it denied both the absolutist nature of civil government and that government was necessitated by the universal incidence of 'restless, selfish, aggressive creatures' who needed taming by authoritative rulers. On the contrary, its necessity arose from a conception of human reason derived from Hobbes's association of rational deliberation with the will and Hume's subordination of reason to passion. What this conception established was that inasmuch as reason was essentially 'deliberative', it could lay claim to no 'demonstrative' certainty. And what it implied was that since reason could not yield 'a common recognition of one, universal truth', political association was consequently instituted not upon principles discoverable by natural reason but upon the purely artificial principle of 'authority'. From these premises the essay construed government in the exclusively legalistic terms of 'steady rules defining offices, duties and procedures'. Indeed, the *authority* of the rules and arrangements comprising the constitution of state was all that held political association together. This meant, on the one hand, that the state was capable of tolerating a diversity of voluntary associations and permitting its members to pursue moral and cultural concerns without legal compulsion. It meant, on the other, that the legal order of the state was autonomous from the independently generated social structure of associations and moral practices comprising the community which the state protected.

The fundamental question which the essay neglected was the *justification* of the much reduced state which it described. It implied that the traditional natural law provided no justification; and it was explicit both that the principle of utility provided no justification either and that so far from conferring legitimacy upon the state, constitutional democracy was antagonistic towards the *moral* aspirations of civil association. These negativities tended, however, to confirm the impression that Mrs Letwin wrote as though the state *required* no external justification. They certainly tended to exclude all consideration of the substantive values in the name of which government exercised its authority, the social, economic and moral ends which the legal order served *instrumentally*, and the conditions under which the consent of its subjects would be given or withdrawn. At any rate, they excluded all discussion of these questions in any terms other than those that imported utilitarian considerations divergent from the moral character attributed to civil association or substantive considerations inconsistent with both the legal formalism upon which its moral character rested and the voluntarist ethical and metaphysical principles from which it was derived. Those exclusions implied that what justified the state and secured the continuing consent of its members to its authority was its capacity to maintain something like the Hobbesian condition of 'peace' – a skeletal concept about which nothing of *moral* significance could be said. That Mrs Letwin did not believe that this implication followed was suggested by the argument of an earlier and important essay which asserted intimate connections between morality and the form of legal order imposed by civil association.

'Morality and Law' revived the aspirations of natural law doctrine in two respects. Firstly, it asserted that to the extent that civil association presupposed a commitment to an exclusive 'conception of what constitutes a civilised life', the connection between morality and civil law was intrinsic. This did not mean that there was an external criterion for judging the morality of law in some sense 'outside of, or distinct from, the law'. On the contrary, the connection which Mrs Letwin was exploring assumed the chief principle of Hobbesian voluntarism: that 'justice' was a quality defined by law, not one it possessed contingently in virtue of the law's rationality or correspondence with a substantive natural law. The assertion did mean, however, that the connection was inherent in the very idea of the rule of law itself since 'the concept of law [was] a moral concept'. Secondly, the essay defended the subordination of communal morality to the public concern of law and the permissibility of enforcing the prevailing moral consensus with legal sanctions. It acknowledged the tension between the aspiration to enforce the uniformity of communal morality and the commitment to the morality peculiar to civil association. Nevertheless, its conclusion was that the rules of any particular civil association *unavoidably* reflected 'the standards of civility that characterise it' and that it was a liberal illusion to pretend otherwise.

The essay attacked liberal illusion on two fronts. In insisting upon the implicit morality of law it rejected the absolute separation of law from morality imposed by the tradition of legal positivism of Austin and Hart. Secondly, it challenged the disingenuousness of the liberal tradition in its assumption of the ethical *neutrality* of law. In fact, instead of achieving neutrality the liberal tradition made very partial, unargued ethical assumptions. This was true of Hume and Bentham, who retained the values of the moral consensus the metaphysical foundations of which they had rejected. And it was true of Mill, whose support for legal restraints upon prostitution implied a commitment to 'a particular conception of what constitutes a civilised life' which he assumed that 'every civilised man must share'.

In attacking liberal illusion the essay conveyed substantial agreement with Casey, Scruton and Cowling. Like Casey and Scruton, Mrs Letwin insisted that the arrangements of law and state, which liberal utilitarianism treated as *means* to some external purpose, embodied *ends* and *values*. And like Cowling, she insisted that liberalism was an ideology whose very exclusive assumptions had to be contested. However, the attack did not implicate Mrs Letwin in their anti-liberal conclusions. Not only was the moral consensus not to be upheld in a confessional form, but, she concluded, 'opposition to theocratic regulation' was essential to the 'moral commitment' presupposed in the commitment to civil association itself. Nor was the consensus to be justified by the sanctions of the substantive natural law prescribed by Aristotle and Aquinas. On the one hand, the post-medieval circumstances of civil association precluded the modern reconstitution of the 'small, homogeneous community' of the Aristotelian *polis*. On the other, a decisive development had taken place fundamentally subversive of the ambition of ethical naturalism to derive law from a conception of the good understood as 'a truth accessible to all human beings who had learned to exercise their rational faculty'. That development had been the distinction between the 'authority and desirability' of law prescribed by Hobbes after the collapse of the metaphysical assumptions about God and nature upon which the traditional natural law depended. What the distinction had sanctioned was the divorce of the obligations imposed by the legal order of the state from the moral consensus of the community embodied in the social order. Not only did Hobbes's distinction define the predicament of the modern state in the sense that it had inspired the illusions of liberalism: the ethically neutral legal order and the severance of law from all attachment to a partial moral consensus. More importantly, Mrs Letwin insisted, all subsequent attempts to collapse Hobbes's distinction and reconstitute the moral consensus previously associated with the natural law had been shattering failures: whereas Bentham's 'calculus of pleasure' restored a consensus without morality by denying the necessity of judging the relative *value* of different human desires, Rousseau's General Will made consensus conditional upon the eradication of the individual particularity of human beings.

'Morality and Law' should be read as a revival of natural law within the context of the post-Hobbesian polity and as a defence of the implicit moral character of the canons of procedural justice which Oakeshott associated with western constitutionalism. The essay avoided reducing those canons to the extreme legal formalism to which 'On Conservative Individualism' capitulated. It claimed instead that law necessarily enforces exclusive forms of communal morality and that it is, in consequence, legitimately *instrumental* to the preservation of the prevailing moral consensus. Nevertheless, the essay left little doubt that the form of communal morality being endorsed was the ethical and cultural consensus of liberalism itself; and the moral *values* being prescribed were those of liberal individualism. In fact, the ethical assumptions of the essay were continuous with both the tenets of Kantian liberalism and the tenets of the natural right tradition of Hobbes and Spinoza: it excluded appeals to a naturalistic ethics and grounded all moral values upon either the will and consent of the individual agent or the collective will of the communal consensus.

Given its repudiation of ethical naturalism and its implication in ethical liberalism, the essay still left unanswered two questions: the ultimate justification of a civil association governed by the canons of legal morality given its *compulsory* character; and the legitimacy of the power and authority it necessarily claims in enforcing the prevailing moral consensus. Particularly, it left it unclear how those questions were to be settled save by an invocation of the authority of entrenched consensual convention, tending to collapse all distinctions between power and authority; or by the incorporation of utilitarian justifications tending to compromise the *moral* weight placed upon the non-instrumental law of civil association.

Mrs Letwin was entirely right to affirm the instrumentality of law in its relation to the moral consensus. Yet it was not clear to what extent she believed that its instrumentality in that respect undermined the distinction between law and the social and economic order preserved by the legal formalism of civil association. In her review of Dworkin's *Taking Rights Seriously* – 'Taking the Law Unseriously'[50] – she was highly critical of an egalitarian jurisprudence which hinged upon the undeniable fact of the law's instrumentality *vis-à-vis* the social order.

The review demonstrated the ideological status of Dworkin's liberalism and the contradictions inherent in his invocation of legal naturalism to defend the rights favoured by left-liberals within western constitutional democracies. Although Dworkin sought to revive the idiom of natural law of Aristotle and Aquinas, his rejection of their metaphysical beliefs in an 'eternal nature' not only deprived rights of their naturalistic grounding – the rejection meant that Dworkin prescribed as 'eternal, indisputable principles of justice' and as fully 'independent of the structure or content of conventional systems' a schedule of rights which were essentially a contingent 'human invention' and about which disagreement was inevitable.

The review also demonstrated the illiberal implications of Dworkin's jurisprudence by invoking the tenets of Oakeshott's legal formalism. Particularly, it argued that Dworkin collapsed the Oakeshottian distinctions between moral principle and positive law and between 'civility' and 'politics'; that by conferring legitimacy upon arbitrary acts of civil disobedience, Dworkin undermined the rule of law itself; that Dworkin misrepresented judicial discretion as an arbitrary declaration of political opinion and obscured the senses in which it presupposed judicial adherence to the procedural law; and that Dworkin misunderstood the nature of 'authorisation' by licensing judges to act as 'unauthorised legislators' in their selection of 'moral principles' to resolve the 'hard cases' covered by no positive law. It argued, finally, that in maintaining that moral principles were both 'objective' and 'indisputable', in the sense that there was only 'one right answer' concerning which 'moral principles' applied in 'hard cases', Dworkin ignored the conflicting moral standards in any given community, any one of which had a claim to be considered as a 'principle' in his sense. In arguing thus, the implications of Dworkin's rejection of 'moral scepticism' for Mrs Letwin were clear: that it was the absence of a universal consensus about moral standards which necessitated a legal order in the first instance; and the principal advantage of the rule of law that it provided uniform conditions of peace for 'people with divergent ideas'.

Mrs Letwin was right to establish the remoteness of Dworkin's liberalism from the tradition of liberal constitutionalism which Oakeshott celebrated, and that Dworkin's liberal credentials were not unquestionable merely because he favoured liberal causes like reverse discrimination and opposed antiliberal legislation against homosexuals and for capital punishment. She was right also to insinuate that Dworkin's liberalism was ultimately the ideology of elitist, bourgeois radicalism – a verdict upon which the Oakeshottian conservative and Marxist would agree.

The problem remained, however, that Mrs Letwin wrote in indifference to two truths upon which Dworkin insisted and with which Scruton and Cowling were in full agreement: that the equality in formal rights enjoyed under the constitution and positive law is meaningless when divorced from the substantial inequalities in the social and economic order which the rule of law legitimises; and that, so far from there being an unconditional 'right to liberty', there exist only those 'rights to particular liberties' conferred in law and exercised in a social order upholding values other than freedom. Certainly the 'right to equal concern and respect' of Dworkin's preference has no greater claim to govern the policies affecting the social order than the cultural or conservative values prescribed by Scruton and Cowling. Certainly also policies like reverse discrimination tend to impose the ends of a preferential conception of social justice at the expense of the ends of a more universal conception of legal justice. However, little is gained by supposing that the perspective of legal formalism adopted by Mrs Letwin can resolve the questions touching the rights and liberties conferred by law in abstraction from a commitment to the kind of social order which the law inevitably reflects and serves.

Given her allegiance to the ethical, political and metaphysical assumptions of liberalism, Mrs Letwin was closer to Dworkin than either Cowling or Scruton. What distinguished her from Dworkin were as much matters of aesthetic preference as issues of doctrine. In fact, she conveyed the impression that Dworkin represented a spirit of enlightened liberalism as alien to Oakeshottian liberalism as the 'philosophe' mentality of Benthamism. The extent to which her involvement in liberal assumptions was informed by unargued aesthetic preferences was apparent in the very Oakeshottian book which she devoted to ethics.

The Gentleman in Trollope provided a systematic doctrine touching upon personal morality, social ethics, politics and religion. It challenged traditional ethics by offering an original formulation of ethical individualism which avoided the dualisms between reason and passion, society and the individual, which, Mrs Letwin argued, had distorted traditional ethics. Although the book was ostensibly a literary study of Trollope, the literary critical dimension was incidental to its doctrinal concerns – and Mrs Letwin acknowledged that no familiarity with Trollope's novels was assumed.

The Gentleman in Trollope was striking for the virtual absence of any historical claims made on behalf of its subject. Not only did the morality of the gentleman presuppose none of the socio-economic stratification appropriate to an aristocratic polity, but the title of gentleman itself 'flourished just because it had nothing to do with "class", as defined by birth, occupation, wealth or rank'. The book thus sought to recover the gentleman from the 'figure of fun' of socio-economic caricature. So far as the considerations of 'birth and rank' were concerned, for instance, the aristocratic ideal was less a matter of holding land or titles than one of the gentleman's sceptical disposition to 'give the labels their due without putting undue faith in them' and to possess 'too much self-esteem for either... arrogance or... servility'. Thus, so far from representing a recession from the Hobbesian liberalism of Oakeshott to the aristocratic constitution of Burke, Mrs Letwin implied that the ethics of the gentleman had no conservative consequences for the social and political order. Although the disposition of the gentleman included an ingrained sense that in politics 'the apocalyptic frame of mind does not signify insight', the book implied that the disposition could be sustained – and the aristocratic ideal realised – within a political and social establishment no more extensive than that of civil association. In fact, the doctrinal core of the book, the two chapters 'The Self-Divided Man' and 'Virtue without Struggle', was a systematic application to ethics of the doctrine of *On Human Conduct*.

In 'The Self-Divided Man' Mrs Letwin challenged the tradition of moral philosophy embracing Plato, Aristotle, Aquinas, Hobbes, Hume, Kant, Hegel, Mill, Marx, Nietzsche and Freud for having promoted the myth of the 'self-divided man'. She insisted that the myth rested upon an untenable dualism between the passions, 'ceaselessly chasing after material things which change and decay', and reason, drawing men 'to the immutable unity that it reveals'. And she concluded that the myth had resulted in both an excessively Kantian ethic, which measured moral goodness in terms of transcendence of 'the conditions of mortal existence', and an excessively Platonic identification of individuality and the 'multiplicity and diversity of the human world' with the world of appearance rather than being. And she concluded that it had resulted, above all, in exactly the kinds of polarisations between individuality and morality and the 'private' and 'public' selves which Oakeshott had first called into question in 'The Tower of Babel'. The subsequent chapter, 'Virtue without Struggle', left it clear that the polarisations were to be avoided only by recourse to the Oakeshottian doctrine rehearsed in 'Nature, History and Morality'. There was the same assumption of the anthropocentric character of human knowledge; the same insistence that its only objective ground was the fragile order imposed by 'the arts, disciplines, skills, manners, habits, institutions, conventions, traditions and rules that constitute civilisation'; and the same conviction that that order posed no threat to human individuality. Ultimately, Mrs Letwin concluded, there was no distinction between the individual's self-knowledge and his participation in civilisation, his submission to its authority representing 'the making of selfhood'. And it was his consistent participation in civilisation that guaranteed the 'integrity' peculiar to the gentleman: 'the connexions that constitute a man's character... unified... by being attached to the same person'. In fact, so far from requiring the unconditional 'authenticity' exclusive of the claims of society in a Kantian or Sartrean sense, the 'integrity' of the gentleman was an 'objectivity' to be realised within the public world.

Although divorced from considerations of social and economic privilege, the ideal of the gentleman was nonetheless an elitist ideal. Whilst it was not anti-democratic in strictly constitutional terms, its implications for politics were obvious, and its ethical assumptions were profoundly anti-democratic. The ideal was antagonistic, particularly, towards the egalitarian spirit of Kant's ethics. The book expressed a powerful rejection of Kant's emphasis upon the conscientious good will; his rationalist concern to establish the moral law upon the foundations of universality; and his dualisms between reason and passion, and between the person as rational agent and the person as beneficiary of unequally distributed social and natural advantages.

In dissenting from Kantian ethics, Mrs Letwin in no sense reverted to Aristotelianism. Whatever the degree of its consonance with Aristotle's emphasis upon practical wisdom and his equation of the virtues with the cultivation of the excellences of character expressed through social activity, the ideal of the gentleman presupposed a rejection on Mrs Letwin's part of both Aristotle's rational teleology and the naturalistic foundations for ethics which was his principal legacy to moral philosophy. Indeed, the metaphysical assumptions of the book were Kantian rather than Aristotelian, and its ethical and political assumptions liberal in the Hobbesian sense. In these respects the book inherited the dissociation of public virtue from the duties of citizenship which had been the principal point of departure of Hobbesian liberalism from the natural law tradition of Aristotle and Aquinas – at the same time as it dissented from the utilitarian, liberalising consequences of the dissociation.

The true precedent for Mrs Letwin's ideal was neither Aristotle nor even Hegel. It was arguably Nietzsche, whose anti-democratic, individualistic and existential ethics represented a dissenting critique of Kant's ethics, collapsing his distinction between the moral and aesthetic, condemning his emphasis upon conscience and dissociating virtue from conformity to universal rules and laws, but asserted from within the ethical and metaphysical perspective provided by Kantian liberalism itself. It is in its relation to this precedent that the ideal of the gentleman should be understood: a personal, rather than fully political, ethics, divorced from the social and economic arrangements which would otherwise lend it coherence and whose persuasiveness was as much aesthetic as moral. There was, moreover, a strong sense confirmed by that precedent that Mrs Letwin's – as much as Casey's — was a conservatism of sentiment. Unlike Casey's, however, Mrs Letwin's conservatism was compromised in virtue of its implications in moral doctrines which had inspired the very political tradition being resisted. This was true of her relation to Hobbesian liberalism. It was true also of the connection she sought to establish between Oakeshottianism and Hume.

In 'Hume: Inventor of a New Task for Philosophy', Mrs Letwin defended Hume's philosophy in terms of the historicist conclusions of 'Nature, History and Morality'. In so defending Hume she made claims on behalf of his philosophy equivalent to the claims which Casey and Scruton made on behalf of Kant and Hegel; conveyed the philosophical parallels between Hume and Oakeshottian conservatism; and implied points of affinity between Humean historicism and the anthropological conclusions of the later Wittgenstein.

In one crucial respect the essay was revisionist in intention. It recovered Hume's empiricism from its modern association with the 'dogmatic empiricism' represented by the logical atomism of Russell and the logical positivism of Carnap and Ayer. In fact, inasmuch as it imposed a distinction between empirical perception and knowledge and reduced human knowledge to the status of mere beliefs generated by customary experience and supported by social convention, the first book of the *Treatise* tended, Mrs Letwin emphasised, to undermine the principal metaphysical claim of both atomism and positivism: the ontological independence of the 'hard sensory core' of 'material atoms' comprising the natural order from the forms of human thought, and the ordering of experience conferred by social convention, which corresponded to it. In another, equally crucial respect, however, the intention of the essay was far from revisionist. It reaffirmed Hume's importance as sceptical subverter of the traditional foundations of both ethical naturalism and the natural law. Hume's ethics and politics presupposed that, so far from being derived from universal human nature, all morality, including "the natural, uncultivated ideas of morality", all institutions and all the municipal laws governing property, contract and crime were a matter of 'artifice' and 'contrivance', in principle 'changeable by human laws' and variable according to the diversity of 'education and human conventions'. Even when Hume characterised the protection of property and the obligation to keep promises as 'laws of nature', he tended to regard them as an 'invention' with no force apart from human convention. The characterisation was not, Mrs Letwin concluded, intended to compromise the fundamental tenets of Hume's ethics: that all values arose from human choices and attitudes; and that there was no natural law independent of the multiplicity of human conventions.

In his anti-naturalism Hume was responding to the dissolution of the naturalistic teleology of Plato and Aristotle. Hume's modernity, Mrs Letwin insisted, did not consist in his relation to atomism and positivism. It consisted, rather, in his closeness to those post-Kantian ethicists like the existentialists who shared his recognition of the contingent arbitrariness of all human knowledge and values and the ultimate groundlessness of all human civilisation once the objective sanctions of God and 'eternal nature' were removed. Indeed, her polemical conclusion was that Hume's context was the collapse of traditional theism and his scepticism 'a description of the world in which, as Nietzsche put it . . . , God is dead'.

In all these respects Hume inherited Hobbes's rejection of the Aristotelian 'cosmic order'. What distinguished Hume from Hobbes – and made him so much closer to Oakeshott – were his negativities towards scientific method and the historicism implied in the *Treatise* and reflected in his *History*. In his identification of science with geometry and his employment of the geometric method to establish universal, necessary and ahistorical 'conclusions about the real requirements of social peace' possessing scientific certainty, Hobbes had, Mrs Letwin concluded, misunderstood the implication of Aristotle's *Rhetoric* which Hume made fundamental to his historicism: that in all reasoning about probable events within the human world, there was no necessary 'truth' but only contingent 'opinion'. The main assumptions of his historicism were spelled out in terms of the Oakeshottian conclusions of 'Nature, History and Morality': that in the absence of God or 'eternal nature', the only objective warrant for human knowledge and values was provided by the conventions, practices, rules and institutions constituting the inevitable continuities generated by historical civilisation itself; and that historical civilisation was autonomous from the natural order in being entirely a human 'invention' and the 'product of a creative act'. What was new was the conclusion that Hume's historicism was inspired by the model of human reasoning sketched in Aristotle's *Rhetoric* in its assumption that the historical world was created from contingent human choices reflecting nothing more 'eternally valid' than relatively stable 'opinion'.

It remains a difficult question to what extent Mrs Letwin's conclusions about Hume undermined the Oakeshottian commitment to civil association conveyed in 'On Conservative Individualism'. There is little doubt that in prescribing the legal morality of civil association she tended to attribute, as much as

Scruton, a universal validity to the political arrangements characteristic of the historically determinate tradition of western constitutionalism. There is equally little doubt that the prescription tended to conflict with the historicist implications of Hume's conservatism, as much as it tended to conflict, in Scruton's case, with his mobilisation of Marxism.

Mrs Letwin may deny that any *prescription* was intended. Nevertheless, throughout her work she has adopted Oakeshottianism as a critical standpoint from which to challenge the moral validity and cultural consequences of the teleocratic tendencies of the modern European state. About Dworkin's subordination of legal justice to the interests of social justice she was polemically explicit. More generally, *The Pursuit of Certainty* established powerful Oakeshottian negativities towards central features of the modern state during the phase of advanced industrialisation from which none of her subsequent essays has significantly departed: the democractisation of the constitution; the ascendancy of statute law at the expense of the common law; the development of the technocratic style of government; the professionalisation of party politics; the redistribution of wealth and resources through fiscal policy and the provision of welfare benefits; the corporatist management of the economy under an increasingly extensive apparatus of law and state; the increasingly *purposive* character of law itself as the interventionist instrument of state policy, social engineering and economic planning.

It is undeniable that the negativities were informed by fundamental moral intuitions of farreaching contemporary significance. What Mrs Letwin was saying – controversially – was that state socialism was antagonistic towards the legal morality inherent in the rule of law, and – rightly – that the moral case for socialism was neither self-evident nor uncontestable. It is undeniable also, however, that all the historical developments connected with socialism from which she dissented just happen to be the features of economic and political life in the modern age and may well be the inevitable consequences of the industrialisation of the economic base of the modern European state.

It is arguable whether the power of Mrs Letwin's Oakeshottian recognitions about law was not diminished by her nostalgia for a style of political activity and moral practice appropriate to the pre-industrial – and pre-Benthamite – age. Certainly the nostalgia conveyed in *The Pursuit of Certainty* and *The Gentleman in*

Trollope tended to align her, in spite of herself, with Casey and Scruton's romantic denunciation of modern materialism and modern philistinism, just as it tended to ignore the actually existing circumstances of advanced industrial society. What is unarguable is that the sceptical, historicist perspective of Humean conservatism provided Mrs Letwin with no critical vantage-point from which to challenge the teleocratic developments of the post-industrial state: at any rate, it provided no vantage-point which did not incorporate unargued preferences that were not as such guaranteed by the historicist perspective. Since historicism was defended precisely because it denied the eternal validity of any particular social, economic or political arrangements, it was unclear upon what moral basis, consistent with the spirit of Hume's metaphysical relativism, the traditions of corporatism and socialism were to be differentiated from the constitutionalist traditions of which Oakeshott's civil association was the abridgement.

In one sense, of course, Mrs Letwin implied that the principle of differentiation was self-evident. Much of her writing has presupposed the truth of Oakeshott's conclusions as to the moral defensibility of civil association and the moral indefensibility of the *compulsory* purposive engagements of the modern state exemplified by socialism, corporatism and 'theocratic regulation'. Although 'Morality and Law' acknowledged the instrumentality of law in its relation to public morality, Mrs Letwin in general upheld the principles of legal formalism underpinning Oakeshott's civil association. To that extent she tended to treat as being morally unproblematic the obvious senses in which the law unavoidably imposes substantive ends and values upon its subjects in indifference to their actual consent – and the equally obvious senses in which civil association is sustained by the imposition of an external authority that is intended to violate the very liberty upon which Oakeshott himself placed such moral weight. At least, her reticence concerning those questions left it unclear upon what principles, consistent with her voluntarist ethical assumptions, she believed that the compulsions exerted by civil association were morally justifiable whereas the statist arrangements of a compulsory enterprise association were not. Whether Mrs Letwin believed that Humean conservatism provided any distinguishing principles is not certain. What is certain is that Hume was a problematic candidate for enlistment in the cause of civil association given his implication in the utilitarian tradition she attacked.

About Mrs. Letwin's relation to utilitarianism it is necessary to say two things: firstly, that she invoked the canons of procedural justice to restore the connections between law and morality destroyed by the positivism of Bentham and Hart and upheld the principles of legal morality embodied in the common law against the subversions of Benthamite utilitarianism; secondly, and perhaps more importantly, that her objections to utilitarianism were as much aesthetic objections to the Benthamite political style as objections to the principle of utility itself. It may well be, as *The Pursuit of Certainty* implied, that Hume's sceptical conservatism lacked the elements of critical rationalism which distinguished the reforming, Benthamite political style. But that does not alter the fact that Hume established the foundations in metaphysics, ethics and politics upon which Bentham and Mill were subsequently to erect their liberal rationalism and that, whatever their differences in matters of degree and tone, all three shared an underlying allegiance to the principles of utilitarianism. In fact, Hume initiated the pursuit of the very utilitarian justifications in morality and politics in dissenting opposition to which Oakeshott's civil association was in many respects defined. Moreover, not only was Hume's consensual utilitarianism continuous with the secularisation, democratisation and collectivisation of the nineteenth and twentieth centuries – it also provided no principles, and certainly not Oakeshottian principles, for resisting the developments to which it led. In his appeal to public utility – particularly in his association of the 'primary and original' obligation imposed by justice with the 'interests' of the governed – Hume imported exactly those purposive considerations into the justification of the state which civil association expressly excluded. In his rejection of natural law in preference for utility, Hume made it inevitable that political action would have to rely upon exactly those consequentialist rationalisations which, Oakeshott insisted, tended to qualify the absolute priority of the procedural rights upheld by legal morality. And so far from denying the legitimacy of the arrangements of enterprise association, Hume's utilitarianism implied that they were in principle as circumstantially defensible as those of civil association; or, at least, that *both* forms of association would have to be justified in terms of their continuing utility.

In all these respects Mrs Letwin's Oakeshottian conservatism was as compromised as Casey's. As much as Casey's mobilisation of Aristotle and Hegel, it involved the sophisticated philosophical assertion of moral and political preferences in the context of a general acceptance of the ethical and metaphysical principles of a political tradition which culminated ultimately in the political and cultural forces being challenged. The degree of arbitrariness which that context conferred upon those preferences was not diminished in Mrs Letwin's case by the general truth of what was concluded in the case of Maurice Cowling: the remoteness of modern philosophical conservatism from the contemporary political situation to which it was a response.

Conclusion: The Significance of Contemporary Conservatism

i

All the writers discussed in this volume wrote in the context of the reversal of the postwar consensus which culminated in the Conservative victory of 1979. Some of them, particularly Casey and Cowling, anticipated it; some of them, particularly Scruton, validated it; and all of them may be understood to have welcomed it. This book offers no historical or sociological conclusions about Thatcherism and the consensus which it superseded. Indeed, it suggests that the contemporary political context that Thatcherism provides is not of especial importance in the reconstruction of the thought of the theorists considered in it. It emphasises that the moral and cultural values underpinning their philosophical conservatism were often prescribed in opposition to the tradition of liberal conservatism of which Thatcherism is an ideologically strident continuation. And the book implies that their work was at its most problematic in leaving it unclear in what practical form their doctrinal conservatism was to engage with the circumstances of contemporary politics. In this connection, it is instructive to consider the work of an historian who is in many ways the laureate of the modern liberal conservatism from which all the theorists dissented: Robert Blake.

Blake is a distinguished historian of acknowledged conservative orientation. He is important because his work demonstrated a grasp of the historical context of conservatism which all the thinkers discussed in this book lacked with the obvious exception of Cowling.

Blake did not share the emphases upon ideology and social structure which aligned Cowling more with Hobbes and Marx than the Whiggish strain of liberal conservatism. On the contrary, what distinguished Blake from Cowling was the absence from his writings of any pressure of dissent from the prevailing assumptions of liberalism. In fact, Blake tended to write in deference to the very orthodoxies of the postwar Churchillian consensus which Cowling challenged throughout his work. In his review of *The Impact of Hitler*, 'The Road to Coalition',[1] he insisted upon the inevitability of what Cowling treated as the contingent outcome of the high political decisions of the late thirties: the destruction of the old Conservative party of Baldwin and Chamberlain by Eden and Churchill, and the eventual liquidation of the British Empire in the period of Russo-American ascendancy after 1945. Writing in 1952 in his introduction to *The Private Papers of Douglas Haig*,[2] Blake asserted the truth of what *The Impact of Hitler* was to question: that Britain's national and imperial interests had demanded resistance to both Imperial and Nazi Germany. So far from regarding American intervention as detrimental to Britain's longterm imperial interests, Blake regarded the interventions of 1917 and 1941 as having been indispensable to the German defeat upon which British survival had depended. In that respect, his conclusion was emphatically Churchillian: 'For both the great Anglo-Saxon powers, the second world war was in a sense a combination of the first, fought with the same objectives against the same principal enemy and with the same ultimate result'.[3]

Like Cowling, Blake has not underestimated the extent to which the contraction of European influence after 1940 threatened the survival of western values or the extent to which the postwar American ascendancy proved antagonistic towards western interests. His *History of Rhodesia*[4] was, in a sense, a book about the vulnerability of the liberal idealism of the west in the period of declining European power. The book placed the Central African Federation in the context of the postwar problem of reconciling the liberalising movement towards decolonisation with the threat to the west posed by international communism and the emergence of the non-aligned third world. It took at face value Huggins's liberal aspiration to use the Federation to create 'a great multi-racial dominion' as a bulwark against both the incipient totalitarianism of African nationalism and the *laager* of Afrikaner South Africa. It recognised the very real extent to which the fulfilment of that aspiration required not democracy but 'European capital, skills, enterprise and technology . . . lifting primitive peoples out of tribal barbarism into prosperity'.[5] And it implied that the dissolution of the Federation represented a tragic defeat for the west, in which the idealism of Huggins and Todd gave way before the majoritarian impetus of African nationalism to a 'bleak and seemingly irreconcilable confrontation between black and white'. Blake did not diminish American responsibility for creating the cultural and political barriers between the west and the third world which the confrontation reflected. His contribution on Eden in MacKintosh's *British Prime Ministers in the Twentieth Century*[6] recognised the responsibility of Eisenhower and Dulles in thwarting Eden's Suez policy and so exposing the longterm vulnerability of western power in the middle east. The recognition did not, however, qualify his concluding judgements that the successful invasion of the canal zone would not have reestablished British ascendancy in the region and that in that respect it had been Eden's tragedy to have failed to 'appreciate the changed status of Britain and France as world powers'.[7]

In none of his writings – not even *The Impact of Hitler* – did Cowling really deny that the changed status of the west in relation to the old European Empires after 1945 was implicit in the prewar situation. Nor did he pretend that the clock could be turned back. But unlike Blake, Cowling wrote in the recognition of both the ultimate cultural arbitrariness of liberal values and their derivative relation to the parochial traditions of western constitutionalism. And his work implied a clear understanding of the inherent self-deception of the liberal idealism for which Blake's *History of Rhodesia* was a lament. In this sense, *The Impact of Hitler* should be read primarily as a pessimistic statement about the precariously exposed position of western liberalism in the context of the much reduced Europe whose decline was initiated in 1940. Its mood of pessimism was not relieved by subsequent statements in *Religion and Public Doctrine* about the longterm prospects of world Christianity in the aftermath of European contraction. Cowling's pessimism in that respect largely explains why he did not share Blake's positive conclusions about British liberal conservatism.

Blake's *The Conservative Party from Peel to Churchill*[8] was a Whig book, and its Whiggism was secular and nonaristocratic. Its theme was the success of the Conservative party as a party of accommodating liberal conservatism in the phase of modern popular democracy initiated in 1832. It thus confirmed the conclusions of Blake's earlier biographical contributions to conservative history: *The Unknown Prime Minister*,[9] which reconstructed Bonar Law's creative role in exploiting the Ulster crisis and Asquithean mismanagement of the war to transform a reactionary Conservative party, split by tariff reform and discredited over diehard resistance to Lords reform, into the commanding party of the consensus that Baldwin inherited in 1923; and *Disraeli*,[10] which emphasised Disraeli's contribution after 1872 to the polarisation of British politics between the reforming radicalism represented by Gladstonian liberalism and the moderate consensus of the satisfied classes that has provided the Conservative party with its bedrock of electoral support ever since.

The liberal conservatism with which Blake was chiefly concerned in *The Conservative Party*, however, was neither Disraelian nor Baldwinian, but Peelite. What Peelism meant was the recovery of the 'centre ground' after the diehardism of Wellington; 'acceptance of the industrial revolution'; 'compromise with the forces of change and adaptation of traditional institutions to the new social demands'; 'compromise with the middle classes'; and a 'libertarian fiscal policy' designed to generate sufficient affluence to neutralise all revolutionary social tensions. Above all, Peelism embodied the lesson of pragmatic conservatism, that 'the old order could not survive if it relied on the narrow foundations of the past'.[11] The lesson had been ignored with disastrous consequences, Blake argued, by Disraeli and Derby in 1846 (in relation to the protection of the landed interest) and by Balfour after 1903 (in relation to the constitution and the emergence of organised labour). But it had been the condition of the political success achieved by Disraeli after 1872, by Bonar Law after 1911, and by the Conservatives in opposition and in office after 1945. In fact, the principal message of *The Conservative Party* was that Peelism represented the essence of conservative wisdom in the circumstances of modern industrial democracy.

It would be wrong to exaggerate the differences between Blake and Cowling. *The Conservative Party* summarised what Cowling was to demonstrate in detail and with polemical emphasis in *The Impact of Labour*: that Baldwin's consensus was a Peelite consensus, dedicated to the defence of property, the rule of law and the constitution against the revolutionary threat posed by Labour 'by making moderate concessions to the forces of change'; that in its anti-socialist intentions the consensus was continuous with the Peelism of the Lloyd George coalition; and that, in party political terms, Baldwinian conservatism involved the consensual ascendancy of the Conservative party, the elimination of the old Liberal party and the institutionalisation of the Labour party. Nevertheless, whereas Cowling in *Religion and Public Doctrine* and 'The Present Position' implied the ideological relevance of Salisbury to the contemporary situation, Blake diminished the prospective political significance of the Unionist coalition over which Salisbury presided after 1886. Despite its electoral success, Blake concluded, Salisbury's consensus was running against the governing political impetus of the period, 'the desire for collectivism, for social reform in the interests of the newly enfranchised rural and urban householders'. And throughout *The Conservative Party* Blake demonstrated that it was Peelism, rather than the Anglican authoritarianism which Cowling admired in Salisbury, that had succeeded in containing that impetus after 1900.

Blake's conclusions about Salisbury left no doubt that the tradition of liberal conservatism represented by Peelism was implicated in the very processes of secularisation and democratisation which Cowling regarded as constituting the central ideological problem for modern conservatism. Throughout *The Conservative Party*, Blake implied that Peelism had functioned with diminishing ideological strain in the context of the secular constitution of modern liberal democracy. He concluded that by the time of Balfour's accession to the party leadership in 1902 'the religious question had ceased to count'. He concluded further that the Conservative party had not only survived the erosion of the old aristocratic constitution after 1832, but that Disraeli and Salisbury had been so successful in uniting the traditional landed interests with the interests of the commercial middle classes that 'by 1900 the Conservatives were the party not just of the land, but of the rich in general'.[12] And he left the general impression that Conservative success after 1951 had depended upon a Disraelian mobilisation of middle class resentment against the levels of austerity and taxation imposed by Labour in conjunction with the Peelite commitment, represented by Butskellism, to the proctection of the welfare state constructed after 1945. In all these respects, the stance of pragmatic Peelism which Blake prescribed was inherently problematic. The difficulty was that Peelism left it unclear upon what precise doctrinal basis the Conservative party was to distinguish itself from the progressive forces it existed to resist, and in the name of which ultimate values resistance was to be conducted. Blake did not deny that there were distinctive conservative values: a preference for 'cautious empirical piecemeal reform'; a 'distrust of centralising officialdom'; the 'rights of property'; the diversity of 'independent institutions' and so on.[13] But those values were the staple of the consensual liberal conservatism against which all the theorists discussed in this book were reacting. Their assertion did little to remove the impression that the fundamental *moral* principles underlying Peelite conservatism were those of the secular and pragmatic utilitarianism which the theorists all rejected on doctrinal grounds.

The Conservative Party concluded that liberal conservatism had operated successfully in the conditions of modern constitutional democracy. To that extent, Blake did not share Oakeshott's recognition of the challenge to the procedural morality of law represented by the progressive democratisation of the constitution after 1832. On the contrary, whereas Oakeshott was polemically revisionist about the relationship between democracy and the moral principles underlying constitutionalism, Blake provided Whiggish statements about the durability of the historic constitution and its responsiveness to the prevailing momentum of popular democracy. 'The Crown and Politics in the Twentieth Century'[14] emphasised Magna Carta and 1688 as decisive phases in the passage from royal absolutism to limited monarchy; and it celebrated the transformation of 'the monarchy from an active force in politics' into the 'impartial pivot upon which the constitution hinges' after the democratising watershed of 1832. *The Office of Prime Minister*[15] traced the survival of the premiership through 'the change from the concept of government as the King's government to that of government as party government' effected in the nineteenth century. And his contribution to Butler's *Coalitions in British Politics*, '1783–1902',[16] demonstrated that the parliamentary constitution had proved capable of accommodating the major party realignments brought about by the Fox-North, Aberdeen and Unionist coalitions.

What Blake was establishing with these statements was that the historic constitution had not been fatally undermined by the rise of popular democracy. He was implying, in fact, what he implied throughout *The Conservative Party*: that the historic constitution, together with the structure of party government, had contained the social polarisations generated by democratic politics in the past and would continue to do so in the future. The statements certainly established Blake's liberal credentials. But they conveyed little of the sense of overriding moral authority which Oakeshott attributed to the constitutional arrangements of civil association; and none of the power of Oakeshott's entirely negative conclusions about the ethics of party politics. In fact, *The Conservative Party* demonstrated that Peelism between 1922 and 1951 had involved a politically unavoidable acquiescence in the drift towards the teleocratic conventions of civil government which Oakeshott had moral reasons to regard as profoundly subversive of the traditions of *societas* he wanted to perpetuate. And the book implied that insofar as that acquiescence had been a precondition of conservative success, the drift would not be reversed in the future.

After *The Conservative Party* Blake made statements about the future of conservatism which departed from the consensual pragmatism of Peelism in the direction of a more ideologically libertarian conservatism. In 'A Changed Climate'[17] he criticised Heath's government for its betrayal in office of the manifesto of 1970 and for its bondage to the postwar orthodoxies of 'planning, high public expenditure, high taxation [and] a rising role for the state'. So far from prescribing a perpetuation of the Peelism embodied in Macmillan's pursuit of the 'middle ground', Blake asserted that conservatism after Heath should pursue liberal conservatism on the assumption that 'there [was] now no middle ground to seek',[18] and that 'paternalism [was] out, along with the welfare consensus'.[19] And in his 1976 paper to the Conservative Philosophy Group, *Conservatism in an Age of Revolution*,[20] Blake announced that a decisive political battle was in prospect to prevent the progressive extension of the welfare state culminating in 'the socialist slum of an East European People's Democracy in which . . . freedom as we know it will become extinct'.[21] To avoid that eventuality, Blake demanded that Thatcherite Conservatism should proclaim the desirability of 'getting government off our backs, setting the people free [and] diminishing bureaucracy'.[22] It is questionable whether Thatcherism has departed radically from the Peelism which Blake defended in *The Conservative Party*. What is not questionable is that his prescription of an ideologically explicit libertarianism distanced his conservatism even further than his Peelism from the conservatism of Casey and Scruton. In fact, *Conservatism in an Age of Revolution* was published at roughly the same moment in the mid-seventies when Casey and Scruton were beginning to mount the Hegelian attack upon liberalism which culminated in the publication of Scruton's *The Meaning of Conservatism* in 1980.

Blake's historical work constitutes a very powerful statement about the possibilities and limitations of intelligent conservative politics in the circumstances of a modern and industrial society. It is discussed at length here because it invites the conclusion that neither the Hegelian *Sittlichkeit*, Salisbury's political Anglicanism nor Oakeshott's *Societas* are to be reconstituted in the modern age, and that they are not viable as objectives of contemporary conservative action. That conclusion invites, in turn, a question fundamental to the concerns of this book: what is the significance of contemporary conservative theory, what saves it from being merely the dissenting intellectual strategy which Cowling adopted in *Religion and Public Doctrine*, the romantic disdain for industrial society which informed the high culturalism of Casey and Scruton and the aristocratic ethics of Mrs Letwin, or a reactionary or nostalgic version of the abstract idealism which Oakeshott denounced in *Rationalism in Politics?* The answer to that question is in part an argument about liberalism, in part an argument about natural law.

ii

What unites the work of Casey, Scruton, Oakeshott, Cowling and Mrs Letwin is the explicitness of their rejection of conventional liberalism. Their unity in this essential respect is not qualified by the truth that the liberalisms which they rejected and the conservatisms which they defended were various and often mutually conflicting. Cowling attacked Mill directly; and *Religion and Public Doctrine* associated the Whiggism of Oakeshott, Churchill, Collingwood and Butterfield with the illusions of liberalism. Oakeshott and Mrs Letwin challenged the tradition of liberal rationalism represented by Bacon, Descartes, Locke and Kant from an historicist perspective; and they challenged the liberal utilitarianism of Bentham and Mill in defence of the procedural morality of the rule of law which they associated with Hobbes, with Hume and with the English Common Law. Casey attacked Kantian liberalism and utilitarianism from the perspectives of Arnoldianism, Aristotelianism, Thomism and Hegelianism. And Scruton's *The Meaning of Conservatism* invoked Kant and Hegel in resistance to Cartesian rationalism, Humean empiricism and Benthamite utilitarianism, and mobilised classical Marxism in the rejection of the economic individualism of Adam Smith and the contractarian tradition of Hobbes and Locke.

The intellectual rigour and moral sincerity with which all five thinkers called into question an entrenched cultural and political consensus should not be underestimated. Nevertheless, what needs to be emphasised is not the fact of their dissent from conventional liberalism, but the extent of their implication in the ruling assumptions of the liberal tradition they sought to challenge.

During his editorship of *The Cambridge Review* Casey wrote with admirable directness about the political character of all moral and cultural values. However, at no stage did he really explain in what precise legal and constitutional form the politicisation of culture was to take place. He repeatedly invoked the Hegelian association of state and civil society. Yet he implied that the association should not be so strict as to compromise either the values of liberal culture which he associated with Arnold and Eliot, or the foundational principle of Kantian autonomy which he derived from Wittgenstein. In fact, it was clear that Casey was not prescribing a politicisation of culture and social morality in either a Leninist or confessional form. On the contrary, he was at his most polemical in attacking the statism which tended to subordinate the independent educational corporations to the egalitarian social policies favoured by the social democratic consensus. To that extent, Casey's high cultural conservatism necessarily involved a defence of liberal values. Indeed, there remains no reason to doubt that he regarded conservatism as entailing the very libertarian principle of 'rolling back the frontiers of the state' which the generally anti-liberal Cowling prescribed in 'The Present Position'.

Since 1982 Scruton has transmitted his conservative doctrine through his *Times* column and *The Salisbury Review*, the latter having acquired under his editorship a substantial transatlantic readership. The period of Scruton's journalism has been treated in this book as a third, liberal phase in the development of his philosophical conservatism after the earlier Kantian and Hegelian phases. The phase has involved significant departures from the earlier position of conciliation with Marxism towards a polemical stance of moral and political opposition to Marxist–Leninism and the bureaucratic and imperialist tendencies of Soviet communism. It has also involved a recession from the Hegelian authoritarianism of *The Meaning of Conservatism* towards the liberal constitutionalism of Oakeshott. The recession towards Oakeshottianism has certainly not represented an alignment with social democracy. However, when it is coupled with his strident anti-Marxism, Scruton's prescription of constitutionalist morality has represented a capitulation to the very ideological liberalism which he rejected in *The Meaning of Conservatism* by appeal to Aristotle, Burke, Hegel, Marx, and Oakeshott himself.

This book has minimised the importance of Oakeshott's relation to Hegel. It has emphasised instead his relation to Hobbes in particular and his allegiance to the tradition of natural right of Bodin, Hobbes, Spinoza and Kant in general. In focusing upon the theory of civil association developed in *On Human Conduct* the book has had two intentions: to present Oakeshott as more liberal than is sometimes conceded; and to suggest a tension between the sceptical historicism which he adopted in the fifties in challenging liberal rationalism and the dimension of rationalist universalism implicit in the moral claims which he advanced on behalf of the tradition of *societas*. In both respects, the general implication is that there is less dividing Oakeshott from opponents like Robert Nozick, John Rawls, H. L. A. Hart and Quentin Skinner than his doctrinally conservative orientation might suggest.

Nozick wrote in an American context, whereas Oakeshott's context was European. To that extent, Nozick neglected the relationship between the rise of modern liberalism and the fragmentation of medieval Christendom, the principal theme of 'On the Character of a Modern European State', and emphasised instead the connections between liberalism and the economic arrangements of modern capitalism. Nevertheless, the 'minimal state' which Nozick defended in *Anarchy, State and Utopia*[23] was limited, much as civil association was limited, to the 'narrow functions of protection against force, theft, fraud [and] enforcement of contracts'.[24] Both Oakeshott and Nozick implied that the canons of procedural or 'transactional' justice operated in defence of individual rights in morally legitimate respects that the teleocratic or 'end-state' considerations of social and distributive justice did not. Both assumed a fundamental distinction between the legal establishment of the state and the social and economic order which it legitimised. Both identified the legal establishment in terms of the monopoly upon all legitimate power claimed by the modern state. Both either concluded (Nozick) or implied (Oakeshott) – problematically – that the monopoly upon power exercised by the state was not a morally indefensible violation of the rights and liberties of its subjects. Both excluded any naturalistic or teleological justifications of the monopoly. And both either insisted (Nozick) or implied (Oakeshott) that any function discharged by the state more extensive than those connected with the legal protection of individual rights necessarily involved an exercise of illegitimate power.

What distinguished Oakeshott from Nozick was not the fact that *Rationalism in Politics* provided a conservative defence of traditionalism against the principles of liberal rationalism of which Nozick was an ideologically articulate American exponent. Rather, it was the fact that Nozick's 'minimal state' was essentially a *Lockean* argument about property, whereas Oakeshott's civil association was essentially a *Hobbesian* argument about law and sovereignty. The difference was in some respects very important. It meant, for one thing, that civil association had fewer anti-distributivist implications than Nozick's 'minimal state', since Oakeshott implied – following Hobbes – that property rights were dependent upon the rules of acquisition, ownership and transference brought into being *by* civil society and were thus alterable by an exercise of legislative sovereignty. It meant, for another, that Oakeshott had fewer difficulties in justifying the monopoly upon legitimate power exercised by the state, since he did not follow Nozick in assuming the existence of a natural law giving rise to a natural right of enforcement and punishment. The difference did not, however, alter the fact that both Oakeshott and Nozick defended a conception of secular government limited by the rule of law in accordance with the principles of the tradition of liberal constitutionalism. Nor did it alter the fact that the ethical assumptions which each made in defending the conception were voluntarist in the classical Hobbesian and Kantian senses. Indeed, the foundational moral presupposition of Nozick's argument for the 'minimal state' was entirely consistent with the ideal of the 'freedom inherent in agency' which provided the moral inspiration of the tradition of *societas*: the 'moral agent capable of guiding its behaviour by moral principles and capable of engaging in mutual limitation of conduct'.[25]

About Rawls, it is necessary to say that in two respects Oakeshott *did* dissent from the conclusions of *A Theory of Justice*.[26] Whereas Rawls argued that the distribution of economic goods and social opportunities was a legitimate concern of law and government, Oakeshott defined the procedural justice governing civil association to the exclusion of every consideration of distributive justice. Secondly, the historicist arguments which Oakeshott advanced against liberal rationalism in the fifties invalidated Rawls's entire strategy in *A Theory of Justice* of reconstructing universally binding principles of justice from the 'original position'. On the one hand, they undermined the dualism inherent in Rawls's abstraction of his rational contractors from their social and historical circumstances. On the other hand, the arguments implied that Rawls's appeal to a perspectiveless Archimedean point, not itself implicated in social and historical contingency, was a rationalist illusion as compromised as the Cartesian method of enquiry which it so much resembled.

Neither point of disagreement was clearcut, however. Oakeshott allowed that civil association could legitimately tax its subjects to finance the maintenance of a judiciary, an army and a bureaucracy. Oakeshott's acceptance of the legitimacy of compulsory taxation in those contexts left it unclear upon what principle he excluded compulsory taxation to finance the more extensive welfare and corporatist enterprises undertaken by modern governments. Moreover, it necessarily involved the minimal considerations of distributive justice connected with assessing how the burden of taxation was to be shared amongst the members of civil association, considerations which Oakeshott excluded *by definition*.

If the historicism of *Rationalism in Politics* undercut Rawls's strategy in *A Theory of Justice*, it also undercut Oakeshott's strategy in *On Human Conduct*. Much of the moral persuasiveness of Oakeshott's arguments about civil association depended upon the tenability of the dualism which he assumed between the formal equality of its members as bearers of a legal personality and the substantial inequalities differentiating them as participants in a social and economic order. This dualism was ultimately no different *in kind* from the Kantian dualisms implicit in Rawls's arguments about the 'original position'. Moreover, at no stage in the argument of 'The Civil Condition' did Oakeshott really explain the derivation of the principles of legal justice governing civil association. The argument of 'On the Character of a Modern European State' implied that they were an abridgement of particular historical traditions of modern European government. But that implication did not support the moral weight which he placed upon the procedural justice of civil association in challenging the legitimacy of those enterprises of modern government associated with the tradition of *universitas*. What divided Rawls from the Oakeshott of *On Human Conduct* was not, in fact, any fundamental difference in procedure: both assumed the existence of universal principles of justice. What divided them concerned the principles which each treated as universal. And in this connection it is important to emphasise similarities rather than disagreements.

In *A Theory of Justice*, Rawls did not assert the priority of distributive justice to the rival commutative and procedural conceptions of justice. On the contrary, he treated considerations of distributive justice as falling under the second principle of justice: the principle that 'social and economic inequalities are to be arranged so that they are both: (a) to the greatest benefit of the least advantaged . . . , and (b) attached to offices and positions open to all under conditions of fair equality of opportunity'.[27] What he did assert was the priority of the first principle of justice, the requirement that 'each person is to have an equal right to the most extensive total system of equal basic liberties compatible with a similar system of liberty for all'.[28] And he insisted, further, that that principle took full 'precedence . . . over the second principle of justice'.[29] Rawls's first principle of justice was a liberal principle of justice; and the maximisation of individual liberty which it prescribed was ultimately the principal moral aspiration of the tradition of liberal constitutionalism to which Oakeshott belonged. Unlike Oakeshott, Rawls took the principle to entail the provision of a democratic constitution. He thus regarded it as an overriding requirement of justice that 'all citizens are to have an equal right to take part in, and to determine the outcome of, the constitutional process that establishes the laws with which they are to comply'.³⁰ But Rawls also took the principle to entail the very requirements of procedural justice which Oakeshott associated with the rule of law. Amongst the requirements of the rule of law – or 'justice as regularity' as he defined it – Rawls included the 'precept that similar cases be treated similarly'; the precept that 'there is no offence without a law'; the requirement that 'laws be known and expressly promulgated'; and the 'precepts defining the notion of natural justice', including the requirements that 'judges . . . be fair, and no man . . . judge in his own case'.³¹ At no stage in *A Theory of Justice* did Rawls claim that the pursuit of social policies designed to satisfy the requirements of the second principle of justice should override the requirements of 'justice as regularity'. To that extent, so far from being a teleocrat in the Oakeshottian sense, Rawls was a constitutionalist who upheld all the demands of the rule of law upon which Oakeshott insisted throughout *On Human Conduct*. Indeed, what was defective about *A Theory of Justice* was not that Rawls sanctioned procedural violations of legal morality to promote distributive justice; but that he assumed that a constitutional democracy governed by the rule of law would operate effectively in the interests of the egalitarian social policies he favoured.

In its conclusions about law and the constitution, *A Theory of Justice* was a liberal book. It was a liberal book in the stronger sense, however, that its ethical assumptions were voluntarist in precisely the respects which Oakeshott shared with Nozick. Rawls intended that the 'original position' would permit the derivation of principles of political association in some sense indifferent to competing 'conceptions of the good'. He intended further that the 'thin theory of the good' which their derivation required would exclude all teleological or perfectionist justifications of the state's authority. And he asserted that the foundational ethical principle of political association was not the *good*, but the principle of *right*. This principle required, firstly, the dualistic assumption that 'the self is prior to the ends which are affirmed by it';³² it required, secondly, the Kantian presupposition that 'the essential unity of the self is already provided by the conception of right'.³³ In both regards, Rawls was affirming the priority of the right to the good. In that respect, the tradition of political philosophy to which he belonged was the tradition to which Oakeshott belonged: the tradition of natural right of Hobbes, Spinoza and Kant. In that respect also, Rawls was endorsing the very principles which Oakeshott regarded in the *Introduction* to *Leviathan* as marking the decisive break with the classical natural law tradition of Aristotle and Aquinas. There were, of course, obvious differences in preferences and emphases between Oakeshott and Rawls – about democracy centrally, and about the nature of political obligation itself (which Rawls virtually neglected altogether). But the differences should not obscure the senses in which they belonged to the same liberal tradition. Nor should they obscure the truth that the ethical principles governing the argument of 'The Civil Condition' were identical with those governing the argument of *A Theory of Justice*.

About Oakeshott's relation to Hart, there remains everything to be said. In one of its aspects, *On Human Conduct* represented a direct challenge to the assumptions of the jurisprudential tradition of which Hart was the most influential postwar exponent. Hart's *Concept of Law*[34] was a restatement of the classical principles of legal positivism. Thus, Hart followed Austin in assuming a fundamental distinction between law and morality and in denying that 'the criteria of legal validity of particular laws used in a legal system must include ... a reference to morality or justice'.[35] In that respect, Hart undercut Oakeshott's conclusion that the canons of procedural natural justice governing civil association guaranteed a connection between law and morality which utilitarianism ignored. In 'Positivism and the Separation of Law and Morals',[36] Hart distinguished the 'justice of law' from 'justice in the administration of law'. And in *The Concept of Law*, he concluded that, whilst the 'inner morality of law' with which Oakeshott was concerned ensured some connection between law and morality, the canons of procedural natural justice were 'unfortunately compatible with great iniquity'.[37] In some respects, the disagreement about procedural justice was fundamental to Oakeshott's polemical concerns in *On Human Conduct*. Certainly Hart wrote without Oakeshott's recognition of the threat which the tenets of Benthamite utilitarianism posed to basic moral intuitions about law and justice; and without Oakeshott's consciousness of the extent of the threat to a stable rule of law posed by the post-Benthamite ascendancy of statute law. Nevertheless, the disagreement between Hart and Oakeshott must be understood in the context of their common allegiance to the tradition of political philosophy stretching back through Kelsen, Austin and Bentham to Hobbes.

Like Oakeshott, Hart rejected the 'teleological conception of nature' of the classical natural law doctrine of Aristotle and Aquinas, together with the metaphysical assumption of 'a Divine Governor of the Universe' which underpinned it. Inasmuch as Hart prescribed a doctrine of natural law, it was the secularised natural law doctrine of Hobbes and Hume, in which 'the modest aim of survival' provided 'the central indisputable element . . . [giving] empirical good sense to the terminology of natural law'.[38] Moreover, Hart and Oakeshott made similar assumptions about the nature of law itself. Both assumed the priority of positive law to natural law. Both implied that all law derived from will and consent. Both asserted a fundamental distinction between legal rules and the rules of customary social morality. Both concluded that all rights presupposed the existence of determinate legal obligations creating them; and that legal obligations presupposed, in turn, the existence of valid legal rules imposing them. And both wrote in acceptance of the principal authoritarian implication of Hobbes's voluntarism: the principle that the validity or authenticity of law was distinguishable from its justice, desirability or morality. Oakeshott affirmed the principle throughout *On Human Conduct*. And the principle informed the elaboration of Austin's jurisprudence which Hart provided in *The Concept of Law*. Thus, Hart demonstrated that there were logical distinctions between different kinds of legal rules which Austin's assimilation of all law to 'commands' of the sovereign obscured. In addition to the *primary* rules imposing specific obligations like those of the criminal law, there were, Hart argued, *secondary* rules stipulating the conditions for the enactment and identification of valid legal rules. In particular, there was a fundamental 'rule of recognition' within any legal system providing 'both private persons and officials with authoritative criteria for identifying primary rules of obligation'. Whereas the criteria included 'reference to an authoritative text; to legislative enactment; to customary practice; to general declarations of specified persons, or to past judicial decisions in particular cases',[39] they did not necessarily include reference to either the justice of law or its morality. In all these respects, so far from involving radical disagreement with Oakeshott, Hart's assumptions about law were identical with the key assumptions about law and state which Oakeshott attributed to Hobbes in the *Introduction* to *Leviathan*.

In obvious senses Hart was a liberal rationalist, whereas Oakeshott clearly was not. Hart's *Law, Liberty and Morality*,[40] for instance, was an unOakeshottian defence of Mill's *On Liberty* which, in denying that it was 'permissible to enforce morality as such', sorted ill with Oakeshott's authoritarian conclusions about social morality in 'The Tower of Babel'. Moreover, Hart intended that the distinction between the validity and justice of law should maximise social criticism of existing law; whereas Oakeshott implied that the distinction had the libertarian consequence of maximising the independence of the legal subject from the constraints imposed by a critical social consensus. Nevertheless, the fact remains that there was little dividing Oakeshott from Hart in their respectively Hobbesian conclusions about law itself. In one sense, Oakeshott was not a legal positivist: he did make the requirements of procedural natural justice central to the morality of civil association. Yet, Oakeshott was closer to Hart than he was to either the Dworkin of *Taking Rights Seriously*[41] or the Finnis of *Natural Law and Natural Rights*,[42] both of whom formulated a version of legal naturalism in open resistance to the legal positivism associated with Austin and Hart.

Dworkin's *Taking Rights Seriously* argued that there were rights antecedent to positive law and that they were derived from the foundational 'right to equal concern and respect'. What was objectionable about the book, from an Oakeshottian perspective, was not simply that it called into question the Hobbesian priority of positive law. It was objectionable, chiefly, because it made a Rousseauesque identification of the political and legal expression of the 'right to equal concern and respect' with the General Will of the social democratic consensus; and because it appeared, in consequence, to sanction the violation of procedural natural justice in the realisation of social justice. In both respects, the book was objectionable because it rejected assumptions about the *positive* character of legal obligation which Oakeshott shared with Hart.

Dworkin's legal naturalism was entirely secular in its metaphysical presuppositions. Finnis's jurisprudence, on the other hand, incorporated Thomist arguments about morality and law. In consequence, Finnis departed radically from the voluntarist and authoritarian principles of the tradition of natural right of Hobbes to which both Oakeshott and Hart adhered. Thus, in 'Some Professorial Fallacies about Rights'[43] and 'The Rights and Wrongs of Abortion',[44] Finnis attacked the voluntarist idiom of natural rights. In 'Reason and Passion: The Constitutional

Dialectic of Free Speech and Obscenity'[45] and 'Natural Law and Unnatural Acts',[46] he developed a naturalistic ethics from the perspective of Thomism. And in 'Reason, Authority and Friendship in Law and Morals',[47] he challenged the positivism of Kelsen and Hart by asserting that jurisprudence was not a value-free science and that the 'enterprise of making and maintaining law [was], centrally, a part of the moral form of life'.[48] What jurisprudence required, Finnis concluded, was a specification of the human ends and purposes served by a legal order. *Natural Law and Natural Rights* provided the specification by relating the rule of law to the 'basic forms of human good', which included life, knowledge, play, aesthetic experience, sociability, practical reasonableness and religion. In a sense, Oakeshott did not dispute Finnis's conclusion that jurisprudence unavoidably made ethical assumptions: his emphasis upon procedural natural justice demonstrated, in fact, that the maintenance of a rule of law rested upon fundamental moral assumptions regarding the liberties and legal capacities of its subjects. Nevertheless, the demonstration was conducted in deference to the ethical principles of Hobbesian voluntarism which Finnis regarded as having been ultimately subversive of the aspirations of the natural law. Moreover, the demonstration was coupled in *On Human Conduct* with an historical recognition that the period of the reformation had culminated in an understanding of the state in which the natural law was deprived of any politically authoritative correlative. The crucial importance of that recognition to Oakeshott's entire position explains the significance of Quentin Skinner.

Unlike Oakeshott, Skinner developed a highly detailed methodology for the understanding of political philosophy. The 'contextualism' which he propounded combined the conclusions of the linguistic philosophy of Austin and Wittgenstein with the doctrines of the hermeneutic tradition of Gadamer and Habermas. What the methodology hinged upon was the principle that the meaning of a text in political philosophy was to be understood in terms of its context, or, as Skinner put it in *The Foundations of Modern Political Thought*, of 'the normative vocabulary which any society employs for the description and appraisal of its political life'.[49] In the key articles 'Meaning and Understanding in the History of Ideas'[50] and ' "Social Meaning" and the explanation of Social Action',[51] Skinner argued that the principle neither entailed a crude causal determinism nor postulated a crudely instrumental relationship between the philosopher and his political context. However, the principle did tend towards the conclusion that political philosophy had an exclusively ideological status. And it was this conclusion which Oakeshott rejected. Thus, in his review of *The Foundations of Modern Political Thought* Oakeshott reiterated the distinction between philosophy and practice first enunciated in *Experience and its Modes*: he insisted that the ideological objectives of a theorist were distinct from his 'philosophical reflexion', the latter being 'concerned with reasons of a different kind from mere justifications or rebuttals of the circumstantial claims of rulers'.[52] Nevertheless, Oakeshott's disagreement about methodology should not obscure the fact of his underlying agreement with Skinner about substantive issues, about Hobbes, for instance, and about the principal characteristics of the modern European state itself.

Skinner did not share Oakeshott's concern with the aristocratic ethics of *Leviathan*. However, his reconstruction of the political context of Hobbes's political thought confirmed the interpretation of Hobbes as secular subverter of the traditional natural law which Oakeshott provided in 'The Moral Life in the Writings of Thomas Hobbes'. Two early articles, 'Hobbes's *Leviathan*'[53] and 'Hobbes on Sovereignty: An Unknown Discussion',[54] followed Oakeshott in challenging Warrender's deontological interpretation of Hobbes's theory of obligation. 'The ideological Context of Hobbes's Political Thought'[55] and 'Conquest and Consent: Thomas Hobbes and the Engagement Controversy'[56] placed Hobbes in the context of the *de facto* theories of legitimacy propounded during the interregnum. What that context established, Skinner concluded, was that Hobbes did not regard civil obligation as being 'derived from any religious sanction, but merely from a self-interested calculation made by each individual citizen'.[57] What it invalidated was the deontological interpretation in which Hobbes was regarded as deriving political obligation from 'the prior duty to obey the laws of nature, in virtue of recognising them to be the commands of God'.[58] And what it demonstrated was that a 'purely rationalist and utilitarian theory of political obligation' was widespread in the seventeenth century and that Hobbes was its ablest and most influential exponent. Oakeshott had polemical reasons of his own for drafting Hobbes in the war against later traditions of rationalism and utilitarianism. Nevertheless, the main upshot of Skinner's work was that Hobbes was of central importance in the process of secularisation by which the modern state came to be grounded in the consent of its subjects, and justified in the utilitarian terms of its capacity to secure 'peace and the protection of its citizens';[59] and that, in the last resort, was also the upshot of Oakeshott's readings of Hobbes. The extent to which Oakeshott was implicated in the process of secularisation was made all the clearer by Skinner's conclusions about the nature of the modern state that Hobbes sought to justify.

The Foundations of Modern Political Thought traced the emergence of the 'modern concept of the state' between the thirteenth and sixteenth centuries. Like Oakeshott, Skinner concluded that the concept was effectively established by the end of the sixteenth century and that the principal contributors to its theoretical elucidation were Dante, Marsiglio, Machiavelli, Luther, Calvin and Bodin. The chief features of the modern state, Skinner asserted, were that it was 'a separate legal and constitutional order' which the ruler had a duty to maintain; that it was 'the sole source of law and legitimate force within its own territory'; and that it was 'the sole appropriate object of its citizens' allegiances'.[60] What its emergence had required was the acquisition by the state of an independent legal sovereignty to the exclusion of the authority of 'any external and superior power' and all 'rivals within its own territories'.[61] The acquisition of sovereignty involved the repudiation of the claims of the Holy Roman Emperor to be 'the sole genuine bearer of *Imperium* in medieval Europe' and the medieval church's 'claims to act as a law-making power coeval with rather than subordinate to the secular authorities'.[62] It involved, further, the erosion of the 'feudal organisation of society' by the incorporation by the state of 'the legal and jurisdictional powers of the Church' and the 'structure of seigneurial rights'. And it involved lastly the principle that the state existed 'solely for political purposes' in the sense that its constitutional powers were 'divorced from the duty to uphold any particular faith'.[63] In all these respects, Skinner attributed to Bodin's *Les Six Livres de la Republique*, for instance, the same underlying conception of the state which Oakeshott attributed to it in 'On the Character of a Modern European State': that the *Republique* was the 'holder of supreme political power within its territories'; that it was the 'institution to which all citizens owe their political allegiances'; and that it was a 'purely civil authority' exercising 'its powers for purely civil ends'.[64]

In his review of *The Foundations*, Oakeshott questioned Skinner's assumption that there was a single 'recognisably modern concept of the state'. Rather, he insisted, there had emerged a variety of disparate concepts, including the confessional state conceived by Luther and Calvin and the technocratic state conceived by Cromwell and Bacon. Certainly Skinner wrote without Oakeshott's emphasis upon the concept of the state as a *universitas* and the extent to which it influenced the development of the modern state. And he implied none of Oakeshott's polemical conclusions regarding the technocratic conventions of modern Government which the tradition of *universitas* inspired. Nevertheless, the fact remains that the modern state described in *The Foundations* was defined in terms of the principal attributes of law and government which Oakeshott associated with the tradition of *societas*. In fact, *The Foundations* was, in a sense, a more extended form of the argument of 'On the Character of a Modern European State'. As such, it served to confirm the senses in which Oakeshott's civil association was an abridgement of the civil constitution of the post-reformation polity. In this respect, it is vital to understand that Oakeshott and Skinner were united in defining the modern state as a legal and constitutional structure capable of comprehending the diversity of its subjects's moral, cultural and religious allegiances, and formally distinguished from the social order which it legitimised. Indeed, the extent of Oakeshott's concurrence with Skinner in identifying the modern state with the dualism between state and morality, culture, religion and social order remains the principal respect in which he is regarded as a liberal theorist of the state in this book. And it remains the single most important respect in which he is distinguished from Cowling and Scruton.

iii

The principles of the modern state that Oakeshott and Skinner enunciated represent the liberal context in which Casey, Scruton, Cowling and Mrs Letwin wrote. All sought to reconstitute the connections between law, morality, politics and the state which the dualisms of the modern post-reformation state undermined. It was in that sense that they were concerned with the claims of the natural law in the modern age. The key figures in this connection were Casey and Cowling.

Oakeshott, Mrs Letwin and Scruton were all concerned with the moral authority attaching to the canons of procedural natural justice. However, they all prescribed a procedural version of legal naturalism whilst either assuming or asserting ethical and metaphysical principles profoundly subversive of the traditional natural law. Oakeshott implied that procedural legal morality governed an association whose structure of authority and obligation reflected all the consequences of Hobbes's rejection of the classical natural law in favour of the foundational principle of natural right. In 'Nature, History and Morality', Mrs Letwin differentiated Oakeshottianism from the classical naturalism of Plato and Aristotle and demonstrated its historicist presuppositions. In *The Pursuit of Certainty*, she associated the procedural morality of the English Common Law with Hume's sceptical conservatism, not withstanding the utilitarian principles of Hume's politics. And in 'Hobbes and Christianity',[65] she developed Hobbes's affinities with Luther in their common rejection of the 'pagan understanding of reason' of Plato and Aristotle upon which Aquinas established a 'natural theology'. Indeed, 'Hobbes and Christianity' served to indicate the extent to which Oakeshott and Mrs Letwin stood in the protestant tradition stretching from Augustine, through Ockham and Luther, to Kant. If that alignment was paradoxical given their anti-puritan sentiments about morality, it was entirely compatible with both their voluntarist and authoritarian assumptions about law and the state and their rejection of classical naturalism.

Scruton's early contribution to moral philosophy, the 1971 article 'Attitudes, Beliefs and Reasons', was a critique of ethical naturalism which defended the emotivist ethics of Ayer and Stevenson in terms of the modified Kantianism of *Art and Imagination*. As such, the article was as continuous with the modern versions of Kantian liberalism provided by Sartre and Hare as it was with Scruton's subsequent Hegelianism. The procedural legal naturalism which Scruton associated with western constitutionalism in *The Salisbury Review* neither required nor involved any retraction of the anti-naturalistic ethical conclusions of 'Attitudes, Beliefs and Reasons'. Nor did it involve the appeal to

Thomism which underpinned Casey's moral doctrine. On the contrary, where Christianity was concerned, Scruton wrote in the tacit acceptance of the post-Cartesian distinction between philosophy and dogmatic theology. Thus, the introduction to *From Descartes to Wittgenstein* expressed the Kantian conviction that philosophy was a *critical* rather than dogmatic procedure, competent to provide a 'rational grounding for theology' but disqualified from validating the *truth* of the metaphysical assumptions about God and nature upon which the universal authority of the Thomist natural law depended. Indeed, the introduction merely indicated the extent to which Scruton assumed – problematically – that legal naturalism was tenable in the post-Kantian context.

Casey is important because he defended a traditional ethical naturalism against the assaults of Kantianism and utilitarianism alike. In this connection, the central texts were Aristotle's *Nicomachean Ethics* and Aquinas's *Secunda Secundae* rather than Hegel's *Philosophy of Right*. On the one hand, Casey rejected the Kantian dualism between nature and morality. On the other, he rejected the Humean justification of the moral virtues in terms of their contingent utility together with the post-Benthamite association of moral reasoning with consequentialist calculation. In focusing upon the traditional virtues of courage, practical wisdom, temperance and justice, Casey was dissenting not only from the Kantian ethical principles underpinning Stevenson's emotivism, Hare's prescriptivism, Sartre's existentialism and Rawls's social democratic egalitarianism. He was dissenting also from the voluntarist ethical principles of the tradition of natural right to which Oakeshott and Mrs Letwin adhered.

Casey's rehabilitation of naturalism was, in fact, inherently problematic. His emphatically Hegelian conclusions about politics were not supplemented by much acknowledgement that the Thomist natural law presupposed the existence of moral restraints upon the sovereign will of the state. On the contrary, Casey tended to follow Hegel in assuming that the will of the state was *absolute*. Moreover, Casey was deafeningly silent about the substantive consequences for politics which really would follow from the reconstitution of the natural law in the context of the modern state; as he was about the conventions of civil government and international law which really would be necessary to reestablish its universal authority. Finally, Casey defended the traditional virtues in deference to the ethics of Hume, whose ethical presuppositions were anti-naturalistic, and in admiration for Nietzsche, whose ethics excluded any metaphysical sanction for human values and derived all morality from the creative will. It was not clear whether either Hume, Hegel or Nietzsche provided adequate doctrinal foundations for the restoration of classical naturalism in any save the *aesthetic* respects which Casey tended to emphasise. It was clear, however, that Casey did not associate the naturalistic derivation of the virtues with either the naturalistic biology of Aristotelian science or the structure of Christian metaphysics underpinning Thomism. Nor did he consider directly, for that matter, whether a naturalistic ethics was viable in the absence of those associations. On the contrary, Casey rejected the secularising, liberalising and democratising tendencies of Kantian ethics from the manifestly post-Kantian perspective provided by the metaphysical assumptions of Hegelian historicism and Wittgensteinian anthropology.

This book has placed great emphasis upon the themes of Wittgenstein's later philosophy in reconstructing the conservative doctrines of Casey and Scruton. Wittgenstein's later philosophy certainly had very persuasive conservative implications: it repudiated the dualism between ethics and nature implicit in the empiricism of the *Tractatus* by grounding all values upon the objective foundations provided by the forms of social life in which they were enacted. However, so far from departing from his initial anti-naturalistic conclusions about ethics, Wittgenstein's post-*Tractatus* thought implied that human values had an entirely conventionalist status. In this regard, Wittgenstein sanctioned neither the universalist claims which Scruton made on behalf of the procedural natural justice of western constitutionalism nor Casey's attempt to reestablish ethical naturalism.

It was not inevitable that Wittgensteinianism should have led Casey and Scruton to Hegelian conservatism. It might easily have led them to a doctrinal liberalism, as it did in the case of a philosopher whom Casey and Scruton both admire: P. F. Strawson. Strawson reviewed *Philosophical Investigations* on its publication,[66] and much of his subsequent work either drew upon Wittgenstein or implied substantial agreement with the conclusions of his later philosophy. *The Bounds of Sense*[67] provided a critical reconstruction of Kant's *The Critique of Pure Reason*. As such, it implied the affinities between Kant and Wittgenstein about which Casey and Scruton were doctrinally explicit. 'Self, Mind and Body'[68] compressed the arguments developed in *Individuals*[69] for rejecting the illusions of Cartesian dualism in favour of the metaphysical priority of the individual person. 'Imagination and Perception'[70] invoked Wittgenstein's remarks about 'aspect perception' in defence of Kant's thesis regarding the status of the imagination as a 'necessary ingredient of perception itself'. And 'Freedom and Resentment'[71] made Kantian affirmations of the priority of the practical to the theoretical reason and the autonomy of human morality from the encroachments of science. In both regards, 'Freedom and Resentment' cohered with the humanistic implications of the later Wittgenstein and furnished Casey and Scruton with conservative arguments for resistance to the deterministic presuppositions of classical Marxism and the utilitarian justifications of criminal punishment. Nevertheless, Strawson wrote without the politically conservative intuitions which informed the work of Casey and Scruton. His reconstruction of Kantian metaphysics in both *Individuals* and *The Bounds of Sense* involved no progression towards Hegelianism. He drew no morally and culturally conservative conclusions from his review of Wittgenstein. And his 'Individual Ideal and Social Morality'[72] celebrated the diversity of individual moral idealism which a liberal – and ultimately secularised – social morality was capable of accommodating. In fact, Strawson's Kantianism was as conventionally liberal in its political orientation as the legal positivism of Hart. At any rate, there was no tension between Strawson's liberalism and the Wittgensteinian character of his metaphysics since both were harmonious with the Kantian assumptions upon which each rested. There were, however, obvious tensions with a moralist like Casey who inherited the metaphysical assumptions of Wittgensteinianism whilst rejecting Kantian ethics in favour of ethical naturalism.

It is important to understand that ethical naturalism did not necessarily involve conservative preferences in morals and politics. The naturalism of Philippa Foot upon which Casey drew in *The Language of Criticism* not only lacked an explicit conservative orientation – it was expounded in the absence of any systematic reflection upon politics whatsoever. Mrs Foot is interesting because the political neutrality of her ethics tends to confirm the conclusion that the Hegelian components of Casey's political conservatism were not guaranteed by the naturalistic foundations of his ethical doctrine.

Like Casey, Mrs Foot rehabilitated ethical naturalism by appeal to Aristotelian and Thomist ethics. In 'Virtues and Vices',[73] she defended the unitary scheme of the traditional virtues derived from Aristotle and Aquinas and asserted its superiority over the rival traditions of Kantian and utilitarian ethics. Against Kant, she insisted that human actions had to 'express' the virtues in addition to being 'in accordance' with them. And against utilitarianism, she insisted that the virtues were *intrinsically* beneficial to human beings in respects which required no further justification in terms of the single utilitarian criterion. Again like Casey, Mrs Foot propounded ethical naturalism in open resistance to the tradition in moral philosophy of Hume and Kant. In 'Hume on Moral Judgement',[74] she challenged the subjectivism implicit in Hume's grounding of the human virtues upon an unargued and contingent sentiment of approval. In 'Morality as a System of Hypothetical Imperatives'[75] and 'Are Moral Considerations Overriding',[76] she demonstrated that the Kantian categorical imperative imposed moral duties which did not necessarily connect with either the fulfilment of human nature or the realisation of the human good. And in 'Moral Arguments',[77] 'Moral Beliefs'[78] and 'Goodness and Choice',[79] she attacked those ethical doctrines like Moore's intuitionism, the emotivism of Ayer and Stevenson and Hare's neo-Kantian prescriptivism for deriving moral values from the voluntarist foundations of human choices and human attitudes. In rejecting the ethical assumptions of liberalism, Mrs Foot recognised that Nietzsche's amoralism posed a threat to the objective authority of moral values which Humean anti-naturalism and Kantian formalism alike were unable to meet. Thus, she concluded in 'Nietzsche: The Revaluation of Values'[80] that the Nietzschean threat could be contained only within the framework provided by the traditional ethical naturalism which Hume and Kant had undermined. Not only was Nietzsche essentially a moralist who assumed a traditional doctrine of the human good, but, she asserted, his entire project of the transvaluation of all values was intelligible only in terms of the teleological structure of ethics underlying Aristotelian rationalism.

Mrs Foot's naturalism should be understood as a critique of the ruling ethical assumptions of the tradition of modern liberalism represented by Hobbes and Kant. However, she wrote without consideration of the implications for politics of her rejection of liberal assumptions about ethics. Unlike Casey, she did not imply the desirability of reconstituting the Aristotelian *polis* in the modern age. Nor did she confront the difficult question of the constitutional form in which the natural law was to be reestablished given the post-Hobbesian secularisation of the modern European state. 'The Problem of Abortion and the Doctrine of Double Effect'[81] and 'Euthanasia'[82] made statements with obviously Thomist bearings upon the connections between law and substantive morality. But the articles did not call into question the secular assumptions of the modern liberal polity in which the connections were to be understood in terms of the consensual calculus of competing individual rights rather than in terms of the perfect duties imposed by the Thomist natural law.

Mrs Foot did not share Casey's doctrinal allegiance to Hegelianism. In consequence, she did not imply that the connections between law and morality were to be guaranteed at the level of *sittlich* relations. Nevertheless, a subsequent article, 'Approval and Disapproval',[83] provided a Wittgensteinian analysis of the attitudes of approval and disapproval in terms of the public criteria for their identification embodied in the containing context of social convention. The article asserted the desirability of regarding morality as a social phenomenon and concluded that the sociological approach would clarify issues in ethics which the post-Kantian emphasis upon the psychology of the individual agent characteristic of emotivism and prescriptivism had obscured. As such, 'Approval and Disapproval' established the basis of an anthropology of morals and tended towards the conclusion that the objectivity of human values was guaranteed by the continuity of the social conventions in which they were enacted. If Mrs Foot avoided associating ethical naturalism with Hegelian historicism in the manner of Casey and Scruton, 'Approval and Disapproval' came close to subordinating a traditionalist naturalism to the requirements of a post-Kantian anthropology from which the metaphysical assumptions of Aristotelianism and Thomism had been removed. In that respect, the article manifested the principal problematic tension underlying Casey's work: the precariousness of the natural law once detached from a universal consensus of belief in its validating metaphysical assumptions. With a philosopher who wrote with an historical awareness of the collapse of the consensus, the tension was even greater: G. E. M. Anscombe.

Elizabeth Anscombe is central because she is both a Wittgensteinian and a defender of ethical naturalism and the natural law. She is important because her work displays many of the doctrinal ambiguities associated with the work of all the thinkers discussed in this book. Unlike Strawson, Miss Anscombe is neither a Kantian nor a liberal. Instead, she insists that Kantian liberalism, no less than the utilitarianism of Mill and Sidgwick, fatally compromised the absolute authority of the moral law. Like Casey, she prescribes ethical naturalism by reference to Aristotelianism and Thomism. And like both Casey and Scruton, she writes in accordance with the anti-metaphysical procedures of the late Wittgenstein. Unlike them, however, she is not an Hegelian in either a doctrinal or procedural sense. On the contrary, her negative conclusions regarding the voluntarist assumptions of Kantian ethics embrace the historicist presuppositions of Hegelian conservatism. Like Cowling, she recognises that the religious question is as much a matter of dogmatic belief in a supernatural object as it is a matter of human morality. In consequence, she implies – problematically, given her adoption of Wittgensteinian procedures – that the post-Kantian metaphysical assumptions of Wittgensteinianism are antagonistic towards the metaphysical assumptions of traditional Christianity. Thus, in 'On Transubstantiation',[84] for instance, she took seriously the metaphysical implications of dogmatic belief in 'the divinity and the resurrection of the Lord'. And in 'Faith',[85] she insinuated that Christian faith involved more than the intensification of ordinary morality to which Kantian ethics led, since for the Christian 'a belief is sometimes the truth, and ... the consequent belief is only then what he means by faith'.

On occasions, Miss Anscombe expressed conclusions corresponding to those of Oakeshott and Mrs Letwin. In 'On Frustration of the Majority by the Fulfilment of the Majority's Will',[36] she questioned the liberal 'conviction of the unique fairness of democracy', implying that democratic procedures neither conferred especial moral authority upon the state nor necessarily expressed the popular will. In 'Authority in Morals',[87] she insisted, much as Oakeshott insisted, that morality was as teachable as chemistry or religious dogma; that moral principles were acquired in practice 'by learning what to do or abstain from in particular situations'; and that the post-Kantian emphasis upon 'personal conscience . . . [as] the supreme arbiter in matters of right and wrong' obscured the dependence of morality upon the authority of social convention. Elsewhere, in 'Rules, Rights and Promises',[88] Miss Anscombe deployed Wittgenstein's arguments about private languages against the epistemological presuppositions of social contract theory. She thus followed Mrs Letwin by upholding Hume's doctrine that promises were not 'naturally intelligible'; that they did not 'naturally give rise to any obligation'; and that their obligatoriness did not arise from some 'peculiar act of mind'. On the contrary, she implied that the obligation imposed by promises presupposed a containing background of social conventions like rules and institutions.

What separated Miss Anscombe from Oakeshott and Mrs Letwin, however, was her conclusion that the authority of social practices required a *teleological* justification. In 'On Promising and its Justice, and Whether it Need be Respected *in Foro Interno*',[89] for instance, she asserted that the convention of promising was justified only as an 'instrument in people's attainment of so many of the goods of common life'. The article 'On the Source of the Authority of the State'[90] was of greater account. Like Oakeshott, Miss Anscombe defined the state in terms of its monopoly upon all legitimate 'institutional, violent coercive power'. Unlike Oakeshott, however, she recognised that the monopoly was *morally* problematic and that, in consequence, it could not be validated exclusively in terms of law itself. On the contrary, she was clear that what was at issue was the *antecedent* entitlement of the state to make and administer law in the first instance. This was why she insisted that the central problem in political philosophy was 'what renders it just to exercise force in . . . requiring what is just'. The problem posed a fundamental question: it undercut not only the Hegelian association of state with the prescriptive authority of civil society advanced by Casey and Scruton – it undercut also the argument of 'The Civil Condition' and 'The Rule of Law' in which Oakeshott neither confronted nor resolved it. Like Oakeshott, Miss Anscombe concluded that the problem was not to be resolved in terms of either the customary authority exerted by the state or the surrender of individual rights to the state by its subjects in a voluntary contract. But she *also* concluded that the problem would have to be resolved in terms of the state's continuous success in 'its performance of a task which is a general human need' – and that conclusion involved exactly the *purposive* justifications of civil authority which Oakeshott excluded from civil association by definition.

As a Wittgensteinian, Miss Anscombe shared the doctrinal negativities of Casey and Scruton towards the tradition of Cartesian rationalism. The negativities were clearest in her most important book: *Intention*.[91] *Intention* rehabilitated the ancient and scholastic doctrine of practical knowledge in reaction against the 'incorrigibly contemplative conception of knowledge' dominating post-Cartesian epistemology and underpinning the dualism of the *Tractatus* between the will and the physical world. The book demonstrated that the concept of an intentional action had to be elucidated in terms of its public criteria rather than the mental processes 'attaching to the action at the time it [was] done'. It concluded that an intentional action was distinguished by the kinds of questions relating to the agent's reasons for acting which had application to it. And it implied that the identification of intentional agency presupposed the public context of institutions, rules and social conventions in a way that excluded the dualism by which 'one can determine one's intentions by making . . . a little speech to oneself'.

In associating practical knowledge with participation in the public world, *Intention* implied the Hegelian conclusions about 'objective freedom' which Casey and Scruton advanced explicitly in relation to institutional morality. It was clear from other statements that Miss Anscombe believed that the rejection of Cartesian dualism had farreaching implications for ethics and politics. In 'War and Murder',[92] she explained the moral errors of the doctrine of 'double effect' in terms of the epistemological legacy of Cartesian dualism. And in 'Two Kinds of Errors in Action',[93] she extended the doctrine of *Intention* to jurisprudence, demonstrating that the attribution of criminal responsibility did not hinge decisively upon the subjective intent of the agent, and that the voluntary element in *mens rea* did not consist simply in 'a mind conscious of doing evil'. Nevertheless, it is vital to understand that *Intention* was not an Hegelian book. So far from being concerned with institutional morality in the Hegelian sense, its principal doctrinal concern was with the foundation of a naturalistic ethics. In this connection, Aristotle's practical syllogism was of crucial importance. What was essential about the practical syllogism, Miss Anscombe argued, was that it was a form of reasoning whose premise had, in principle, to include some characterisation of its object as a desirable object of human want 'for the reasoning to lead to any action'. What it indicated was that moral reasoning presupposed some substantial conception of human goods, like health and pleasure, which corresponded to the natural wants and needs of the human agent. And what it provided was the basis for the reconstruction of an entirely naturalistic ethics. The urgent importance of reviving ethical naturalism in the contemporary situation was the theme of Miss Anscombe's brilliantly polemical essay 'Modern Moral Philosophy'.[94]

'Modern Moral Philosophy' was an avowedly revisionist essay. For the purposes of this volume, it needs to be read as a meditation upon the implications of the post-Hobbesian fragmentation of ethical culture which Oakeshott celebrated and to which Casey, Scruton and Cowling were responding. The essay demonstrated the precariousness of absolute moral values like justice and honesty in the context of the modern predominance of Kantian and utilitarian ethics. It insisted that their equidistance from ethical naturalism was a more significant fact about the traditions of Kantian and utilitarian ethics than their distance from each other. And it exposed the inadequacy of the liberal traditions of post-reformation ethics and the arbitrariness of the historical assumptions upon which they rested. Thus, Miss Anscombe questioned Butler's exaltation of conscience, because it neglected the truth that 'a man's conscience may tell him to do the vilest things'; Hume's severance of 'facts' from 'values', because it precluded the passage from 'is' to 'owes' as surely as the passage from 'is' to 'ought'; and the vacuous formalism of Kant's ideal of 'legislating for oneself'. Above all, she attacked the consequentialism of Sidgwick and subsequent English philosophers for their unquestioning acceptance of the principle that 'the "right action" means the one which produces the best possible consequences'. Sidgwick's consequentialism was pernicious for two reasons. It was pernicious, firstly, because it recognised no morally relevant distinction between the 'foreseen and intended consequences' of voluntary actions. It was pernicious, secondly, because it undermined the absolute authority of the prohibitions on treachery, adultery, murder and perjury enshrined in the 'Hebrew-Christian ethic' by entailing that even the 'prohibition such as that on murder does not operate in the face of some consequences'. In fact, Sidgwick's legacy to moral philosophy had been to legitimise the moral reasoning about consequences which permitted the conclusion that it was 'morally right' in certain circumstances to adopt the procedure of 'the judicial execution of the innocent'. Not only was Miss Anscombe clear that it was its conclusion as to the permissibility of that procedure which constituted the fatal defect of ethical utilitarianism; she was clear also that the deontological premises of Kantian ethics did not exclude the conclusion either. Indeed, such was the conclusiveness of the distinction between human morality and nature imposed by Hume and Kant, that a *moral decision* about the desirability of adopting the procedure could be made in full agreement that the procedure was, in respect of the circumstantial facts concerning its application, inherently 'unjust'. In that respect, Kantian ethics sanctioned what the neo-Kantian ethics of Hare entailed: that the 'man who makes an absolute decision that injustice is "wrong"' was disqualified from criticising 'someone who does not make the decision as judging falsely'.

In challenging both Kantianism and consequentialism, 'Modern Moral Philosophy' implied that naturalism provided the foundations for the reconstruction of the kind of coherent ethics formerly associated with the notion of a system of absolute moral prohibitions. It was not clear, however, how the foundations were to be rebuilt given Miss Anscombe's diagnosis of the predicament of contemporary ethics. She insisted that in the Hebraic-Christian tradition such prohibitions had had a foundation in the moral law prescribed by God who imposed them as unconditional requirements. But she also insisted that the moralists whom she attacked had had to write in the recognition that the metaphysical beliefs associated with a deontological moral law had been fatally undermined. The notions of 'moral obligation' and 'moral law' favoured by Kant were, in fact, 'survivals' from the 'earlier conception of ethics' and were 'only harmful without it'. Butler's Protestantism, Humean sentimentalism, Kantian rationalism and liberal utilitarianism, Miss Anscombe was implying, were responses to the vacuum created by the erosion of the metaphysical assumptions underlying the doctrine of 'God as a lawgiver'. In that regard, 'Modern Moral Philosophy' insinuated that the secularised naturalism derived from Aristotle, rather than Thomism, would have to provide the antidote to consequentialism and Kantian formalism in the future. Aristotle was instructive, firstly, because his ethics lacked the voluntarist notions of 'illicit', 'unlawful' and moral obligation underlying post-Kantian ethics. His ethics were instructive, secondly, because they provided reasons for rejecting the Kantian emphasis upon the relationship between the psychological experience of being 'morally bound' and the will of the agent. And they were instructive, lastly, because, in denying centrality to the Kantian doctrine of the autonomy of the will, they gave centrality instead to the human virtues for which a teleological justification in terms of human 'function' and 'needs' was indispensable.

'Modern Moral Philosophy' is important because its argument subverted the ethical assumptions of the traditions in political philosophy to which Oakeshott, Scruton, Mrs Letwin and Casey all adhered. The brutality of its conclusions about justice left little doubt that Hume and Kant were not to be enlisted in the cause of reestablishing connections between law and morality without considerable historical strain since the essay demonstrated that each was responsible for having undermined them. The essay ignored Hegel. The implication, however, was clear: insofar as Hegelianism inherited the Kantian assumption of the metaphysical autonomy of human morality from nature, its historicism was simply a less individualistic, more communitarian and less utilitarian reflection of the fundamental predicament of modern moral philosophy. In calling into question the ascendancy of post-Hobbesian ethics, Miss Anscombe was indirectly challenging the ethical principles underlying the post-reformation polity which Oakeshott and Skinner described. She implied that the principles of Hobbesian voluntarism were inadequate as a basis of resistance to the creeping utilitarianism which Oakeshott associated with the rise of modern teleocracy. On the contrary, she concluded that consequentialism was ultimately an extension of the dissociation of ethics from nature implicit in the tradition of natural right of Hobbes and Kant, and a result of the collapse of the Aristotelian and Thomist teleology which Oakeshott assumed as his point of departure. She implied further that resistance to consequentialism required a fully naturalistic account of human needs which the formalism of Oakeshott's legal naturalism excluded by definition. With both implications, 'Modern Moral Philosophy' confirmed from its Aristotelian perspective two conclusions which this book has advanced regarding Oakeshott's theory of civil association: that Oakeshott's invocation of procedural natural justice was implicated in precisely the dualisms between substantive morality and the legal arrangements of the modern state which constituted the central problem concerning the relationship of ethics to politics; and that the ruling assumptions of the modern liberalism which Oakeshott derived from Hobbes were continuous with the drift towards the utilitarianism which he was doctrinally determined to reject. In connection with Oakeshott, 'Modern Moral Philosophy' nevertheless left one problem unresolved: how the aspirations of ethical naturalism were to be fulfilled in a plausible political context given the bondage of the modern European state to the Hobbesian assumptions which Oakeshott associated with the tradition of *societas*, and the utilitarian assumptions which he associated with the tradition of *universitas*.

Like Oakeshott, Miss Anscombe wrote with the doctrinal intention of impugning the legitimacy of certain conventions of modern government. This was so particularly with regard to the practices of modern warfare. In the 1939 article 'The Justice of the Present War Examined',[95] she predicted that the British strategies of naval blockade and aerial bombardment would violate the principle of the Thomist natural law prohibiting the deliberate killing of innocent noncombatant civilians. In the 1958 article 'Mr Truman's Degree',[96] she condemned Truman's deployment of atomic weapons against Japan on the ground that it had breached the Thomist requirements for a just war in exactly that respect. And in 'War and Murder', she distinguished murder from legitimate killing in a just war; and concluded that pacifism, unlike the more discriminating Thomist natural law, sold the pass to an unconditional consequentialism by failing to affirm the *unique* injustice of the 'deliberate killing of the innocent, whether for its own sake or as a means to some other end'. 'Mr Truman's Degree' did not hesitate to associate the illegitimacy of modern warfare with the predominance of the ethical doctrines which were to be reviewed systematically in 'Modern Moral Philosophy'. On the one hand, the post-Kantian emphasis upon the 'supreme value' of acting from a 'motive of duty' sanctioned the conscientious violation of the moral law in the waging of war. And on the other, the pragmatic violation of the natural law was justified by the utilitarian conclusion that 'the "prima facie duty" of securing some advantage might outweigh the "prima facie duty" of not killing the innocent'. In both respects, Miss Anscombe was asserting in connection with modern warfare what Oakeshott asserted in connection with modern technocracy: that the conditions of modern advanced industrial society had undermined the traditional bonds between law, morality and the exercise of political power. Her convictions on that score were in some regards as morally compelling as Oakeshott's. Her Thomist conclusions about the injustice of modern war were damaging to Scruton, for instance, since he assumed that the preservation of the constitutionalist morality of the west was legitimately defended by the possession of nuclear weapons whose deployment would inevitably breach the requirements of the natural law. In other regards, however, Miss Anscombe's conclusions were as problematic as Oakeshott's. Not only did they fail to engage with the circumstances of the modern world; or, at any rate, with the conventions of post-Napoleonic and post-industrial warfare. They also left it unclear in what sense the natural law gave rise to a legitimate order of government capable of enforcing it other than the order provided by the legally sovereign state of the post-reformation polity which was, in important senses, the political manifestation of the predicament of modern ethics.

It is true that 'On the Source of the Authority of the State' concluded that civil authority required a teleological justification. Nevertheless, the state whose authority the essay vindicated in purposive terms was neither the Aristotelian *polis* nor the Hegelian *staat*. On the contrary, it was a state understood principally in the legalistic idiom of Hobbes and Austin favoured by Oakeshott, Hart and Nozick. Like Oakeshott, Miss Anscombe identified the state in terms of law and its jurisdiction; defined civil authority in terms of 'a regular right to be obeyed in a domain of decision'; and assumed that the primary task of civil government was to maintain the peace by providing an administration of justice competent to settle 'accusations of infringements of law' and 'complaints (in respect of wrongs) and claims (in respect of rights)'. Again in common with Oakeshott, Miss Anscombe insisted that the legal relations brought into being by the state involved implicit moral considerations, and, hence, that the 'intrinsic limits' to civil authority arose not from any contractual constraints upon 'a transfer of individual rights' to the state, but from the formal principles underlying the rule of law itself. In fact, she claimed as emphatically as Oakeshott that there was no absolute distinction between principles of 'legal authority, legal validity and legal obligation' and those of 'moral authority, moral validity and moral obligation'. With that claim, she was dissenting from the utilitarian separation of law and morality underlying the tradition of legal positivism, as surely as 'Modern Moral Philosophy' dissented from the consequentialist implications of Sidgwick's ethics and the autonomy of morality from nature asserted by Hume and Kant. It was in this sense that 'On the Source of the Authority of the State' promoted the cause of natural law doctrine in the understanding of law and the state, just as 'Modern Moral Philosophy' promoted the cause of ethical naturalism in the context of contemporary ethics. Thus, Miss Anscombe concluded that there were minimal procedural requirements of natural justice governing the rule of law which utilitarian and voluntarist assumptions about morality undermined in the senses made plain in 'Modern Moral Philosophy'. In particular, it remained the case that 'the enactment of a law by which it was an offence to go on living (though one had committed no other offence) [was] not a possibility for legitimate government', in the sense that its subject was inherently incapable of being 'guilty under the law creating the offence'.

The principles of procedural natural justice which Miss Anscombe defended did not constitute a particularly substantive version of natural law; nor did they imply any very extensive connections between the state and the moral practice of its subjects. The principles were not connected by Miss Anscombe with the enforcement of virtue in the Aristotelian sense, or with the enforcement of communal morality in the Hegelian sense. On the contrary, they were understood to govern an association which was less the public context for the exercise of the moral and political virtues that Aristotle and Hegel associated with citizenship, than the narrowly protective establishment of law and obligation of the Hobbesian tradition. Moreover, the principles were entirely secular in both their derivation and their metaphysical assumptions. Miss Anscombe did not imply that they required the political context provided by the confessional state. On the contrary, she distinguished the compulsory legal arrangements of the modern state from all voluntary 'corporative associations' the authority of whose rules and offices was 'weight-relative to free decisions'. And that was a fundamental distinction entailing the crucial distinctions between church and state on the one hand, and civil obligation and religious confession on the other, underlying the post-Hobbesian polity which Oakeshott celebrated.

Miss Anscombe is important, firstly, because her work demonstrates the full range of difficulties concerning the revival of natural law doctrine in the modern situation. The difficulties were partly about reconciling the claims to objectivity and universality advanced by the traditional natural law with the liberal, consensual and secular assumptions of the modern state. And they were partly a matter of reconstructing the metaphysical foundations of the natural law in the post-Kantian situation in which Miss Anscombe herself was implicated by reason of her doctrinal adherence to Wittgensteinianism. Miss Anscombe is important, secondly, because her work implies that the Thomist natural law imposes conditions for the reconstitution of the connections between law, morality and the state which are not necessarily satisfied by either the legal proceduralism of Oakeshott or the Hegelian conservatism of Casey. In both respects, her work defined the central problem to which Cowling's work must be understood as a response.

Casey is interesting chiefly because he associated the revival of ethical naturalism with Hegelian conservatism. Accordingly, his work tended to imply that ethical naturalism would survive in the post-Kantian context in virtue of its accommodation with anti-naturalistic traditions like Hegelianism and Wittgensteinianism. Unlike Casey, Cowling did not contribute to moral philosophy in an analytical idiom. Nevertheless, he remains central because *Religion and Public Doctrine* implied that the historicism which Casey and Scruton associated with Hegel and Wittgenstein, and the libertarianism which Oakeshott and Mrs Letwin associated with Hobbes and Hume, were as much implicated in the problematic process of secularisation as liberal rationalism itself. In that regard, *Religion and Public Doctrine* should be read as a prolonged meditation upon the moral, cultural and political issues raised by the kinds of tension reflected in Casey's work between Thomism on the one hand, and Hegelianism and Wittgensteinianism on the other. Indeed, the question which Cowling's work posed was fundamental: upon what foundations were the connections between law, morality and politics to be reconstituted in the secular post-Kantian context of which Hegelianism and Wittgensteinianism were manifestations.

The projected second volume of *Religion and Public Doctrine*[97] confirms the senses in which the connections had been eroded by the secularisation of English life, and the senses in which the post-Peelite Conservative party was disqualified from functioning as the agent of their reconstitution. Whereas the defenders of Christianity discussed in the first volume of *Religion and Public Doctrine* – Salisbury, Hoskyns, Smyth, Enoch Powell and Edward Norman, for instance – assumed that rechristianisation was realisable in terms of Church-State Anglicanism, those discussed in Volume Two did not. Thus, the Tractarian attitudes considered in Part One – of Keble, Pusey, Froude, Manning and Newman – involved the rejection of the post-reformation assumptions governing the Anglican regime restored in 1661. And the defenders of Christianity discussed in Part Four – Belloc, Chesterton, Graham Greene and Copleston, for instance – espoused Roman Catholicism rather than Erastianism as the only religion capable of combatting secular modernity. Cowling insists that the Tractarian demand for rechristianisation was political as well as religious. The demand was, in fact, a response to both the secularising erosion of the Anglican regime initiated by Catholic emancipation in 1829 and the democratising erosion of the aristocratic constitution begun in 1832. To that extent, the Tractarian thinkers were invoking the regime destroyed by Wellington and Peel by extending the 'counter-revolutionary Christianity' established by Burke's critique of Jacobinism after 1789. To that extent also, they were prescribing rechristianisation in dissenting opposition to the processes of accommodation with secular modernity which Robert Blake associated with the tradition of liberal conservatism of Peelism established after 1832. Not only did the fact of Tractarian dissent from Peelism imply the remoteness of the project of rechristianisation from contemporary conservatism; but, so far as conservative action was concerned, the crucial judgement about the regime which

Burke defended was that what was 'held up for conservation by even the most conservative of subsequent thinkers' was 'the Jacobinism which Burke attacked'.

This book has suggested that the conservative theorists with whom it deals failed to reconstitute the connections between law, morality and the state. It has suggested further that they failed either because of an adherence to the underlying ethical and metaphysical principles of the liberal tradition they sought to challenge; or because of a sense, which Cowling's work endorses, that the liberalising drift towards secularisation was not to be reversed. Whether the theorists were alone in believing the connections to be of crucial importance, and whether Wittgensteinianism, Hegelianism and procedural legal naturalism have been adopted as bases for their reconstitution in doctrinally *nonconservative* contexts are questions to which, it is hoped, a further volume will provide the answer.

Notes

PREFACE

1. Anthony Quinton, *The Politics of Imperfection: the Religious and Secular Traditions of Conservative Thought in England from Hooker to Oakeshott* (London: Faber & Faber, 1978).
2. Ibid., pp. 16–17.

CHAPTER 1: WITTGENSTEIN AND CONTEMPORARY CONSERVATISM

1. Ludwig Wittgenstein, *Tractatus Logico-Philosophicus*, trans. D. F. Pears and B. F. McGuinness (London: Routledge & Kegan Paul, 1961).
2. Ibid., Proposition 6.53.
3. Ibid., Prop. 6.41.
4. Ibid., Prop. 6.52.
5. Ibid., Prop. 6.42.
6. Ibid., Prop. 6.421.
7. Ibid., Prop. 6.373.
8. Ibid., Prop. 6.374.
9. Ibid., Prop. 6.423.
10. Ludwig Wittgenstein, *Philosophical Investigations*, trans. G. E. M. Anscombe (Oxford: Blackwell, 1953).
11. Ibid., no. 23.
12. Ibid., no. 66.
13. Ibid., no. 40.
14. Ibid., p. 213.
15. Ibid., p. 197.
16. Ibid., no. 580.
17. Ibid., no. 581.
18. Ibid., no. 583.
19. Ibid., no. 613.
20. Ibid., no. 615.
21. Ibid., no. 627.
22. Ibid., no. 143.
23. Ibid., no. 150.
24. Ibid., no. 144.
25. Ibid., no. 320.

26. Ibid., no. 143.
27. Ibid., no. 198.
28. Ibid., no. 242.
29. Ibid., no. 217.
30. Ibid., no. 199.
31. Ibid., no. 282.
32. Ibid., no. 284.
33. Ibid., no. 303.
34. Ibid., no. 258.
35. Ibid., no. 271.
36. Ibid., no. 404.
37. Ludwig Wittgenstein, *Lectures and Conversations on Aesthetics, Psychology and Religious Belief*, ed. Cyril Barrett (Oxford: Blackwell, 1966).
38. Ibid., p. 14.
39. Ibid., p. 51.
40. Ibid., p. 45.
41. Ibid., p. 54.
42. Ibid., p. 57.
43. Ludwig Wittgenstein, *On Certainty*, trans. Denis Paul and G. E. M. Anscombe (Oxford: Blackwell, 1974).
44. Ibid., no. 115.
45. Ibid., no. 472.
46. Ibid., no. 283.
47. Ibid., no. 342.
48. Ibid., no. 95.
49. Ibid., no. 83.
50. Ibid., no. 94.
51. Ibid., no. 238.
52. Ibid., no. 110.
53. Ibid., no. 509.

CHAPTER 2: JOHN CASEY

1. *The Language of Criticism* (London: Methuen, 1966).
2. Ibid., p. 56.
3. 'The Autonomy of Art', in Godfrey Vesey (ed.), *The Royal Institute of Philosophy Lectures*, vol. VI: *Philosophy and the Arts* (London: Macmillan, 1973) pp. 65–87.
4. Ibid., p. 80.
5. Ibid., p. 84.
6. 'Beauty, Truth and Necessity', *The Times Literary Supplement* (2 January 1976) 14–18.
7. 'T. S. Eliot: Language, Sincerity and the Self', in *Proceedings of the British Academy*, vol. LXIII (London: Oxford University Press, 1978) pp. 95–124.
8. *The Cambridge Review*, 1975–9 (Cambridge: Heffers).
9. Ibid., 98, no. 2233 (1976) 161–3.
10. Ibid., 99, no. 2235 (1976) 29–32.

11. Ibid., 100, no. 2241 (1977) 25–7.
12. Ibid., 99, no. 2237 (1977) 99–100.
13. Ibid., 100, no. 2240 (1977) 1–4.
14. Ibid., 97, no. 2228 (1975) 3.
15. Ibid., 99, no. 2234 (1976) 12–14.
16. Ibid., 100, no. 2246 (1978) 1–3.
17. Ibid., 100, no. 2251 (1979) 164–7.
18. Ibid., 100, no. 2248 (1979) 61–4.
19. Ibid., 99, no. 2238 (1977) 129–31.
20. Ibid., 100, no. 2243 (1978) 93–6.
21. Ibid., 100, no. 2242 (1978) 80–5.
22. *The Salisbury Review*, 1 (Autumn 1982) 23–8.
23. *The Cambridge Review*, 97, no. 2228 (1975) 18–20.
24. Ibid., 100, no. 2245 (1978) 159–61.
25. 'Tradition and Authority', in Maurice Cowling (ed.), *Conservative Essays* (London: Cassell, 1978) pp. 82–100.
26. Ibid., p. 94.
27. 'Actions and Consequences', in John Casey (ed.), *Morality and Moral Reasoning* (London: Methuen, 1971) pp. 155–206.
28. Ibid., p. 194.
29. Ibid., p. 198.
30. 'Human Virtue and Human Nature', in Jonathan Benthall (ed.), *The Limits of Human Nature* (London: Allen Lane, 1973) pp. 74–91.
31. 'Attacking Scholarship', *The Spectator* (19 November 1983) 22–3.
32. 'Emotion and Imagination', *The Philosophical Quarterly*, 34, no. 134 (January 1984) 1–14.
33. I refer to an unpublished manuscript on the traditional virtues which Dr Casey kindly showed me.
34. 'After Virtue', *The Philosophical Quarterly*, 33, no. 132 (July 1983) 296–300.
35. 'The Noble', in A. Phillips Griffiths (ed.), *The Royal Institute of Philosophy Lectures*, vol. XVI: *Philosophy and Literature* (Cambridge University Press, 1984) pp. 135–53.

CHAPTER 3: ROGER SCRUTON

1. *Art and Imagination* (London: Methuen, 1974).
2. *The Aesthetics of Architecture* (London: Methuen, 1979).
3. *The Politics of Culture and Other Essays* (Manchester: Carcanet Press, 1981).
4. *The Aesthetic Understanding* (London: Methuen, 1983).
5. *The Meaning of Conservatism* (London: Penguin, 1980).
6. *A Dictionary of Political Thought* (London: Macmillan, 1982).
7. *From Descartes to Wittgenstein: a Short History of Modern Philosophy* (London: Routledge, 1981).
8. *Kant* (Oxford University Press, 1982).
9. *Fortnight's Anger* (Manchester: Carcanet Press, 1981).
10. 'Attitudes, Beliefs and Reasons', in John Casey (ed.), *Morality and Moral Reasoning*, (London: Methuen, 1971) pp. 25–100.

11. Ibid., p. 99.
12. *Art and Imagination*, p. 9.
13. Ibid., p. 148.
14. Ibid., p. 98.
15. 'Philosophy and Literature', rpt. in *The Politics of Culture*, pp. 80–7.
16. 'Sense and Sincerity', *Times Literary Supplement* (17 October 1975), rpt. in *The Politics of Culture*, pp. 22–30.
17. 'The Impossibility of Semiotics', *London Review of Books* (7 February 1980), rpt. in *The Politics of Culture*, pp. 31–43.
18. 'Deconstruction and Criticism', BBC Radio Talk 1980, rpt. in *The Politics of Culture*, pp. 44–9.
19. 'The Semiology of Music', *Cambridge Review* (2 June 1978), rpt. in *The Politics of Culture*, pp. 75–9.
20. 'Adrian Stokes', *Spectator* (5 August 1972), rpt. in *The Politics of Culture*, pp. 148–51.
21. 'Marxism in Architecture', *Times Literary Supplement* (25 July 1980), rpt. in *The Politics of Culture*, pp. 167–73.
22. 'Morality and Architecture', *Encounter* (November 1978) and *Cambridge Review* (1981), rpt. in *The Politics of Culture*, pp. 157–66.
23. David Watkin, *Morality and Architecture* (Oxford: Clarendon Press, 1977).
24. 'Beckett and the Cartesian Soul', in Peregrine Horden (ed.), *Philosophy and Fiction* (All Souls College, 1983), rpt. in *The Aesthetic Understanding*, pp. 222–41.
25. 'Aesthetic Education and Design', in *The Aesthetic Understanding*, pp. 189–221.
26. 'Art History and Aesthetic Judgement', in *The Aesthetic Understanding*, pp. 166–78.
27. 'Recent Aesthetics in England', *Architectural Association Quarterly*, 13 (1981), rpt. in *The Aesthetic Understanding*, pp. 3–13.
28. 'Photography and Representation', *Critical Inquiry*, 7 (1981), rpt. in, and 'Fantasy, Imagination and the Screen' in, *The Aesthetic Understanding*, pp. 102–26; 127–36.
29. 'Absolute Music'; 'Programme Music'; 'The Nature of Musical Expression', in Stanley Sadie (ed.), *The New Grove Dictionary of Music*, rpt. and rev. in *The Aesthetic Understanding*, pp. 37–40; 41–8; 49–61.
30. 'Understanding Music', *Ratio*, 25, 2 (1983), rpt. and rev. in *The Aesthetic Understanding*, pp. 77–100.
31. 'The Ideology of the Market', *Cambridge Review* (29 June 1979), rpt. in *The Politics of Culture*, pp. 200–4.
32. 'Academic Freedom', *Cambridge Review*, 100, no. 2240 (1977).
33. 'The Ideology of Human Rights', *Times Literary Supplement* (14 March 1980), rpt. in *The Politics of Culture*, pp. 205–9.
34. 'Humane Education', *The American Scholar* (September 1980), rpt. in *The Politics of Culture*, pp. 220–9.
35. 'Poetry and Politics', *PN Review*, 17, (7 March 1980), rpt. in *The Politics of Culture*, pp. 210–19.
36. 'The Politics of Culture', in Maurice Cowling (ed.), *Conservative Essays* (London: Cassell, 1978) pp. 101–16.
37. Ibid., p. 113.

38. Ibid., p. 109.
39. 'The Significance of Common Culture', *Philosophy*, 54 (January 1979) 51–70.
40. *The Meaning of Conservatism*, p. 73.
41. Ibid., p. 99.
42. Ibid., p. 36.
43. Ibid., p. 30.
44. Ibid., p. 36.
45. *From Descartes to Wittgenstein*, p. 284.
46. 'Editorial', *The Salisbury Review*, 1 (Autumn 1982) 37–9.
47. 'Editorial: The Tory Opportunity', *The Salisbury Review*, 4 (Summer 1983) 46–7.
48. Ibid., pp. 46–7.
49. Ibid., pp. 46–7.
50. Ibid., 6 (Winter 1984) 42–3.
51. Ibid., 5 (Autumn 1983) 46.
52. Ibid., 4 (Summer 1983) 46–7.
53. *The Times* (21 February 1984) 12.
54. Ibid., (4 January 1983) 10.
55. Ibid., (22 March 1983) 12.
56. Ibid., (21 June 1983) 10.
57. Ibid., (5 July 1983) 10.
58. Ibid., (24 May 1983) 12.
59. Ibid., (26 April 1983) 12.
60. Ibid., (19 July 1983) 12.
61. *The Salisbury Review*, 2 (Winter 1983) 13–15.
62. *The Times* (6 September 1983) 10.
63. *The Salisbury Review*, 1 (Autumn 1982) 37–9.
64. Ibid., 2 (Winter 1983) 42–3.
65. *The Times* (17 May 1983) 12.
66. Ibid., (31 May 1983) 12.
67. Ibid., (28 February 1984) 14.
68. Ibid., (6 December 1983) 12.
69. 'Antonio Gramsci', *The Salisbury Review*, 6 (Winter 1984) 18–21.
70. 'Rudolf Bahro', *The Salisbury Review*, 5 (Autumn 1983) 21–5.
71. *The Times* (12 April 1983) 12.
72. Ibid., (29 March 1983) 12.
73. Ibid., (1 February 1983) 14.
74. Ibid., (15 February 1983) 12.
75. *The Salisbury Review*, 4 (Summer 1983) 47.
76. *The Times* (13 September 1983) 12.
77. Ibid., (27 September 1983) 14.
78. Ibid., (1 November 1983) 14.
79. Ibid., (3 January 1984) 10.
80. *The Salisbury Review*, 3 (Spring 1983) 46–7.
81. *The Times* (15 November 1983) 12.
82. *The Salisbury Review*, 3 (Spring 1983) 46.
83. *The Times* (19 April 1983) 12.
84. Ibid., (23 August 1983) 8.

85. Ibid., (15 November 1983) 12.
86. Ibid., (5 April 1983) 10.
87. Ibid., (31 May 1983) 12.
88. Ibid., (8 March 1983) 14.
89. Ibid., (11 October 1983) 12.
90. 'Michel Foucault', *The Salisbury Review*, 3 (Spring 1983) 21–7.
91. 'Ronald Dworkin', *The Salisbury Review*, 2 (Winter 1983) 25–9.
92. 'E. P. Thompson', *The Salisbury Review*, 1 (Autumn 1982) 12–15.
93. 'Raymond Williams', *The Salisbury Review*, 4 (Summer 1983) 23–8.

CHAPTER 4: MICHAEL OAKESHOTT

1. *Experience and its Modes* (Cambridge University Press, 1933).
2. 'John Locke', *Cambridge Review*, LIV (1932–3) 72–3.
3. 'The New Bentham', *Scrutiny*, I (1932–3) 114–31.
4. *The Social and Political Doctrines of Contemporary Europe* (Cambridge University Press, 1939).
5. 'The Activity of Being an Historian', in T. D. Williams (ed.), *Historical Studies I* (London: Bowes & Bowes, 1958) pp. 1–19, rpt. in Michael Oakeshott, *Rationalism in Politics and Other Essays* (London: Methuen, 1962) pp. 137–67.
6. *On Human Conduct* (Oxford University Press, 1975).
7. 'Present, Future and Past'; 'Historical Events: the Fortuitous, the Causal, the Similar, the Correlative, the Analogous and the Contingent'; 'Historical Change: Identity and Continuity', in *On History and Other Essays* (Oxford: Blackwell, 1983) pp. 1–44, 45–96, 97–118.
8. 'Religion and the Moral Life', *The 'D' Society Pamphlets*, no. II (Cambridge: Bowes & Bowes, 1927) 1–13.
9. 'The Importance of the Historical Element in Christianity', *The Modern Churchman*, XVIII (1928–9) 360–71.
10. 'On Being Conservative' (1956), in *Rationalism in Politics*, pp. 168–98.
11. 'The Tower of Babel', *Cambridge Journal*, II (1948–9) 67–83, rpt. in *Rationalism in Politics*, pp. 59–79.
12. *On Human Conduct*, pp. 81–6.
13. *Introduction*, in Michael Oakeshott (ed.), Hobbes's *Leviathan* (Oxford: Blackwell, 1946), as rpt. in Michael Oakeshott, *Hobbes on Civil Association* (Oxford: Blackwell, 1975) pp. 1–74.
14. *Experience and its Modes*, p. 347.
15. 'The Concept of a Philosophical Jurisprudence', *Politica*, III (1938) 203–22, 345–60.
16. 'Contemporary British Politics', *Cambridge Journal*, I (1947–8) 474–90.
17. 'The Political Economy of Freedom', *Cambridge Journal*, II (1948–9) 212–29, rpt. in *Rationalism in Politics*, pp. 37–58.
18. 'The Authority of the State', *The Modern Churchman*, XIX (1929–30) 313–27.
19. 'Thomas Hobbes', *Scrutiny*, IV (1935–6) 263–77.
20. *Hobbes on Civil Association*, p. 60.

21. Ibid., p. 62.
22. Ibid., p. 45.
23. 'Political Education' (Cambridge: Bowes & Bowes, 1951) 1–28, rpt. in *Rationalism in Politics*, pp. 111–36.
24. 'The Study of "Politics" in a University' (1961), in *Rationalism in Politics*, pp. 301–33.
25. *Rationalism in Politics*, pp. 327.
26. 'Political Laws and Captive Audiences', in G. R. Urban (ed.), *Talking to Eastern Europe* (London: Eyre and Spottiswoode, 1964) pp. 291–301.
27. *Rationalism in Politics*, p. 187.
28. Ibid., p. 187.
29. 'The Moral Life in the Writings of Thomas Hobbes' (1960), in *Rationalism in Politics*, pp. 248–300.
30. 'The Masses in Representative Democracy' (1957), as rpt. in William F. Buckley, Jr (ed.), *American Conservative Thought in the Twentieth Century* (New York: Bobbs-Merrill, 1970) pp. 103–23.
31. 'The Claims of Politics', *Scrutiny*, VIII (1939–40) 146–51.
32. 'The Voice of Poetry in the Conversation of Mankind' (London: Bowes & Bowes, 1959) 1–63, rpt. in *Rationalism in Politics*, pp. 197–247.
33. 'The Idea of a University', *The Listener*, XLIII (1950) 424–6.
34. 'The Universities', *Cambridge Journal*, II (1948–9) 515–42.
35. Ibid., p. 541.
36. 'Learning and Teaching', in R. S. Peters (ed.), *The Concept of Education* (London: Routledge & Kegan Paul, 1967) pp. 156–76.
37. 'A Place of Learning', *The Colorado College Studies*, 12 (Jan. 1975) 6–27.
38. 'Rational Conduct', *Cambridge Journal*, IV (1950–1) 3–27, rpt. in *Rationalism in Politics*, pp. 80–110.
39. 'Rationalism in Politics', *Cambridge Journal*, I (1947–8) 81–98, 145–57; rpt. in *Rationalism in Politics*, pp. 1–36.
40. *Rationalism in Politics*, p. 15.
41. Ibid., p. 109.
42. Ibid., p. 103.
43. Ibid., p. 103.
44. Ibid., p. 109.
45. Ibid., p. 71.
46. Ibid., p. 71.
47. Ibid., p. 74.
48. Ibid., p. 63.
49. Ibid., p. 78.
50. Ibid., p. 79.
51. Ibid., p. 4.
52. 'The Vocabulary of a Modern European State', *Political Studies*, XXIII (June–September 1975) 319–41; (December 1975) 409–14.
53. 'Talking Politics', *National Review*, 27, no. 47 (5 December 1975) 1345–7, 1423–8.
54. 'The Rule of Law', in *On History and Other Essays*, pp. 119–64.
55. *Hobbes on Civil Association*, p. 43.
56. *On Human Conduct*, p. 158.
57. Ibid., p. 158.

58. *On History*, p. 140.
59. *On Human Conduct*, p. 153.
60. Ibid., p. 317.
61. Ibid., p. 110.
62. *On History*, p. 159.
63. *Hobbes on Civil Association*, p. 37.
64. *On History*, p. 157.
65. Ibid., p. 136.
66. Ibid., p. 139.
67. *On Human Conduct*, p. 132.
68. *On History*, p. 150.
69. 'The Vocabulary of a Modern European State', p. 327.
70. *On Human Conduct*, p. 154.
71. 'The Vocabulary of a Modern European State', p. 333.
72. *On Human Conduct*, p. 155.
73. 'Talking Politics', p. 1424.
74. *On Human Conduct*, p. 151.
75. *On History*, p. 143.
76. 'Talking Politics', p. 1427
77. *On History*, p. 156.
78. *On Human Conduct*, p. 155.
79. *On History*, p. 163.
80. *On Human Conduct*, p. 229.
81. Ibid., p. 202.
82. Ibid., p. 255.
83. Ibid., p. 261.
84. Ibid., p. 273.
85. Ibid., p. 268.
86. Ibid., p. 287.
87. Ibid., p. 271.
88. Ibid., p. 297.
89. Ibid., p. 301.
90. Ibid., p. 312.
91. 'The Tower of Babel', in *On History and Other Essays*, pp. 165–94.

CHAPTER 5: MAURICE COWLING AND SHIRLEY ROBIN LETWIN

1. *The Nature and Limits of Political Science* (Cambridge University Press, 1963).
2. *Mill and Liberalism* (Cambridge University Press, 1963).
3. *Religion and Public Doctrine in Modern England* (Cambridge University Press, 1980).
4. *The Nature and Limits of Political Science*, p. 131.
5. Ibid., p. 206.
6. Ibid., p. 207.
7. Ibid., p. 74.

8. *Mill and Liberalism*, p. 98.
9. Ibid., p. 130.
10. *1867, Disraeli, Gladstone, and Revolution: the Passing of the Second Reform Bill* (Cambridge University Press, 1967).
11. *The Impact of Labour 1920–24: the Beginning of Modern Politics* (Cambridge University Press, 1971).
12. *The Impact of Hitler: British Politics and British Policy 1933–40* (Cambridge University Press, 1974).
13. *The Nature and Limits of Political Science*, p. 185.
14. Ibid., p. 119.
15. *The Impact of Labour*, p. 414.
16. 'The Present Position', in Maurice Cowling (ed.), *Conservative Essays* (London: Cassell, 1978) pp. 1–24.
17. Ibid., p. 17.
18. *Religion and Public Doctrine*, p. xii.
19. Ibid., p. 280.
20. Ibid., p. 161.
21. 'The Achievement of Friedrich A. Hayek', in Fritz Machlup (ed.), *Essays on Hayek* (London: Routledge & Kegan Paul, 1977) pp. 147–67.
22. *The Pursuit of Certainty* (Cambridge University Press, 1965).
23. Ibid., p. 121.
24. 'Morality and Law', *Encounter* (November 1974) 35–43.
25. *The Gentleman in Trollope: Individuality and Moral Conduct* (London: Macmillan, 1982).
26. Ibid., p. 222.
27. Ibid., p. 225.
28. Ibid., p. 222.
29. Ibid., p. 239.
30. Ibid., p. 231.
31. Ibid., p. 237.
32. Ibid., p. 239.
33. 'Rationalism, Principles and Politics', *The Review of Politics*, 14 (1952) 367–93.
34. Ibid., p. 369.
35. 'Representation Without Democracy: The Webbs' *Constitution*', *The Review of Politics*, 16 (1954) 352–75.
36. Ibid., p. 375.
37. *The Pursuit of Certainty*, p. 302.
38. Ibid., p. 308.
39. Ibid., p. 309.
40. Ibid., p. 94.
41. Ibid., p. 102.
42. Ibid., p. 59.
43. 'Nature, History and Morality', in R. S. Peters (ed.), *The Royal Institute of Philosophy Lectures*, vol. VIII: *Nature and Conduct* (London: Macmillan, 1975) pp. 229–50.
44. Ibid., p. 249.
45. Ibid., p. 244.
46. Ibid., p. 247.

47. Ibid., p. 248.
48. 'Hume: Inventor of a New Task for Philosophy', *Political Theory*, 3, 2 (May 1975) 134–58.
49. 'On Conservative Individualism', in Maurice Cowling (ed.), *Conservative Essays* (London: Cassell, 1978) pp. 52–68.
50. 'Taking the Law Unseriously', *Encounter* (October 1977) 76–82.

CONCLUSION: THE SIGNIFICANCE OF CONTEMPORARY CONSERVATISM

1. Robert Blake, 'The Road to Coalition', *Times Literary Supplement* (25 July 1975) 839.
2. Robert Blake (ed.), *The Private Papers of Douglas Haig 1914–19* (London: Eyre & Spottiswoode, 1952).
3. Ibid., p. 59.
4. Robert Blake, *A History of Rhodesia* (London: Methuen, 1977).
5. Ibid., p. 282.
6. Robert Blake, 'Sir Anthony Eden', in John P. MacKintosh (ed.), *British Prime Ministers in the Twentieth Century*, vol. II (London: Weidenfield & Nicolson, 1977) pp. 73–117.
7. Ibid., p. 113.
8. Robert Blake, *The Conservative Party from Peel to Churchill* (London: Eyre & Spottiswoode, 1970).
9. Robert Blake, *The Unknown Prime Minister: the Life and Times of Andrew Bonar Law* (London: Eyre & Spottiswoode, 1955).
10. Robert Blake, *Disraeli* (London: Eyre & Spottiswoode, 1966).
11. *The Conservative Party*, p. 69.
12. Ibid., p. 272.
13. Ibid., p. 271.
14. Robert Blake, 'The Crown and Politics in the Twentieth Century', in Jeremy Murray-Brown (ed.), *The Monarchy and its Future* (London: Allen & Unwin, 1969) pp. 11–28.
15. Robert Blake, *The Office of Prime Minister* (Oxford University Press, 1975).
16. Robert Blake, '1783–1902', in David Butler (ed.), *Coalitions in British Politics* (London: Macmillan, 1978) pp. 1–24.
17. Robert Blake, 'A Changed Climate', in Lord Blake and J. Patten (eds), *The Conservative Opportunity* (London: Macmillan, 1976) pp. 1–12.
18. Ibid., p. 12.
19. Ibid., p. 8.
20. Robert Blake, *Conservatism in an Age of Revolution* (London: Papers of the Conservative Philosophy Group, 1976).
21. Ibid., p. 22.
22. Ibid., p. 23.
23. Robert Nozick, *Anarchy, State and Utopia* (Oxford: Blackwell, 1974).
24. Ibid., p. ix.
25. Ibid., p. 48.
26. John Rawls, *A Theory of Justice* (Oxford University Press, 1971).

27. Ibid., p. 302.
28. Ibid., p. 302.
29. Ibid., p. 244.
30. Ibid., p. 221.
31. Ibid., p. 235–9.
32. Ibid., p. 560.
33. Ibid., p. 563.
34. H. L. A. Hart, *The Concept of Law* (Oxford University Press, 1961).
35. Ibid., p. 181.
36. H. L. A. Hart, 'Positivism and the Separation of Law and Morals', *Harvard Law Review*, 71 (1958) 593–629.
37. *The Concept of Law*, p. 202.
38. Ibid., p. 187.
39. Ibid., p. 97.
40. H. L. A. Hart, *Law, Liberty and Morality* (Oxford University Press, 1963).
41. Ronald Dworkin, *Taking Rights Seriously* (London: Duckworth, 1977).
42. John Finnis, *Natural Law and Natural Rights* (Oxford University Press, 1980).
43. John Finnis, 'Some Professorial Fallacies about Rights', *The Adelaide Law Review* 4 (December 1972) 377–88.
44. John Finnis, 'The Rights and Wrongs of Abortion', *Philosophy and Public Affairs* 2 (1973) 117–45.
45. John Finnis, 'Reason and Passion: the Constitutional Dialectic of Free Speech and Obscenity', *University of Pennsylvania Law Review*, 116 (December 1967) 222–43.
46. John Finnis, 'Natural Law and Unnatural Acts', *Heythrop Journal*, 11 (1970) 365–87.
47. John Finnis, 'Reason, Authority and Friendship in Law and Morals', in B. Y. Khanbhai, R. S. Katz and R. A. Pineau (eds), *Jowett Papers 1968–69* (Oxford: Blackwell, 1970) pp. 101–24.
48. Ibid., p. 124.
49. Quentin Skinner, *The Foundations of Modern Political Thought*, vol. I: *The Renaissance* (Cambridge University Press) p. xii.
50. Quentin Skinner, 'Meaning and Understanding in the History of Ideas', *History and Theory*, 8 (1969) 3–53.
51. Quentin Skinner, ' "Social Meaning" and the Explanation of Social Action', in Peter Laslett, W. C. Runciman and Quentin Skinner (eds), *Philosophy, Politics and Society*, Series IV (Oxford University Press, 1972) pp. 136–57.
52. Michael Oakeshott, 'Review Article: *The Foundations of Modern Political Thought* – Quentin Skinner', *Historical Journal* 23, 2 (1980) 449–53.
53. Quentin Skinner, 'Hobbes's *Leviathan*', *Historical Journal* 7, 2 (1964) 321–33.
54. Quentin Skinner, 'Hobbes on Sovereignty: an Unknown Discussion', *Historical Journal* 8, 2 (1965) 213–18.
55. Quentin Skinner, 'The Ideological Context of Hobbes's Political Thought', *Historical Journal*, 9, 3 (1966) 286–317, as rpt. in Maurice Cranston and Richard S. Peters (eds), *Hobbes and Rousseau: a Collection of Critical Essays* (New York, Doubleday, 1972) pp. 109–42.
56. Quentin Skinner, 'Conquest and Consent: Thomas Hobbes and the

Engagement Controversy', in G. E. Aylmer (ed.) *The Interregnum: the Quest for Settlement 1646-60* (London: Macmillan, 1972) pp. 79–98.
57. *Hobbes and Rousseau*, p. 116.
58. Ibid., p. 136.
59. *The Interregnum*, p. 94.
60. *The Foundations of Modern Political Thought*, vol. I, p. x.
61. *The Foundations of Modern Political Thought*, vol. II: *The Age of the Reformation*, p. 351.
62. Ibid., p. 351.
63. Ibid., p. 352.
64. Ibid., p. 358.
65. Shirley Robin Letwin, 'Hobbes and Christianity', *Daedalus* (Journal of the American Academy of Arts and Sciences), (Winter 1976) 1–21.
66. P. F. Strawson, 'Wittgenstein's *Philosophical Investigations*', *Mind*, 63 (1954), as rpt. in P. F. Strawson, *Freedom and Resentment and Other Essays* (London: Methuen, 1974) pp. 133–68.
67. P. F. Strawson, *The Bounds of Sense* (London: Methuen, 1966).
68. P. F. Strawson, 'Self, Mind and Body', *Common Factor*, 4 (1966), rpt. in *Freedom and Resentment*, pp. 169–77.
69. P. F. Strawson, *Individuals* (London: Methuen, 1959).
70. P. F. Strawson, 'Imagination and Perception', in Lawrence Foster and J. W. Swanson (eds), *Experience and Theory* (Massachusetts University Press, 1970), rpt. in *Freedom and Resentment*, pp. 45–65.
71. P. F. Strawson, 'Freedom and Resentment', *Proceedings of the British Academy*, 48 (1962), rpt. in *Freedom and Resentment*, pp. 1–25.
72. P. F. Strawson, 'Individual Ideal and Social Morality', *Philosophy*, 36 (1961), rpt. in *Freedom and Resentment*, pp. 26–44.
73. Philippa Foot, 'Virtues and Vices', in Philippa Foot, *Virtues and Vices* (Oxford: Blackwell, 1978) pp. 1–18.
74. Philippa Foot, 'Hume on Moral Judgement', in David Pears (ed.), *David Hume* (London: Macmillan, 1963), rpt. in *Virtues and Vices*, pp. 74–80.
75. Philippa Foot, 'Morality as a System of Hypothetical Imperatives', *Philosophical Review*, 81, no. 3 (July 1972), rpt. in *Virtues and Vices*, pp. 153–73.
76. Philippa Foot, 'Are Moral Considerations Overriding', in *Virtues and Vices*, pp. 181–8.
77. Philippa Foot, 'Moral Arguments', *Mind*, 67 (1958), rpt. in *Virtues and Vices*, pp. 96–109.
78. Philippa Foot, 'Moral Beliefs', *Proceedings of the Aristotelian Society*, 59 (1958–9), rpt. in *Virtues and Vices*, pp. 110–31.
79. Philippa Foot, 'Goodness and Choice', *The Aristotelian Society Supplementary Volume* (1961), rpt. in *Virtues and Vices*, pp. 132–47.
80. Philippa Foot, 'Nietzsche: the Revaluation of Values', in R. C. Solomon (ed.), *Nietzsche: a Collection of Critical Essays* (New York: Doubleday, 1973), rpt. in *Virtues and Vices*, pp. 81–95.
81. Philippa Foot, 'The Problem of Abortion and the Doctrine of Double Effect', *Oxford Review*, 5 (1967), rpt. in *Virtues and Vices*, pp. 19–32.
82. Philippa Foot, 'Euthanasia', *Philosophy and Public Affairs*, 6, no. 2 (Winter 1977), rpt. in *Virtues and Vices*, pp. 33–61.

83. Philippa Foot, 'Approval and Disapproval', in P. M. S. Hacker (ed.), *Law, Morality and Society: Essays in Honour of H. L. A. Hart* (Oxford: Clarendon Press, 1977), rpt. in *Virtues and Vices*, pp. 189–207.
84. G. E. M. Anscombe, 'On Transubstantiation', *Pamphlet of the Catholic Truth Society* (London: 1974), rpt. in G. E. M. Anscombe, *Ethics, Religion and Politics: Collected Philosophical Papers, Volume III* (Oxford: Blackwell, 1981) pp. 107–12.
85. G. E. M. Anscombe, 'Faith', in *Ethics, Religion and Politics*, pp. 113–20.
86. G. E. M. Anscombe, 'On Frustration of the Majority by the Fulfilment of the Majority's Will', *Analysis*, 36, 4 (1976), rpt. in *Ethics, Religion and Politics*, pp. 123–9.
87. G. E. M. Anscombe, 'Authority in Morals', in John Todd (ed.), *Problems of Authority* (London: Darton, Longman & Todd, 1962), rpt. in *Ethics, Religion and Politics*, pp. 43–50.
88. G. E. M. Anscombe, 'Rules, Rights and Promises', *Mid-West Studies in Philosophy*, 3 (Morris, Minnesota, 1978), rpt. in *Ethics, Religion and Politics*, pp. 97–103.
89. G. E. M. Anscombe, 'On Promising and its Justice, and Whether it Need be Respected *in Foro Interno*', *Critica* (Mexico), 3, 7/8 (1969), rpt. in *Ethics, Religion and Politics*, pp. 10–21.
90. G. E. M. Anscombe, 'On the Source of the Authority of the State', *Ratio*, 20 (1), (1978), rpt. in *Ethics, Religion and Politics*, pp. 130–55.
91. G. E. M. Anscombe, *Intention* (Oxford: Blackwell, 1957).
92. G. E. M. Anscombe, 'War and Murder', in Walter Stein (ed.), *Nuclear Weapons: a Catholic Response* (London and New York: 1961), rpt. in *Ethics, Religion and Politics*, pp. 51–61.
93. G. E. M. Anscombe, 'Two Kinds of Error in Action', *Journal of Philosophy*, 60 (1963), rpt. in *Ethics, Religion and Politics*, pp. 3–9.
94. G. E. M. Anscombe, 'Modern Moral Philosophy', *Philosophy*, 33 (1958), rpt. in *Ethics, Religion and Politics*, pp. 26–42.
95. G. E. M. Anscombe, 'The Justice of the Present War Examined', from G. E. M. Anscombe and Norman Daniel, *The War and the Moral Law* (Oxford: 1963), rpt. in *Ethics, Religion and Politics*, pp. 72–81.
96. G. E. M. Anscombe, 'Mr Truman's Degree' (Oxford: 1957), rpt. in *Ethics, Religion and Politics*, pp. 62–71.
97. I refer to an unpublished version of *Religion and Public Doctrine: Volume Two – Tensions* which Mr Cowling kindly showed me.

Name Index

Anscombe, G. E. M., 229–38
St Thomas Aquinas
  G. E. M. Anscombe and, 229, 235–6
  Casey and, 16, 30, 224–5
  S. R. Letwin and, 173, 189, 195, 223
  Oakeshott and, 100, 126–8
  Scruton and, 61
Aristotle, 227
  G. E. M. Anscombe and, 229, 231–4, 236–7
  Casey and, 16, 31, 32, 36–42, 224
  S. R. Letwin and, 172–3, 183–4, 189, 195, 197
  Oakeshott and, 100, 126–8
  Scruton and, 53, 59, 61, 76
Arnold, Matthew, 15, 16
  Casey on, 20, 36–7
Asquith, H. H.
  Cowling on, 153–5
Attlee, C. R., 88–9
  Cowling on, 159–61, 164
  Oakeshott and, 95
Austin, John, 236
  H. L. A. Hart and, 216–18
  S. R. Letwin and, 189
  Oakeshott and, 103, 126
  Scruton and, 61, 76
Ayer, A. J., 227
  Cowling and, 145
  S. R. Letwin and, 196
  Scruton and, 45, 223

Bacon, Francis
  Oakeshott on, 113, 139, 222
  Scruton on, 57
Bahro, Rudolf
  Scruton on, 75

Baldwin, Stanley
  Blake on, 205
  Cowling on, 153–7
Barthes, Raymond, 28
Beckett, Samuel
  Scruton on, 55
Bennett, Jonathan, 33
Bentham, Jeremy, 61, 91
  Oakeshott on, 93, 119
  S. R. Letwin on, 177–9, 189–90, 200
  Scruton and, 76
Berlin, Sir Isaiah, 162, 171
Blake, Robert, Lord, 202–9, 239
Blackstone, William
  S. R. Letwin on, 178–9
Bodin, Jean
  Oakeshott on, 130, 136, 138
  Skinner on, 221–2
Bradley, F. H.
  Oakeshott and, 94–5, 115–16
Burke, Edmund
  Casey and, 36, 41
  Cowling on, 239–40
  S. R. Letwin on, 172, 176, 183, 193
  Oakeshott and, 103, 140
  Scruton on, 59
Butler, Joseph
  G. E. M. Anscombe on, 232–3
Butler, R. A. B.
  Cowling on, 159–60
Butterfield, Sir Herbert
  Cowling on, 167

Callaghan, James
  Casey on, 25
  Cowling on, 161, 164
Calvin, Jean

Name Index

Skinner on, 221
Carnap, Rudolf
　S. R. Letwin on, 196
Carter, Jimmy, 57
Casey, John, 1, 5, 12–14, 15–42, 46,
　　91–2, 161, 163, 208–9, 113–15,
　　229–32, 234, 238–9
Chadwick, Owen
　Cowling on, 166
Chamberlain, Neville
　Cowling on, 156–9
Churchill, Sir Winston S.
　Cowling on, 156–60, 168–9, 203
Coleridge, S. T., 36–7
Collingwood, R. G., 36, 52, 94, 110
Cowling, Maurice, 1, 91, 144–71,
　　202–7, 209–10, 222, 229, 232,
　　238–40
Croce, Benedetto, 46–7, 110
　Casey on, 22

Derby, Edward Stanley, 14th Earl of
　Blake on, 205
　Cowling on, 151–2
Descartes, René, 1, 13, 14
　Casey on, 40
　S. R. Letwin and, 184–6
　Oakeshott on, 113–14
　Scruton on, 54–5, 63, 66–8
　Wittgenstein and, 3–4, 7, 10
Disraeli, Benjamin
　Blake on, 205–6
　Cowling on, 151–2
Dworkin, Ronald, 218
　S. R. Letwin on, 191–2
　Scruton on, 87

Eden, Sir Anthony, 90
　Blake on, 204
　Cowling on, 156–9
Eliot, T. S., 31
　Casey on, 24

Finnis, John, 218–19
Foot, Philippa, 226–9
　Casey on, 18–19
Foucault, Michel
　Scruton on, 87
Freud, Sigmund
　Casey on, 18, 31
　Scruton on, 51
　Wittgenstein on, 9
Frye, Northrop, 17, 20

Gladstone, W. E.
　Blake on, 205
　Cowling on, 151–3, 169
Godwin, William
　Oakeshott on, 119
Gramsci, Antonio
　Scruton on, 75

Haig, Sir Douglas, 1st Earl
　Blake on, 203
Halifax, E. F. L. Wood, 3rd
　　Viscount
　Cowling on, 156–9
Hampshire, Sir Stuart, 15, 31
Hare, R. M., 223, 227, 233
　Casey on, 18–19
Hart, H. L. A., 91, 216–18, 236
　S. R. Letwin and, 189, 200
　Oakeshott and, 103, 126, 142,
　　216–18
　Scruton and, 76
Hayek, F. A., 79, 119, 162, 176
　S. R. Letwin on, 171
Heath, Edward, 90
　Blake on, 208
　Cowling on, 159–60
Hegel, G. W. F., 12–14, 229, 236–7
　Casey on, 23–4, 29–31, 36–42
　Casey and, 15–16, 25–6, 28, 34–5,
　　224–5
　S. R. Letwin and, 186, 193
　Oakeshott on, 99, 102, 136–7
　Oakeshott and, 94–5, 110, 112,
　　115–18, 128
　Scruton on, 46–7, 51, 66–9
　Scruton and, 51–5, 58–9, 60–6,
　　78–80, 91, 223–4
Hitler, Adolf
　Cowling on, 156–9, 203–4
　Scruton on, 75
Hobbes, Thomas
　G. E. M. Anscombe and, 234–7
　Casey and, 36, 41
　S. R. Letwin on, 188–90, 197, 223

S. R. Letwin and, 172–3, 187–8
Oakeshott on, 99–103, 108–10, 136, 138
Oakeshott and, 106–9, 110, 122–4, 126–8, 130, 132, 223
Scruton on, 60, 68–9
Scruton and, 61, 65, 76, 91
Skinner on, 220–1
Hooker, Richard, x–xi, 61
Huggins, Sir Godfrey, Lord Malvern
Blake on, 203–4
Hume, David, 2, 13, 16, 91
G. E. M. Anscombe on, 230, 232–3
Casey and, 18–19, 32, 37, 39–40, 225
Philippa Foot on, 227
S. R. Letwin on, 171–3, 177–80, 180–3, 186–7, 196–8, 223
Oakeshott on, 136
Scruton and, 46

John Paul II
Casey on, 26
Johnson, Samuel, 20
Joyce, James, 31

Kant, Immanuel
G. E. M. Anscombe on, 229, 232–4
Casey and, 16, 20–1, 30, 32–3, 38–41, 224–5
Philippa Foot on, 227–8
S. R. Letwin on, 179, 193–5
S. R. Letwin and, 172–4, 183, 186, 223
Oakeshott on, 109, 136
Oakeshott and, 94–6, 127, 130, 211–12, 215–16
Scruton on, 46–56, 60, 66–9
Scruton and, 45, 57–8, 61–2, 65, 78–80, 91, 223–4
Strawson on, 225–6
Wittgenstein and, 3, 5, 8–9, 10, 12–14
Kelsen, Hans, 76, 103, 126

Laing, R. D., 28
Scruton on, 78
Laski, Harold, 103
Law, Andrew Bonar

Blake on, 205
Cowling on, 153–5
Leavis, F. R.
Casey on, 15, 20, 28, 36–7
Scruton on, 51
Lenin, V. I.
Oakeshott on, 139
Scruton on, 174–5
Letwin, Shirley Robin, 1, 12–13, 171–201, 223, 229–30, 234, 238
Lévi-Strauss, Claude
S. R. Letwin on, 184
Lloyd George, David
Cowling on, 153
Locke, John
Oakeshott on, 93, 119, 130, 136
Scruton on, 60–1, 76, 91
Luther, Martin
S. R. Letwin on, 223
Oakeshott on, 136, 138
Skinner on, 221

MacDonald Ramsay
Cowling on, 153–5
Machiavelli, Niccolo, 105, 151
Oakeshott on, 119
Skinner on, 221
MacIntyre, Alasdair
Casey on, 39
Macmillan, Harold, 90
Blake on, 208
Cowling on, 159, 161
Marx, Karl
Casey on, 29–31, 39
S. R. Letwin on, 184
Oakeshott on, 105–6, 139
Scruton on, 57–9, 75
Mill, J. S., 36, 218, 229
Cowling on, 147–9
S. R. Letwin on, 177, 179–81, 189
Oakeshott on, 93, 131, 136
Scruton on, 60–2, 69, 91
Montaigne, Michel de, 171
Montesquieu, Charles de
Oakeshott on, 136
Scruton on, 76
Moore, G. E., 227
Scruton on, 44, 67
Morley, John, 152

Name Index

Murry, J. Middleton, 20

Newman, J. H., 145
Nietzsche, Friedrich, 227
   Casey and, 16, 41–2, 225
   S. R. Letwin and, 193–5, 197
   Oakeshott and, 94, 106, 109, 117–18, 127, 136
Norman, Edward
   Cowling on, 166–7
Nozick, Robert, 27, 40, 91, 142, 211–13, 236
   Oakeshott and, 211–13

Oakeshott, Michael, 1, 12–14, 41, 61, 65–6, 79–80, 93–143, 145–50, 167–8, 171, 176–7, 183–7, 191–2, 194, 199–201, 208, 211–23, 229–30, 232, 234–8
Ockham, William of, 223

Pascal, Blaise, 171
   Oakeshott on, 136
Peel, Sir Robert
   Blake on, 205–9
   Cowling on, 152, 239
Pickthorn, Kenneth
   Cowling on, 167
Plato
   S. R. Letwin on, 172, 183, 194, 197
   Oakeshott on, 100
Plumb, J. H.
   Cowling on, 167–8
Popper, Sir Karl, 79, 162, 171, 176
Powell, J. Enoch
   Casey on, 26–8
   Cowling on, 160
   Scruton on, 82–3

Quinton, Anthony, Lord, x–xi

Rawls, John, 33–5, 40, 91, 142
   Oakeshott and, 213–16
Richards, I. A., 20, 36
Rousseau, Jean-Jacques
   S. R. Letwin on, 190
   Oakeshott and, 118, 133
   Scruton on, 69

Russell, Bertrand
   S. R. Letwin on, 196
   Scruton on, 67

Salisbury, Robert Cecil, 3rd Marquis of
   Blake on, 206
   Cowling on, 169–70
Sartre, Jean-Paul, 127, 223
   S. R. Letwin on, 182–3
   Scruton on, 78
Scruton, Roger, 1, 5, 12–14, 43–92, 161, 163, 208–11, 222–5, 229–32, 234, 236, 238
Sidgwick, Henry
   G. E. M. Anscombe on, 229, 232–3
Skinner, Quentin, 219–22, 234
   Oakeshott and, 219–22
Smith, Adam
   Scruton and, 60, 210
Smyth, Charles
   Cowling on, 167
Spinoza, Benedict de
   Casey on, 31, 37–8
   S. R. Letwin and, 172
   Oakeshott on, 136
   Scruton and, 65
Stalin, Josef
   Scruton on, 74
Stevenson, C. L., 227
   Scruton on, 45, 223
Stokes, Adrian
   Scruton on, 51, 52
Strawson, P. F., 31, 225–6
   Casey and, 225–6
   Scruton and, 225–6

Talmon, J. L., 79, 162, 171
Todd, Sir Garfield
   Blake on, 204
Thatcher, Margaret, 56, 160–1
Thompson, E. P.
   Scruton on, 87–8
Trollope, Anthony
   S. R. Letwin on, 174–5, 193–5
Truman, Harry S., 235

Ullmann, Walter
   Cowling on, 166

Watkin, David, 54
  Scruton on, 51
Webb, Beatrice & Sidney, 139
  S. R. Letwin on, 176–7
Welbourne, Edward
  Cowling on, 168
Williams, Raymond
  Scruton on, 88
Wittgenstein, Ludwig, 1–14, 219, 225–6, 228
  G. E. M. Anscombe and, 229–31, 238
  Casey on, 17–24, 31, 34
  S. R. Letwin and, 186
  Oakeshott and, 1, 113–14
  Scruton on, 46–51, 55, 63, 67–8
Wilson, Sir Harold, 89
  Cowling on, 161, 164

Subject Index

absolutism, ethical, 32–5
   see also naturalism, ethical; virtues
adjudication, and law, 76, 129
   see also constitutionalism; judicial independence; justice, legal, natural and procedural; law, the rule of
aesthetic attitude, 46, 48–9
   see also Kantian aesthetics
aesthetic interest, 50–1, 55–6
   see also Kantian aesthetics
aesthetics
   Casey on, 16–24, 29, 36–8
   Oakeshott on, 110–11
   Scruton on, 46–51, 51–6
   Wittgenstein on, 2–3, 8–9
   see also expressionism; Kantian aesthetics; practical criticism
Anglicanism, 94, 206
   Cowling on, 166–71, 239
   see also Christianity; church; religion; secularisation; theocracy
appeasement, 156–9
architecture, 51–6
aristocracy, aristocratic ethics
   Casey on, 39–42
   S. R. Letwin on, 176–7, 182–3, 193–5
   Oakeshott on, 108–10, 117–18
   see also justice, as a virtue; nobility, the noble; obligation
Aristotelianism, 210, 229, 236–8
   Casey and, 16, 37–9, 42
   S. R. Letwin and, 172, 184, 189–90, 195
   Oakeshott and, 100–1, 108–9, 126–8
   Scruton and, 53–4, 61, 76

   see also constitutionalism; natural law; naturalism, ethical; teleology; Thomism; virtues
authoritarianism, 28, 68, 173, 175, 216–18, 223
   Oakeshott on Hobbes and, 99–101
   see also law, the rule of; legal positivism; natural right; voluntarism
authority, 2, 12
civil authority, 212, 215–18; 230–1, 236–8: Casey on, 27, 29–31; S. R. Letwin on, 187–90; Oakeshott on, 100–1, 106–8, 123–31 (*passim*); Scruton on, 60–1, 68–9
customary, institutional, social and traditional authority: Casey on, 25–6, 29–31, 33–4; S. R. Letwin on, 185–7, 196–7; Oakeshott on, 103–5, 112–15; Scruton on, 58–9, 63–4
moral and religious authority, 229–30: Casey on, 26, 33–4; Oakeshott on, 115–17

Benthamism, 198–200, 216
   S. R. Letwin on, 177–9, 189–90
British Empire, 89, 203–4
   Cowling on, 156–60, 170
   Oakeshott on, 139
   Scruton on, 73, 84–5, 89
   see also colonisation; *universitas*
Butskellism, 70, 156, 159–60

Calvinism, 138, 221
Cambridge Review, 25–9, 90
capital punishment, 70, 192
Central African Federation, 203–4

certainty, 66
  Wittgenstein on, 10–12
Christianity, 38, 78, 204, 206, 229,
    239–40
  Cowling on, 147, 165–71, 239–40
  S. R. Letwin on, 174–5, 181
  Oakeshott on, 94–5, 117–18, 138
  see also Anglicanism; church;
    religion; secularisation;
    theocracy; *universitas*
church, 78, 238–40
  Casey on, 26–7
  Cowling on, 147, 166–71
  S. R. Letwin on, 175
  Oakeshott on, 94–5, 101, 135
  Scruton on, 78
  see also Anglicanism; Christianity;
    religion; secularisation;
    theocracy; *universitas*
civil association, 65–6, 168, 211–22
    (*passim*), 229, 239
  Cowling on, 149, 168
  S. R. Letwin on, 187–90,
    197–200 (*passim*)
  Oakeshott on, 99–102,
    121–43 (*passim*)
  see also constitutionalism; justice,
    legal, natural and procedural;
    law, the rule of; natural law;
    natural right; *societas*; state
civil law
  S. R. Letwin on, 188–92 (*passim*)
  Oakeshott on, 100–1, 106, 108–9,
    122–3, 128, 136–9
  Scruton on, 62–3
  see also authoritarianism;
    authority; justice, legal and
    procedural; law, the rule of;
    legal positivism; obligation;
    voluntarism
civil society, 64–5, 69, 79, 99
  see also 'objective spirit'; *Sittlichkeit*;
    social contract
classism, 75
collectivism, 200, 206
  Oakeshott on, 138–9, 142
colonisation, 203–4
  Casey on, 28
  Oakeshott on, 139

Scruton on, 73–4
see also British Empire
common law, 210
  S. R. Letwin on, 177–9
  Scruton on, 62–3, 73–4, 76–7, 81,
    83
  see also constitutionalism; justice,
    legal, natural and procedural;
    law, the rule of
confessional state
  see under theocracy
consensus, 73, 131, 189–90
  see also constitutionalism
consequentialism, 18–20, 29, 32–5,
    224, 232–4
  see also utilitarianism
Conservative party, 89–90, 202–9,
    239
  Cowling on, 150–71 (*passim*)
  Scruton on, 56, 70–2
constitutionalism, 63, 142–3, 210–11
  Scruton on, 72–6, 79–85 (*passim*)
  see also civil association; civil law;
    judicial independence; justice,
    legal, natural and procedural;
    law, the rule of; legitimacy;
    natural law; *societas*
constitutionality
  see under constitutionalism
contextualism, 219–21
contract, 76–7
courage, 38, 108
crime, 76–7
culture, 16, 23–4, 29, 36–7, 51, 54–5,
    57–9, 110–12, 138, 179
  see also education; 'objective
    spirit'; traditionalism

democracy, 28, 200, 204–8, 229–30
  Casey and, 40–2
  Cowling on, 150–60
  S. R. Letwin on, 177–81, 198
  Oakeshott on, 108–10, 122, 131–2,
    139
  Scruton on, 61–3, 73–4
  see also civil association;
    constitutionalism;
    majoritarianism; teleocracy;
    universitas

Subject Index

determinism, 30–1, 64, 184, 226
dualism, 3–4, 6, 14, 24, 39–41, 54, 58–9, 63, 101, 112–14, 193–4, 214–16, 231–2
  Scruton on, 66–69
  see also intention; liberalism; 'objective spirit'; practical knowledge; rationalism; will

education, 13, 20, 185, 196–7
  Casey on, 25–6, 31, 35–6
  Oakeshott on, 103–5, 110–13, 115–17
  Scruton on, 55–7, 62
  see also culture; traditionalism
emotivism, 223–4, 227
  Scruton on, 44–6
empiricism, 2, 4
  Casey and, 15, 17, 21, 23–4, 38, 40
  S. R. Letwin and, 196–7
  Oakeshott on, 103
  Scruton on, 66–8
  Scruton and, 46–7, 54
empiricist aesthetics
  Casey on, 16–18, 20–4
  Scruton on, 46–51, 55–6
Enlightenment, 118–19
enterprise association, 61
  Oakeshott on, 124–43 (*passim*)
  see also universitas
equity, 77, 80, 129, 178
establishment, 64–5, 99, 123, 128, 149, 212, 221–2
  see also civil association; constitutionalism; state
eudaimonia, 53
existentialism, 184–5, 224
expressionism, 15, 51
  Casey on, 20–4, 36–7
  Oakeshott on, 110–11
  Scruton on, 55, 58–9
  see also aesthetics; culture; dualism; 'objective spirit'; practical knowledge

Fabianism, 176–7
Falklands war, 70–2, 164
fascism, 86

feminism, 78
feudalism, 41–2, 123, 134–5, 138–9, 221–2
  see also aristocracy, aristocratic ethics; *universitas*
free market economics, 132, 171, 181, 211
  Scruton on, 56–7, 60, 71, 73
  see also laissez-faire economics
friendship, 61

general will, 69, 190, 218
gentleman
  S. R. Letwin on, 174–6, 192–4
  see also aristocracy, aristocratic ethics; nobility, the noble
Gould Report, 56

historicism, 12, 14, 16, 34–5, 38–9, 45, 55, 64, 173, 211, 217, 225, 228–9, 234, 238
  S. R. Letwin and, 173, 183–6, 196–7 (*passim*)
  Oakeshott and, 94, 102, 117–21 (*passim*), 143–5 (*passim*)
human rights
  Scruton on, 57, 63, 72, 76
  see also justice, legal, natural and procedural; law, the rule of; natural law; rights

idealism, 5, 43, 91–2
  Casey on, 21–4, 36–7
  Oakeshott and, 114–15
  Scruton on, 66–9
  Scruton and, 46–7
ideology, 4, 37–8, 56–7, 80–5 (*passim*), 96, 102–4, 115–17, 119–21 (*passim*), 144, 147–51 (*passim*), 161, 220
  see also liberalism; Marxism; practical knowledge
imagination, 5, 8–9
  Casey on, 23–4, 36–7
  Scruton on, 46–51, 55–6
  see also expressionism; Kantian aesthetics
immigration, 70
individualism, 62, 146–7

Casey and, 28–31
S. R. Letwin and, 177–9, 187–8, 190
Oakeshott and, 99, 101, 108–9
see also authoritarianism; civil association; Kantian liberalism; liberalism; natural right; voluntarism

intention, 6, 17, 30, 33, 68–9, 231–2
see also dualism; practical knowledge; will

Ireland, 28
Israel, 28

judicial discretion, 129, 191
judicial independence, 129, 179
Scruton on in relation to constitutionalism, 73–4, 76–7
see also adjudication, and law; constitutionalism; justice, legal, natural and procedural; law, the rule of; natural law

justice
as a virtue, 224, 232–4: Casey on, 38; S. R. Letwin on, 182; Oakeshott on, 108–9; see also naturalism, ethical; nobility, the noble; obligation
distributive: Casey and, 35–6; S. R. Letwin and, 178; Oakeshott on, 131, 139; Oakeshott in relation to Nozick and Rawls on, 212–16; see also socialism; teleocracy; *universitas*
institutional: Casey on, 25, 30; see also 'objective spirit'; *Sittlichkeit*
legal, 61, 230–1: S. R. Letwin and, 172–3; Oakeshott on, 106–8, 128; Oakeshott on Hobbes and, 100–1; Oakeshott in relation to Rawls and, 214–15; **Oakeshott in relation to H. L. A. Hart and, 216–18**; see also authoritarianism; civil law; law, the rule of; legal positivism; natural right; nominalism; obligation; sovereignty; voluntarism
natural, 31, 46, 179, 188–92, 230–4, 236–7: Oakeshott on, 104, 125, 131; Oakeshott in relation to Hart, Dworkin and Finnis on, 216–19; Scruton on, 64, 73–6 (*passim*), 80–1; see also Aristotelianism; common law; constitutionalism; judicial independence; law, the rule of; legitimacy; natural law; Thomism
procedural, 236–7: S. R. Letwin on, 188–92; Oakeshott on, 125–8; Oakeshott in relation to Rawls, Hart, Dworkin and Finnis on, 216–19; Scruton on, 75–6; see also civil association; constitutionalism; judicial independence; law, the rule of; natural law
revolutionary, 74–5
social, 25, 40, 198, 212, 218: Oakeshott and, 112; Scruton on, 64; see also socialism; teleocracy

Kantian aesthetics
Casey and, 20–2
Scruton on, 46–56
see also aesthetic attitude; aesthetic interest; aesthetics; imagination

Kantian liberalism, 95, 195, 210, 223, 226, 228–9
Casey and, 41–2
Oakeshott and, 95
Oakeshott in relation to Nozick and Rawls and, 213–17
Scruton and, 45–6, 60–2, 76, 80
see also constitutionalism; law, the rule of; liberalism; natural right; voluntarism

Labour party, 71, 85–90
Cowling on, 153–65 (*passim*)
Oakeshott and, 97–8

Subject Index

see also socialism
laissez-faire economics, 177
  Oakeshott and, 131–2
  Scruton and, 64
  see also free market economics
language games, 4–8, 10–12, 18, 34, 68
  see also 'objective spirit'; private languages; rules, rule-following
law, the rule of, 62–3, 88–90, 236–8
  S. R. Letwin on, 180–1, 188–92
  Oakeshott on, 106–9, 122–31 (*passim*), 142–3
  Oakeshott in relation to Rawls, Hart, Dworkin and Finnis on, 214–19
  see also civil association; constitutionalism; justice, legal, natural and procedural; legitimacy; natural law; natural right; sovereignty
legal morality
  see under civil association; constitutionalism; justice, legal, natural and procedural; law, the rule of; natural law
legal positivism, 76, 79, 226, 236–7
  S. R. Letwin and, 189–90
  Oakeshott and, 103, 126, 216–18
  see also authoritarianism; authority; civil law; justice, legal and procedural; natural right; sovereignty; teleology; will
legitimacy, 61, 68–9, 230–1, 235
  Oakeshott and, 130–1, 211–12
  Scruton and, 72–3
  see also constitutionalism; justice, legal, natural and procedural; law, the rule of; natural law
Leninism
  see under Marxism–Leninism
liberal conservatism, 202–9
  Oakeshott and, 97–8
  see also liberalism
Liberal party, 151–5, 204–5
liberalism, 2, 13–14, 209–22 (*passim*), 225–8 (*passim*), 234–5

Casey on, 27, 29–31, 36–42 (*passim*)
Cowling on, 144–50 (*passim*), 160–3, 168–9
S. R. Letwin and, 171–3, 178–80, 187–93 (*passim*), 195, 200
Oakeshott on, 100–3, 105–6, 111–12, 118–19
Oakeshott and, 126, 136–7, 142–3
Scruton on, 56–66, (*passim*), 72–5 (*passim*), 82–5
Scruton and, 45–6, 48, 52, 54, 77–81
  see also civil association; constitutionalism; ideology; individualism; Kantian liberalism; law, the rule of; natural right
Lutheranism, 138, 221, 223

majoritarianism, 72, 109, 122, 229
  see also democracy
Marxism, 51–2, 102–3, 106, 120, 143, 150–1, 184, 211
  Casey on, 29–31
  Cowling on, 161
  S. R. Letwin on, 193
  Oakeshott on, 139
  Scruton on, 56–9, 64–5
  see also Marxism–Leninism; socialism
Marxism–Leninism, 139, 143, 210
  Scruton and, 74–5, 79, 86–8
  see also Marxism; socialist legality
'minimal state', 27–8, 40, 211–13
Moralitat, 115

NATO, 83–5, 89
  see also Western Alliance
nationalism, 27–8, 123, 203
natural law, 216–19, 223–5, 237–8
  Casey and, 16, 31, 39
  S. R. Letwin and, 172–3, 181, 183, 189–91, 196–7
  Oakeshott on, 99–103, 104, 108, 126–8, 131
  Scruton on, 57, 64, 75–6, 81
  see also Aristotelianism; constitutionalism; justice,

legal, natural and procedural; law, the rule of; legitimacy; rights; teleology; Thomism
natural right, 31, 39, 57, 172–3, 223–5, 228
  Oakeshott on, 99–103, 104, 107, 123, 126–8, 136–7
  Scruton on, 60, 62, 69, 75–6
  see also authoritarianism; authority; justice, legal, natural and procedural; nominalism; obligation; social contract; *societas*; voluntarism; will
naturalism, ethical, 16, 78, 183–4, 223–5, 227–9, 232–5
  Casey on, 18–19, 32–5, 38
  Scruton on, 44–6
  see also absolutism, ethical; Aristotelianism; natural law; natural right; Thomism
'naturalistic fallacy', 32, 44
necessary unity of consciousness,
  see under 'transcendental unity of apperception'
nobility, the noble, 79
  Casey on, 39–42
  Oakeshott on, 108–9
  see also aristocracy, aristocratic ethics; gentleman
nominalism, 99–103, 151, 172
  see also authoritarianism; natural right; scepticism; voluntarism
nomocracy, 135

'objective spirit', 14, 16, 38, 80, 115, 171, 180
  Casey on, 30–1
  Scruton on, 54
  see also civil society; culture; *Sittlichkeit*; traditionalism
obligation, 27, 41, 62, 66, 69, 76–7, 220, 230, 232–4 (*passim*), 238
  S. R. Letwin on, 187–90 (*passim*)
  Oakeshott on, 100–1, 108–9, 123–31 (*passim*), 216–18
  see also authority; law, the rule of; natural law; natural right; social contract; voluntarism; will
'original position', 33–4, 40, 213–16

Peelism, 204–9
phenomenology, 46, 55
photography, 56
phronesis, 38, 224
  see also practical knowledge
polis, 42, 61, 126–7, 189, 236
  see also Aristotelianism; natural law; 'objective spirit'
pornography, 27–9, 59
positive law
  see under civil law; justice, legal; law, the rule of; legal positivism; nominalism; statute law; voluntarism
positivism, 2–4, 67, 196
practical criticism, 16–22, 29, 36–7, 51
  see also aesthetics; expressionism; Kantian aesthetics
practical knowledge, 3–4, 6–7, 185–6, 231–2
  Casey on, 22–4, 38
  Oakeshott on, 113–17 (*passim*), 121
  Scruton on, 50–5 (*passim*), 58–8, 66–8
  see also dualism; expressionism; 'objective spirit'; *phronesis*; rationalism
prescriptivism, 224, 229
  Casey on, 18–19
private languages, privacy, 2, 7–8
  Scruton on, 66–9
  see also language games; rules, rule-following
promises, promising, 63, 196, 230–1
property, 162–3, 168, 207
  Oakeshott on, 212
  Scruton on, 60, 86
  see also right
psychoanalysis, 9, 18, 31, 52–3

racialism, 75
  Casey on, 27–8

Subject Index

rationalism, 1–4, 16–17, 68, 80–1, 91–2, 220
  Cowling on, 145–50 (*passim*)
  S. R. Letwin on, 171–3, 176–9, 183–6, 196–8
  Oakeshott on, 100–1, 112–21 (*passim*), 141–2
  see also liberalism; practical knowledge; traditionalism
realism, 2–4, 196
reformation, 41, 149, 198, 211, 232–4
  Oakeshott on, 121, 127, 134–40 (*passim*), 221–2
  see also Christianity; church; religion; secularisation; theocracy
religion, 9–10, 26, 36, 78, 224, 229
  Cowling on, 149, 165–71, 238–40
  S. R. Letwin on, 174–6
  Oakeshott on, 94–5, 99, 138, 221–2
  see also Christianity; church; secularisation; theocracy
Rhodesia, 203–4
right, 30–1, 60–1, 215–16
  see also natural right; property; will
rights, 228
  Casey on, 28–31
  S. R. Letwin on, 173, 191–2
  Oakeshott on, 101, 125–6, 131–4 (*passim*), 212–13, 215–16
  Scruton on, 57, 62–3, 73–4, 76, 87
  see also constitutionalism; human rights; individualism; justice, legal, natural and procedural; natural law; natural rights; obligation; voluntarism
Roman Catholicism, 239
  Casey on, 26
rules, rule-following, 8, 17, 191, 194
  Oakeshott on, 112–18 (*passim*)
  see also language games; practical knowledge; private languages; rationalism; traditionalism

Salisbury Review, 70–5, 82–5, 210, 222
scepticism, x, 100–1, 171
science, 1–5, 8–10, 16–17, 46, 49, 52, 92, 185–6

  Oakeshott on, 112–14, 119–20
  see also rationalism; scientism
scientism, 148–9
  S. R. Letwin on, 176–7, 197
  Oakeshott on, 105–6, 119–20
  see also rationalism
secularisation, 126–7, 200
  Cowling on, 166–71, 206, 238–40
  see also Anglicanism; Christianity; church; reformation; religion; *societas*; theocracy
self-ascription, 17, 31
  see also 'transcendental unity of apperception'
semiology, 51, 52
sincerity, 51
  Casey on, 20, 22–3, 37
Sittlichkeit, 14, 39, 65, 115, 186, 209, 228
  see also civil society; 'objective spirit'
social contract, 230–1, 236–7
  S. R. Letwin on, 172, 178, 182, 186
  Oakeshott on, 100–1, 130, 210–16, (*passim*)
  Scruton on, 60–2, 68–9
  see also authority; liberalism; natural law; natural right; obligation; voluntarism
social engineering, 25, 59, 128, 198
socialism, 25, 208
  Cowling on, 153–66 (*passim*)
  S. R. Letwin on, 176–7
  Oakeshott on, 97–8, 120, 138–9, 142–3
  Scruton on, 64, 70–1, 79, 85–91
  see also teleocracy; *universitas*
socialist legality, 74
societas, 134–42 (*passim*), 208–9, 211, 222
  see also civil association; liberalism; natural right
South Africa, 74, 204
sovereignty, 27–8, 82
  Oakeshott on, 99–103, 107, 123–5, 135–7, 221–2
  see also authoritarianism; civil association; legal positivism;

societas; voluntarism; will
Soviet Union, 106, 138, 157, 211
    Scruton on, 74–5, 82–5
Stalinism, 74, 79
state, 26–8, 51–3, 57, 149, 230–1, 236–8
    Casey on, 30–1
    S. R. Letwin on, 187–8
    Oakeshott on, 99–102, 106–7, 123–42 (*passim*), 213–14, 221–2
    Scruton on, 60–6, 68–9
    see also civil association; civil society; justice, legal, natural and procedural; law, the rule of; *polis*; social contract; *societas*; sovereignty
statism, 142, 210
statute law, 178–9, 198, 216
    Scruton on, 76–7, 81
    see also civil law; law, the rule of; legal positivism
structuralism, 36
succession, 73
    see under constitutionalism

taxation, 70–1, 139, 163, 206, 208, 213
teleocracy, 135, 138–43 (*passim*), 198–200, 208, 234–5
    see also enterprise association; *universitas*
teleology, 94, 183–4, 216–17, 230–1
    teleological ethics, 234
    teleological justifications of moral and civil authority, 236–7: Casey on, 40, 42; S. R. Letwin on, 187–8; Oakeshott on, 126–8, 212, 216–17; Scruton on, 65
    see also Aristotelianism; naturalism, ethical; teleocracy; *universitas*; virtues
temperance, 38, 224
Thatcherism, 70–2, 90–1, 160–6 (*passim*), 202
theocracy, 36, 78–9, 210, 236–8
    S. R. Letwin on, 175, 189–90
    Oakeshott on, 95, 101, 107, 138, 221–2

    see also Anglicanism; Christianity; church; reformation; religion; secularisation; *universitas*
Thomism, 16, 30, 210, 219, 227–9, 234, 236, 238
Times, The
    Scruton and, 70–8 (*passim*), 82–8 (*passim*), 210
tort, 76–7
trades unions, 56, 65, 90
traditionalism, x, 13–14, 146
    Casey on, 29–31
    S. R. Letwin on, 185–6, 197–8
    Oakeshott on, 103–5, 112–21 (*passim*)
    Scruton on, 54–5, 58–9, 60–6 (*passim*)
    see also authority; culture; dualism; historicism; liberalism; 'objective spirit'; practical knowledge; rationalism
'transcendental unity of apperception', 8–9, 24, 31, 54, 66–8
    see also self-ascription
Turkey
    Scruton on, 72–3

Unionism, 28, 170
United States, 28, 56, 89–90, 203–4, 211–12
    Cowling on, 156–9
    Oakeshott on, 120
    Scruton on, 70, 82–5
    see also Western Alliance
universitas, 134–42 (*passim*), 222
    see also enterprise association; *universitas*
utilitarianism, 13–14, 207, 216, 223, 227, 229, 232–8 (*passim*)
    Casey on, 16, 20–1, 29–35 (*passim*), 40
    Cowling on, 147–9
    S. R. Letwin on, 172–3, 177–80, 186–90, 199–200
    Oakeshott on, 102–3, 111–12, 125–6, 131, 139–40, 142–3
    Scruton on, 53–4, 61–3

see also consequentialism; legal positivism; teleocracy

virtues, 227–8
  Casey on, 16, 32–5, 38–9, 42, 224–5
  see also Aristotelianism; naturalism, ethical; Thomism
voluntarism, 68–9, 76–7, 80, 173, 189–90, 234–5
  Oakeshott and, 99–103, 122–4, 127–8, 130–1, 212–19 (*passim*)
  see also authoritarianism; liberalism; nominalism; obligation; sovereignty; will

Warsaw Pact
  Scruton on, 82–5

welfare state, 70, 89–90, 198, 206, 208, 213–15
  Oakeshott on, 126, 138–9
  Scruton on, 73–4
  see also justice, distributive; socialism
Western Alliance, 165, 203–4
  Cowling on, 157
  Scruton on, 70, 72–3, 82–5
  see also NATO
will, 3–4, 6, 80, 234–5
  S. R. Letwin on, 172–3
  Oakeshott on, 100–3, 126–7, 130
  Scruton on in relation to aesthetics, 49–50
  see also dualism; legal positivism; sovereignty; voluntarism